BEYOND THE REACH OF SENSE

Beyond the Reach of Sense

AN INQUIRY INTO
EXTRA-SENSORY PERCEPTION

by

Rosalind Heywood

WITH AN INTRODUCTION BY
J. B. RHINE
The Parapsychology Laboratory, Duke University

A Dutton  *Paperback*

NEW YORK
E.P. DUTTON & CO., INC.
1974

Contents

Acknowledgements

I WOULD like to record my gratitude to the experts who have kindly read the summaries of their work and views which I have made here, and in particular to Mr. Guy Wint, without whose help and advice this book would never have been written.

The following authors and publishers have kindly given permission for the inclusion of copyright material in this book: Dr. W. Grey Walter and Messrs. Gerald Duckworth and Co., Ltd. for an extract from *The Living Brain*; Sir George Thomson and the Cambridge University Press for extracts from *The Foreseeable Future*; Dr. H. J. Eysenck and Penguin Books Ltd. for an extract from *Sense and Nonsense in Psychology*; Upton Sinclair and Messrs. T. Werner Laurie Ltd. for an extract from *Mental Radio*; T. S. Eliot and Messrs. Faber and Faber Ltd. for extracts from *Four Quartets*.

I must also thank the President and Council of the Society for Psychical Research for permission to quote extensively from its records. But the Society as such holds no corporate views and is in no way responsible for those expressed by me.

Introduction

THIS is not just another book on ESP. While the title, BE-YOND THE REACH OF SENSE, is an appropriate description, eight chapters of the book take up the very old question of post-mortem survival and the attempts to investigate it scientifically. This is proper enough, since the belief in survival assumes an existence "beyond the reach of the senses," and also because the evidence Mrs. Heywood reviews has to be judged as to whether it is better interpreted as telepathy (a form of ESP) from discarnate spirit personalities or telepathy from the *living*. Mrs. Heywood is not taking a firm stand; she is allowing the reader to judge for himself, if he can, how decisive the evidence is. But at least the reader will see that if it is difficult to make up one's mind on the strength of this evidence as to whether there is proof of survival, his position would indeed be much worse without it.

Why should the subject of ESP be brought to the fore by a long review of the investigation of this question of discarnate agency? Because historically that was the way it happened. It was the great stir over the claims of the Spiritualists that communication with the dead could be demonstrated that led to the formation of the Societies for Psychical Research, the study of mediumship, and the investigation of various types of ESP as possible explanations of the way the medium obtained her information.

One of the best chapters of this book is the story of the development of the Society for Psychical Research in London in 1882, which was followed by similar societies in other countries. It is well told, not only with the authority of a person long associated with the SPR as a council member but with the warmth of human interest that is a special contribution of the author herself.

Perhaps the book may seem to some workers on the Continent and in the U.S.A. to be a bit English in its viewpoint. But we very much need a good book about the English work. England is definitely the Mother Country of psychical research or, as we now say, parapsychology; and who else but an Englishman could so well catch the spirit of this stirring development of the last seventy-five years as she has done it? Besides, we already have books about ESP and parapsychology in general as developed on this side of the Atlantic, and others are on the way.

Much of the charm of this account of parapsychology as the author has reviewed it is in the many pleasant little touches and anecdotes; here and there a remark is quoted or an incident related that adds much to the general appreciation and enjoyment of this field of inquiry. If that could be contagious, it would be a blessing in itself.

J. B. Rhine

BEYOND THE REACH OF SENSE

CHAPTER I

An Unrecognised Faculty

MAN is a born explorer and in this era of expanding science new marvels appear on his horizon every day. Not least of the mysteries surrounding him is his own nature and here of recent years he has made great headway. Biologists are laying bare the secrets of inheritance through Mendelian genes, the chemical equilibrium of the body and that superb electrical instrument, the brain. Psychologists are probing ever deeper into the astonishing complexities of mental states. But we still have far to go. Take, for example, the nature of memory. Every man alive is remembering all the time. Yet nobody knows how he does it, although there are plenty of theories. And take consciousness itself. We know that impacts from the exterior world on the senses travel by way of the nervous system to the brain. But what happens next? How are these impacts translated into consciousness? Again, nobody knows.

One line of research has recently come on a possible clue to some of these mysteries, and it may eventually help to throw light on others, such as man's relation to space and time. This clue is the confirmation of an age-old belief, which had long been cast aside as nonsensical since it would not fit in with the concepts of current science. In both England and America experiments conducted under rigid scientific conditions have now shown that it is possible for one human being to become aware at a distance of another's thoughts or feelings, in conditions strictly controlled to ensure that no knowledge of them could have been acquired by sensory means. The evidence provided by these experiments is far more impressive than is generally realised. They are based on a prosaic procedure which is seen at its simplest in "card guessing." There are two guinea-pigs, A, the agent, and P, the percipient. The experimenters ask A to look through a pack of cards, which has been put up in random order, one by one, while P, from a position in which he cannot see the cards and is not in sensory contact with A, recites their order. Certain percipients, though not hitting every nail on the head, can get that order right to a degree of correctness astronomically beyond the bounds of chance. In the earliest tests agent and percipient were in the same room, but a comparable level of results has been obtained with the two in separate towns, even in separate countries. This curious faculty has become known as telepathy.

Once it had been shown by experiment that in this direct fashion, at a distance, one human being could become aware of another's thoughts or feelings, the next question was: could he also get information about inanimate objects of which there was no mental image in any mind? Further experiments were devised which demonstrated that certain percipients could report, with an equivalent degree of correctness, the order of packs of cards which was unknown to anybody, since they had been mechanically shuffled. Experiments have also shown that not only can the limitations of space be thus overcome, but apparently those of time as well, for some percipients have been able to call through packs of cards, with the same order of accuracy, in advance. In other words, they appear to exercise precognition. Telepathy and precognition have also appeared to function in controlled experiments involving the reproduction of simple drawings at a distance.

What it all comes to is this. Evidence has been produced that man is a creature who can make contact with distant events by an unknown process, which does not involve the use of sight or hearing or touch or taste or smell, and which to some extent at least is independent of time.

Experimental research into the nature of this strange faculty is still at a very early stage and is hampered by the fact that the laws which govern it are not yet known. But the simple discovery that it exists could lead to a revolution in thought about the nature of living creatures and their relation to their environment. In 1894 the first Lord Balfour wrote that no event which easily finds its niche in the structure of the physical sciences, even one so startling as the destruction of the earth by some unknown celestial body, ought to excite half as much intellectual curiosity as the fact that Mr. A. can communicate with Mr. B. by extra-sensory means. Why then has so little been heard of this fact now that at last it seems to have been confirmed by detailed experiment? Why is it not acclaimed as a momentous discovery? This is a question of great psychological interest. It is true, of course, that the faculty has little practical value, for it is elusive, sporadic and unreliable. Even the few who sometimes exercise it cannot predict without fail who will win the Derby or how Kaffirs will stand next week, though one day they may conceivably learn to do so. But to the enquiring mind the most absorbing of all questions is "What is life?", and here is a new flicker of light on a faculty possessed by the living. Why then is it ignored?

There seem to be two main reasons. The first is that we accept without question certain hypotheses on which both our practical activities and our scientific theories are based. We take it for granted that every event has a cause which precedes it, and that no event can have an effect before it has happened; also that for any event to influence another there must be some transfer of energy between the two. Most of us nowadays also take it for granted that consciousness is no more than an aspect of physical processes, that it is non-existent apart from a physical brain, and that it can only become aware of its surroundings through the medium of a physical nervous system. In other words, we do not accept that mind can be separated from body. These assumptions fit in with the whole enormous body of information acquired through the natural sciences, and are believed in by most educated men in the twentieth century as implicitly as Christians believe in Heaven. To traditional science, then, claims for telepathy or precognition are a heresy greater than that of Copernicus and too absurd to be taken seriously. When mooted to the physicist, Helmholtz, he cried in horror: "Neither the testimony of all the Fellows of the Royal Society, nor even the evidence of my own senses, would lead me to believe in the transmission of thought from one person to another independently of the recognised channels of sense". And if, said an American scientist, these alleged facts were genuine and real, the labours of science would be futile and blind.

The second reason why these facts about the make-up of man are so widely ignored by men of science is that before the modern techniques of experiment were devised the evidence in their favour was anecdotal and scarcely watertight. A mother's sudden awareness that her distant son was drowning; a wife's vision of her dying husband; a man's consciousness that his friend was in desperate need; an apparition giving warning of danger; foreknowledge of an unexpected event; these were the kind of phenomena which aroused contempt in the majority and detached curiosity in but few. Yet they were sometimes reported by reasonable and educated persons, often enough indeed for a small number of open-minded men to doubt whether they could be attributed solely to chance, fraud or fevered imagination. But they were not evidence, collected in a scientific manner, and until the power of receiving extra-sensory impacts could be tested experimentally its existence could always be denied, for each spontaneous case could be assessed separately, and, however watertight its corroboration, dismissed as chance coincidence. Moreover, it was not difficult to prove that many claims for so-called supernatural events were impostures, and natural contempt was aroused by the fact that these were—and still are—uncritically accepted by the many who, in Carlyle's bitter words, hunger and thirst to be bamboozled.

It is a natural instinct to revolt against the unknown, particularly against an unknown which has in the past been labelled abnormal, supernatural, uncanny, and has been associated with fraud and superstition throughout the ages. But a bank-note is no less a bank-note because there are forgeries. And for the faculty of extra-sensory awareness of events distant in space and time there is now testimony far stronger than that on which many historical facts are accepted. At the same time it must be remembered that even in less controversial subjects there is usually a time lag between discoveries which run counter to current belief and their general acceptance, and there are signs that in psychical research too the mental climate is slowly beginning to modify. In 1949 Professor Sir Alister Hardy, F.R.S. gave a presidential address to the Zoological Section of the British Association to which he added this epilogue: "There is another matter which I feel it only right to mention if one is not to be intellectually dishonest. There has appeared over the horizon something which many of us do not like to look at. If it is pointed out to us we say: 'No, it can't be there, our doctrines say it is impossible.' I refer to telepathy —the communication of one mind with another by means other than by the ordinary senses. I believe that no one who examines the evidence with an unbiased mind can reject it . . . It is perhaps unorthodox for a zoologist to introduce such a topic; but I do so for a reason. If telepathy has been established, as I believe it has, such a revolutionary discovery should make us keep our minds open to the possibility that there may be so much more in living things and their evolution than our science has hitherto led us to expect."

Professor Hardy's views were not derided, denied or ignored to the extent that similar observations had been in the past. This may have momentous implications. Once it is accepted as possible that a human being can respond to impacts from a distance which do not reach him by means of the senses, and can sometimes even respond to them before in physical time they have been set in motion, many hitherto unquestioned assumptions must come up for review. Humdrum guessing through packs of cards may be an undramatic first step along a route whose end may confirm the intuition of Blake when he wrote

> This life's five windows of the soul
> Distort the heavens from pole to pole
> And teach us to believe a lie
> When we see with, not through, the eye.

But it must not be thought that the findings of psychical research are a matter of mysticism or poetry. In substance they are thoroughly down-to-earth. What it comes to, fundamentally, is that new data have been made precise and science must in future take note of them in its attempts to explain the nature of the universe.

The interpretation of these data calls for an almost superhuman impartiality and detachment. To study a living organism is far harder than to study inanimate matter. And who can hope, when dealing with man's own nature, to be the perfect detective, unaffected by the mental climate in which he lives or by hopes and fears as to what he may find? What he does find, indeed, may depend on what he is, and his interpretation of it is only too likely to fit his previous theories.

Psychical research is the name given to the study of such data. This short sketch is an attempt to disperse a little of the smoke screen which has kept the man in the street in ignorance that this research is going on. What exactly are the discoveries which its pioneers claim to have made? What kind of men are they? What credence can we put in what they tell us? One unexpected point emerges dramatically from the records. The pioneers have included outstanding men of their generations: philosophers, mathematicians, chemists, biologists, physicists, classical scholars. Among the first were Henry Sidgwick, Rayleigh, Crookes, Barrett, J. J. Thomson, A. J. Balfour, William James, Henri Bergson, L. P. Jacks. Many have also been pioneers along other lines of research. J. J. Thomson, for instance, revolutionised physics by his discovery of the electron. And among their successors today are men of comparable stature.

The explorations made by these eminent heretics and their struggles to get their findings accepted as more than fairy gold are as romantic as tales of the search for hidden treasure. Side trails lead into a mist, deceptions are unmasked, the most subtle of clues lie around. But the full record is too long and involved to compress into a short non-technical study. For this reason landmarks on the central trail, the trail which ended in the confirmation of extra-sensory powers in man by orthodox methods of detection, will alone be included. Serious psychical researchers use orthodox methods. They have always been cautious men, proceeding slowly, testing and re-testing each foothold as they go. A satirist said of one of them that he only knew two words: I doubt. But now they seem to have reached a cleft in the rock, no wider, it is true, than an arrow slit, but opening on to remote and alluring vistas.

CHAPTER II

What is *Psi*?

IN most forms of research new findings can usually be described in modifications of existing terms, but in psychical research there are drawbacks to this procedure. Some traditional names have unfortunate associations with fraud and superstition; the word clairvoyant, for instance, is liable to stand for fake fortune-tellers at village fairs. Existing terms, moreover, may carry implications about the nature of the findings which may be incorrect. In consequence researchers tend to seek neutral and impersonal names for psychic phenomena.

Psi, the twenty-third letter of the Greek alphabet, is now widely used as a blanket name for the psychic in general; that is, for the whole family of apparent phenomena and experiences, real or alleged, for which no physical cause has as yet been discovered. It includes not only extra-sensory communication, for which the evidence is coercive, but other phenomena for which the quality of the evidence varies—apparitions, dowsing, poltergeists, 'other world' experiences and certain physical phenomena which some people claim to produce by psychic means.

To find a name both scientifically respectable and noncommittal for the *psi* faculty of extra-sensory communication has proved difficult. It was first labelled paranormal cognition. But the implications of the word paranormal are misleading, for there is no reason to suppose that there is anything beyond the normal, in other words, outside the laws of nature, about it. Mass experiments have suggested that it is widespread in a very rudimentary form. And on the whole it is the normal and healthy people who seem to do best in such experiments. The faculty is paranormal only in the sense that its cause is not perceptible to human senses or to their extensions, scientific instruments. The word cognition, too, is inaccurate when applied to the *psi* process, for this takes place below the threshold of consciousness and there is no means of being sure that the impacts received do always seep up to the surface.

Nowadays the name usually given to this *psi* faculty is extra-sensory perception, although the word perception also implies awareness of an impact. However, the phrase has been telescoped into ESP and as this abbreviation trails no obvious clouds of unwished-for associations it seems to have come to stay. ESP is the form of *psi* with which we shall have most to do.

As the result of experimental work during the last twenty-five years it has become customary to speak of four variants of ESP. The best known of these, direct awareness of the mental state of another person, has been given the name telepathy. Direct awareness of a physical event has, oddly enough, been allowed to retain the traditional name, clairvoyance. Fore-knowledge of the future, apart from rational inference, is known as precognition and similar knowledge of the past as retrocognition. Such a verbal division into classes is useful for purposes of study, but we must not be led into assuming that the four are separate faculties. To many researchers it is beginning to seem a more probable guess that they are examples of a single faculty manifesting itself in different situations.

There are a number of difficulties special to research into ESP, over and above the crucial one that we are ignorant of the laws which control it and so cannot produce it to order. No more than the ultimate constituents of matter can it be studied directly, and as it appears to function in another relation than the one we know to time and space our language itself may be an unsuitable tool to deal with it. We may well be asking the wrong questions. Professor H. H. Price, holder of the Wykeham Chair of Logic at Oxford, has suggested that "we may have to ... puzzle ourselves not about extra-sensory perception but rather about normal sense-perception, treating it *not* as normal but rather as a sub-normal and biologically explicable limitation imposed upon an inherent and aboriginal omniscience."[1] If that should be so, our question ought to be: how are the

[1] *Journal* S.P.R., March 1943.

ordinary processes of sense-perception and everyday consciousness switched off?

Little as we know about what ESP is, we have some idea of what it is not. Lord Rayleigh suggested that any hypothesis of physical radiations, of 'mental radio' from physical brain to physical brain, could be ruled out, since all known physical types of energy fall off inversely as the square of the distance from the source; and ESP apparently is unaffected by distance. Nor can the occasional 'arrival' of extra-sensory perceptions before they are 'sent' be squared with our present view of the nature of physical radiations. Physically transmitted messages, even ordinary speech and writing, must be encoded at one end and decoded at the other, and demand special transmitting and receiving mechanisms. No signs of these have been found in the human body.

If the percipient himself is asked to describe the process of ESP he can give little help. When it surfaces it either seems to him to come 'out of the blue' or to be accompanied by an awareness of conditions indescribable in ordinary terms to those who have not shared them. He is therefore liable to speak in terms which seem nonsensical to the investigator. This surfacing sometimes seems to be delayed—we may guess that it often fails altogether—and the manner in which it takes place is as mysterious as the manner in which the impacts are transmitted from the originating cause to the percipient's subconscious mind. Even the word 'transmitted' is an example of the difficulties of language in psychical research, for it conveys the idea of movement in space which may well be misleading. There are also drawbacks to the word subconscious, which has acquired a number of specific associations. In this book it will be taken to mean quite simply 'beyond the threshold of consciousness.' Two points should be noted. The form in which all ESP finally reaches surface consciousness seems to vary with the temperament or mood of the percipient. And the originating cause is not *reproduced*. It is only *represented*, sometimes sharply and accurately, sometimes in a vague and shadowy way, sometimes, particularly in dreams, by symbols. These may have a practical purpose, for the study of spontaneous cases of ESP

suggests that when surfacing it has to evade a kind of censorship, and to conceal itself in a symbol would be a means of
doing just that. Such a censorship may arise from the desire to
defend commonsense realism, but it may also be biologically
useful, since a means of information which takes little account
of the difference between time past, present or future would
have certain defects, were the information a warning of the
imminent arrival of a hungry lion or a fast car. Without it,
too, man might be swamped, dazed, drowned in an avalanche
of impressions. The terrifying sense of disintegration under
excess of experience which can be induced by such drugs as
mescalin or lysergic acid is well known.

The hypothesis that ESP has to evade a censorship fits in
with the curious fact that in many recent experiments at card-
and picture-guessing some of the guinea-pigs made a habit of
scoring hits, not on the target aimed at, but on the preceding
or subsequent ones. It also provides a possible explanation for
the absurd and irrelevant devices employed—at times apparently with surprising success—by soothsayers of old and
sensitives today. To focus the attention of the conscious mind
on a bundle of bones, or on tea-leaves, cards, a crystal, or the
lines of a hand, may be a means of evading the censor. It may
also tend to still the restless activity of that mind, as a ruffled
pool is stilled when the wind dies down and so becomes
translucent to the mysteries in its bed. Contemplatives from
both East and West have always affirmed that such a process of
"stilling" is the first step towards any extension of awareness.

CHAPTER III

Psi in the Past

THROUGHOUT the ages there have been reports of spontaneous *psi* phenomena: visions of long-past battles, premoni-
tions, haunted houses, apparitions of the living and the dead.
It would be absurd to take these as facts. It would also be
absurd to ignore them altogether, for whether they come from
ancient Egypt or modern Africa, from a spiritualist séance in
Bayswater or the Pacific Islands, they bear a marked family
resemblance, and they are, oddly enough, less lurid and
dramatic than the invented 'supernatural' events of fiction.

Both the Bible and the classics abound in such records. The
Prophet Elisha is said to have tapped the military secrets of
the King of Syria by telepathy. "Will ye not show me,"
complained the King, "which of us is for the King of Israel?"
"None, my Lord, O King," replied his servants, "but Elisha,
the Prophet that is in Israel, telleth the King of Israel the words
thou speakest in thy bedchamber." And there is a famous test
set by King Croesus of Lydia to discover which of seven Greek
and Egyptian Oracles was the most skilled. On a given date he
sent embassies to the Oracles, with instructions to ask them all a
hundred days later, "What is King Croesus, son of Alyattes,
now doing?" Those were good times to apply such tests. The
priestess could not cheat by getting a friend at court to telephone, cable or radio the right answer. She had to rely on her
telepathic power or on guess work. And, however she did it,
on this occasion the Pythia at Delphi hit the mark by announcing that she could smell a lamb and a tortoise being cooked together in a brazen pot. The King had indeed chosen this
improbable occupation as a test, and he then, not unnaturally,
chose the Delphic Oracle as his adviser. Her subsequent
ambiguous statement, that his campaign would end in the
destruction of a great army, he took as predicting victory for

himself. But it was in fact his own army that was destroyed. Similar misfortunes are not unknown in modern days when the ambiguous counsel of humbler Sybils in Oxford Street is similarly misinterpreted.

The test set by Croesus differed from modern research in a basic way. Today we seek to confirm the existence and study the nature of *psi* phenomena. He was merely testing the relative skills of the Oracles, for in those days the fact of divination, as it was called, was accepted without question, —and accepted, too, as supernatural, and therefore very much not a subject for investigation. Alone among the ancients Aristotle and Democritus ventured to question whether after all it might not have a natural origin, and they found no serious successors until the eighteen fifties. But though belief was strong, interest was discouraged. The Christian Church laid a ban on all matters connected with psychical research. They were of the devil and to be avoided at all costs. Even St. Augustine of Hippo recounts how a very sick man, who was desperately longing for a visit from a priest, correctly described in advance the priest's journey to his home. But St. Augustine did not take this simple exercise of ESP as a sign of the man's intense desire for his spiritual adviser, but, coupled with the fact that he had convulsive seizures, as a sign of diabolical possession.

But since ESP appears to be a normal faculty in man, it naturally continued to crop up spontaneously here and there in spite of the Church's disapproval, and being an excellent source of profit, it also continued to be faked. Serious interest in it never died out, although driven underground by the Church. From classical times until the nineteenth century we hear of groups of intellectuals—Neo-Platonists, Alchemists, Rosicrucians, Renaissance scholars, the Cambridge Platonists and others—getting together in secret to indulge in occult practices. The populace, too, believed obstinately in witch-craft, and some witches seem to have had genuine gifts, though many of the phenomena produced by them would today be recognised as no more than hysterical symptoms. But the intellectuals were not scientific investigators. What they sought

20

was illumination—or power—and the poor were after little more than material help.

About the middle of the seventeenth century the winds of modern science began to blow. From then on educated people grew more and more to doubt the existence of *psi* phenomena, although there were exceptions. Among these were the Wesley family, highly intelligent people, who were much troubled by occurrences they believed to be supernatural. Swedenborg, too, an outstandingly competent man where things of this world were concerned, took what he believed to be his own *psi* experiences in 'another world' seriously enough to base a whole theology on them. He was, incidentally, the first man to suggest that, like the physical, that world was subject to natural law. There are records of several incidents, such as his apparent awareness that a distant house was being burnt down, which convinced the philosopher Kant that at least he exercised ESP about mundane events. Kant commented, "Philosophy is often much embarrassed when she encounters certain facts which she dare not doubt yet will not believe for fear of ridicule."

During the eighteenth and nineteenth centuries reports of *psi* were increasingly regarded by the scientifically educated as dangerous folly. To understand the depth of this hostile feeling we must remember the picture of the universe which had developed out of Newton's three laws of motion and his theory of gravitation. On the basis of these the mathematicians who followed him believed that they had managed to explain everything in the universe. It was one great physical mechanism. Its basic constituents were tiny atoms, as solid as billiard balls, whirling around in an all-pervading aether, and this aether, said Lord Kelvin, was the most indubitable fact of our experience. The atoms were whirling in strict obedience to the laws of cause and effect, so much so that Laplace said that had a supreme mathematician been given the distribution of all the particles in the primitive nebula, he could have deduced the whole future history of the world.

This discovery of mathematical harmony must have aroused a joyous serenity in the minds of nineteenth century scientists.

They had climbed out of the bog of superstition and vague metaphysics, out of the irrational, on to clear uplands of law and order. The universe was comprehensible. Its processes were predictable. No miracles of magic could interfere with the majestic inevitability of natural law. It was sheer nonsense to suggest that man could communicate by means other than the senses, could even at times foresee the future in other ways than by rational inference from known facts. How could an effect precede its cause? These were all tales told by idiots and signified nothing whatever.

The attitude of the Victorian scientist to *psi* was summed up in an outburst by the fiery Lord Kelvin. Clairvoyance and the like, he declared, were the results "of bad observation chiefly, somewhat mixed up with the effects of wilful imposture, acting on an innocent trusting mind." As for "that wretched superstition of animal magnetism and table-turning and spiritualism and mesmerism and clairvoyance of which we have heard so much . . ." in his view they were only fit for the rubbish heap.

Lord Kelvin lumped together several very different phenomena. Mesmerism was the name then given to hypnotism, because its discovery was attributed to Anton Mesmer, a Viennese physician who had made many cures in the later eighteenth century through what he erroneously believed to be a flow of 'animal magnetism' from doctor to patient. Hypnotic trance had in fact been known for thousands of years but, oddly enough, it does not appear that Mesmer himself induced it in his patients. This seems to have been done accidentally by one of his pupils, the Marquis de Puységur, in carrying out Mesmer's treatment. However that may be, both master and pupils were condemned as quacks, although they had come upon a genuine fact in nature.

Their successors also got short shrift. In 1842 a London surgeon, W. S. Ward, amputated a leg at the thigh under 'mesmeric trance' and read a paper about it to the Royal Medical Society. This was in the days before anaesthetics, but the Society, far from welcoming such release from pain, struck Ward's paper off its minutes and accused the unfortunate patient of being an impostor. They said that he was merely pretending that he felt no pain. In the early forties London University ordered one of its Professors, Dr. Elliotson, to cease his hypnotic experiments, but he refused to do so and resigned his chair. A Dr. Esdaile in India read of Elliotson's work and between 1845 and 1859 he did over a hundred operations with the patient under hypnotic anaesthesia. But medical journals refused to publish his reports. In 1900 hypnotism was still dismissed as futile quackery. It is now one of the official benefits of the National Health Service.

Among the phenomena which aroused Lord Kelvin's anger were spiritualism and table-turning. Spiritualism was one of the factors which first stimulated serious scientific investigation into *psi* phenomena, and it still remains part of the background against which psychical research goes on. But it is a peculiar background. The desire for wonders and to peep 'behind the veil' lies deep in human nature, and it was probably inevitable that something should take the place of the occultism and witchcraft of past ages. In the nineteenth century it did so with a vengeance. In 1848 in America, among simple and illiterate people, Spiritualism was born. It first sprang into some prominence when the relatives of two girls, the Fox sisters, claimed that they could communicate with the spirits of deceased human beings by means of raps. The relatives made a good thing out of this and we are unlikely ever to know if there was any element of true *psi* in the phenomena produced by the girls. But their claim fell on fertile soil, and their successors multiplied—and prospered—exceedingly, for many people rejoiced at the thought of communicating with the dead.

The Spiritualist cult soon spread from America to England and on all sides persons appeared who not only undertook to transmit messages from the 'other side' by means of raps, but fell into trances during which they purported to converse personally with the deceased. Some were entirely honest, others were shameless frauds, making a good thing out of the longing of the bereaved for continued contact with their lost friends and relatives. In any case, honest or fraudulent, the spiritualists triumphantly filled the gap left by the occultists and witches of old and succeeded in making an impression, not only on the simple and credulous, but on some highly educated and outstanding people. A number of these—Elizabeth Barrett Browning, for instance, some of the famous "Souls" of the nineties and Victor Hugo—found that they need not resort to professional mediums to get mysterious messages, but could produce them themselves by such activities as automatic writing, planchette and table-turning. In consequence they took to these with great enthusiasm, to the immense disdain of contemporary scientists. Yet their behaviour was less foolish than it sounds. For they did get apparent messages from some source which was not that of their conscious minds. And they had little conception of the subconscious, of its love of drama, or of its power of storing up memories of observations which the surface mind had never consciously made or had forgotten. Neither did they know that a number of normal persons, by means of techniques varying from the inducement of slight dissociation to deep trance, can cause statements to emerge from beneath the threshold of consciousness which are quite unexpected by their surface selves. And since it is beneath that threshold that ESP appears to function, it is not surprising that at times they achieved items of information which to them genuinely appeared to come from 'the beyond'. They were thus encouraged to accept as coming from an exterior source much else which probably originated in their own subconscious as a result of wishful thinking or frustration.

The different methods most commonly used to evoke such up-wellings from the subconscious require to be noted. Automatic writing is one. A good many people can hold a pencil resting on a sheet of paper, with the result that after a number of attempts it will write without its owner being conscious of what is written. What it writes is usually incoherent and meaningless—but not always. A second method of communication with the subconscious is to make use of what is called a Ouija Board (from the French Oui and the German Ja). The board is highly polished and on it are painted the letters of the alphabet. On top of it is placed a smaller board, heart-shaped and mounted on tiny castors which enable it to slide about. If two or more persons place their finger-tips very lightly on this smaller board, in many cases it will slide without being consciously pushed, so that the apex of the heart moves from letter to letter, forming words and sometimes sentences. If a pencil is attached to the apex of the heart and a blank sheet of paper is placed on the board, coherent writing will sometimes take place. This form of the apparatus is known as a planchette.

A third, though laborious, method of communication with the subconscious is for several persons to rest their fingers lightly on a three-legged table, which, for some, in response to unconscious pressure, will tip up and tap with one leg, so many times for each letter of the alphabet. This was Lord Kelvin's abhorred table-turning. A fourth method is for a person to talk aloud while in a state which may range from slight dissociation to deep trance. In this trance the normal personality is sometimes apparently replaced by another, and it can be brought on voluntarily by certain men and women—nowadays mostly by women—who then talk and behave as if they were somebody else. Even their handwriting may be different.

The phenomena of trance and of lesser automatisms seem to be inherent in human nature, for they were recorded in the literature of Greece and Rome and travellers have reported them from India, China and elsewhere and also from primitive societies. In classical times a priestess was thought to be possessed by a god, and other persons by their daemons or their familiar spirits, which were not supposed to be those of human beings. It was through the Witch of Endor's familiar that King Saul, although he had forbidden such practices, attempted to consult the dead prophet, Samuel. But in our civilisation persons who can produce this trance personality are usually spiritualists, and spiritualists believe that it is the spirit of a human being who has died. The entranced persons they call a Medium —a medium of communication with departed spirits—and the personality taking possession they call a Control, because they believe that it controls the Medium's body in order to transmit messages from the spirit world.

Automatisms and trance-mediumship can only too easily be simulated by mercenary pseudo-psychics, but in the spate of such activities which occurred in the second half of the nineteenth century there was clearly something which demanded explanation over and above the mass of fraud and folly. At the same time sporadic reports of apparitions continued. These reports were to be the starting point of modern and scientific research into *psi* matters, for, in the middle of the century, a group of intelligent young men at Cambridge, who were especially fascinated by apparitions, came to the conclusion that too much smoke was caused by the 'supernatural' for there to be no fire behind it. They repeated the question asked by Aristotle and Democritus two thousand years before: What if supernatural phenomena do occur and what if they are not supernatural after all, but normal and subject to natural law? This question was the seed from which modern psychical research has grown.

CHAPTER IV

The Background to Psychical Research

THE question of apparitions, said Dr. Johnson, is one of the most important, whether in theology or philosophy, that could come before the human understanding. So too thought the group of young Cambridge intellectuals to whom it had occurred that *psi* might be a genuine natural phenomenon, and they set about taking practical steps to find an answer to it. The first was to found a University Society which, braving ridicule, they called the Ghost Society. One of its founding members was Edward White Benson, later Archbishop of Canterbury, who, according to his son, A. C. Benson, was always more interested in psychic phenomena than he cared to admit; and it was joined a few years later by his younger cousin, Henry Sidgwick. Now and again a rare personality will colour his whole environment, and to his contemporaries it will seem as absurd to question his integrity and intellectual honesty as to question that night follows day. Sidgwick grew to be such a man, and it was his wise guidance which set the pattern and standards for psychical research in later years. He was the son of a clergyman and went to school at Rugby, where he was both happy and successful. In 1855 he went on to Trinity College, Cambridge, where he read classics and mathematics. His academic career was a string of triumphs. In 1857 he won a Craven Scholarship, in 1858 he shared the Browne Prize for Greek and Latin epigrams with G. O. Trevelyan. In 1859 he was first in the classical tripos and thirty-third wrangler in the mathematical tripos. In the same year he won the First Chancellor's Medal and was elected a Fellow of Trinity.

So far all was sunshine. But in the sixties Sidgwick's honesty drove him into the clouds. Fellows of Trinity had to declare themselves "bona fide members of the Church of England," which entailed signature of the Thirty Nine Articles. But recent discoveries had made it hard to accept these as demanded by a Church which still believed that in B.C. 4004 the world was created in a week. Sidgwick did his best. With desperate earnestness he studied Hebrew and Arabic, theology and philosophy. But the Christianity of the day and the new scientific knowledge were like oil and water. They would not mix. So he resigned his Fellowship and Assistant Tutorship, although his less fiercely upright colleagues thought such drastic behaviour more than unnecessary and it also cost him severe material loss. But his standards were absolute. "I happen to care little," he wrote to a friend, "what men in general think of me individually; but I care very much what they think of human nature. I dread doing anything to support the plausible suspicion that men in general, even those who profess lofty aspirations, are secretly swayed by material interests."

Trinity did not at all wish to lose a man who so uncompromisingly displayed such Christian virtues, so they created a lectureship in Moral Science, without theological conditions, and appointed him to it. This gave him some income, which enabled him to live until 1875, when the College appointed him Praelector in Moral and Political Philosophy. He later became Knightsbridge Professor of Moral Philosophy, a post he held until he died.

From the time Sidgwick joined the Ghost Society, so we learn from his letters, he collected records of apparent spontaneous *psi*, and these, together with every other type of *psi* phenomenon, he assessed with most careful dispassion. No judge could have endeavoured more scrupulously to give its just weight to every particle of evidence, either for or against. Quite early on he studied the automatic writings of a friend, Mr. Cowell, but they both came to the conclusion that there was nothing in the scripts beyond the contents of his own mind. The experience, however, gave Sidgwick a first glimpse of the astuteness of the human subconscious, for he and Cowell put various tests to the purported author of the scripts, and the blarney by which he tried to account for his failure to pass them was of great ingenuity.

28

In the sixties Sidgwick began to enquire into the newly fashionable spiritualism, but the first professional medium he went to was a depressing augury for the future. She was, he said, a complete humbug. And all he obtained from the many mediums he investigated during the next twenty years was a little circumstantial evidence, none of it quite watertight, and a lot of obvious fraud. He called it a very dreary and disappointing chapter in his life. But still he never quite lost his belief that there was something behind mediumship. "I don't know what," he commented in a letter. "Have tried hard to discover, and find that I always paralyse the phenomena. My taste is strongly affected by the obvious humbug mixed with it, which at the same time my reason does not over-estimate."

To Sidgwick it was a great puzzle that he never witnessed successful physical mediumship in watertight conditions when a number of intelligent persons assured him that they had done so. He felt he might have found a clue to the answer in a curious story told him at a dinner party by the great Italian, Mazzini. Mazzini had once seen a group of people gazing into the sky, and, seeing nothing himself, he asked one of them what they were looking at. "The cross—don't you see it?" replied the man. Mazzini could see no cross, though all the others assured him they could do so. But one man appeared more intelligent than the rest and he looked puzzled. Mazzini asked him what he saw. "The cross," he answered, "There!" Mazzini shook his arm and said, "But there is no cross." The man's face cleared, as if he were awaking from a dream. "No," he said, "as you say, there is no cross at all." And they walked away together, leaving the others to watch the—at least physically—illusory cross. Could this sort of collective hallucination, Sidgwick wondered, throw light on reports of other physical *psi* phenomena?

In these preliminary canters before the serious hunt for *psi* Sidgwick soon found a congenial companion. In 1860 a young man, Frederic Myers, went up to Trinity to read classics, and Sidgwick happened to become his tutor. Myers was a brilliant scholar and a poet of some distinction, and he seemed set for a successful literary career. But, like Sidgwick, he was more than a scholar, for he also persistently asked basic questions and would not be content with answers which did not account for all the facts. The two were marked out to be friends. They were living, we must remember, at a tense moment, at a water-shed of history when the traditional view of man's nature as composed of body, soul and spirit was being challenged as never before by Darwinian theory and other discoveries of science. To both, the question of all questions was the same: What is Man? What is his destiny? Neither could accept the traditional answers, but neither felt that the whole picture was covered by the new answers of science. Nevertheless the poet in Myers delighted in the ordered beauty of scientific method. An interrogation of nature, he called it, entirely dispassionate, patient, systematic, which can often elicit from her slightest indications her deepest truths. "This method," he said with a flash of insight, "has never yet been applied to the all-important problem of the existence, the power, the destiny of the human soul."

Sidgwick and Myers met again in 1869, when Myers went back to Cambridge to examine for the Moral Science Tripos. He had been wondering with increasing earnestness whether *psi* phenomena could provide any clues to the great question, and he wrote years later of that meeting: "I felt drawn in my perplexities to Henry Sidgwick as somehow my only hope. In a starlight walk which I shall not forget, I asked him, almost with trembling, whether he thought that when Tradition, Intuition, Metaphysics had failed to solve the riddle of the Universe, there was still a chance that from any actual observable phenomena—ghosts, spirits, whatsoever there might be— some valid knowledge might be drawn as to a World Unseen. Already, it seemed, he had thought that this was possible; steadily, though in no sanguine fashion, he indicated some last grounds of hope: and from that night onwards I resolved to pursue this quest, if it might be, at his side."

These phrases are of a particular time and setting and may draw a smile in the twentieth century, but the passionate determination that prompted them will be valued in any age. Myers had his wish. He did investigate whatever there might be with tireless enthusiasm until he died. But first he equipped himself for the task by the study of biology and psychology and in every other way possible within the mental framework of the time.

Sidgwick's determination was no less. "I sometimes feel," he wrote to Myers in 1872, "with somewhat of a profound hope and enthusiasm that the function of the English mind, with its uncompromising matter-of-factness, will be to put the final question to the Universe with a solid passionate determination to be answered which *must* come to something."

The enthusiasm of Sidgwick and Myers drew in another Cambridge man, Edmund Gurney. He too was a distinguished classical scholar, and he soon became a great asset to them, for he had more leisure than the others and he was also found to have a natural gift for psychological experiment, especially in hypnosis. Being of a meticulously thorough temperament, he came to the conclusion, on discovering this, that he could not do his best work without professional knowledge. So he trained as a doctor, studying both in London and at Cambridge, and then, like Myers, he gave the rest of his life to the search for *psi*.

These three, Sidgwick, Myers, and Gurney, formed a nucleus, and more than a nucleus. They were also a magnet. The great physicist, Lord Rayleigh, was drawn in, and so were Arthur Balfour, later to be Prime Minister, and his brother Gerald, who in later years was also in the Cabinet. Their sister, Eleanor Balfour, was working at research under Lord Rayleigh at the Cavendish Laboratory, and she too came in and with her romance, for in this way she met Sidgwick. They were kindred spirits, both being profoundly concerned with the same two vital yet unpopular subjects, psychical research and the higher education of women. In 1876 they were married and worked at their enthusiasms together until Sidgwick died in 1900. Afterwards Eleanor continued to play a major part in psychical research until her own death many years later in 1930.

To go back to the seventies. Here were some of the best brains in Cambridge peeping at *psi* round the door. The same thing was happening at Oxford where the Phantasmological Society was formed. In the seventies too, William Barrett,

Professor of Physics at the Royal College of Science in Dublin, was forcing his scientific colleagues to take a reluctant glance at hypnotism. He submitted a paper to the British Association for the Advancement of Science on experiments in hypnosis which he had been conducting for thirteen years and in which the hypnotised subject had shown signs of *psi*. The Biology Section of the Association was thoroughly shocked at such heresy and would have nothing to do with the paper, but Alfred Russel Wallace, the biologist, who, independently of Darwin, had propounded the theory of evolution, protested with vigour against attempts to exclude from investigation occurrences reported by intelligent and disinterested observers, merely because they did not fit in with current knowledge. Eventually, by Wallace's casting vote, Barrett was allowed to read his paper to the anthropological sub-section, and when he had finished he appealed to the British Association to form a committee of investigation. But this was too much. They would not do it. They would not even publish the paper. Nevertheless, although unpublished, it caused a lot of talk.

In 1871 interest was aroused by a statement in the quarterly *Journal of Science* by the pioneer physicist, Sir William Crookes, that he had been investigating spiritualistic phenomena. In London a group called the London Dialectical Society was formed with the object of giving a hearing to 'subjects which are ostracised elsewhere, especially those of a metaphysical, religious, social or political character'. Its members invited Thomas Huxley to join them in an investigation of spiritualistic phenomena, but he put them firmly in their place. He was no more interested in their offer, he said, than he would be to listen in to the chatter of old women and curates in a distant cathedral town. Here once again emotional fear of *psi* seems to have driven dispassion out of the window, for it was Thomas Huxley who wrote in a letter to Charles Kingsley: "Sit down before fact like a little child, be prepared to give up every preconceived notion, follow humbly to wherever and to whatever abysses nature leads or you shall learn nothing."

The Dialectical Society did not achieve any outstanding work, but its members originated an idea which was the embryo of some productive experiments later on. They sought to 'educe' supernormal faculties among themselves; that is, it occurred to them that without having recourse to professional spiritualist mediums, it might be possible to study *psi* by experimental 'thought transference', automatic writing and so on, among ordinary people.

Meanwhile Myers, Lord Rayleigh and A. J. Balfour had joined Sidgwick in the study of spiritualism at first hand, and they experimented in their own homes with a number of mediums. It was not a happy experience, for apart from the sordid and deliberate fraud which they often struck, it must have felt like leaving the green lawns of the Backs for mouldy cellars to pass from the rarefied air of Cambridge society to the semi-hysterical emotionalism of the average séance. We get a glimpse of the effort it entailed from a comment by William James, that Myers' passion for truth was strong enough "to carry him into regions where either intellectual or social squeamishness would have been fatal. So he 'mortified' his *amour propre*, unclubbed himself completely and became a model of patience, tact and humility wherever investigation required it." He was largely rewarded, for not only did he collect valuable information about *psi*, he also became a pioneer psychologist. In the days when Freud was working as a youthful student in a physiological laboratory in Vienna, Myers was making a prolonged study of hitherto unrelated phenomena: genius with its sudden 'out of the blue' flashes of creative thought; sleep with its occasional telepathic and precognitive dreams; hypnotic trance; and automatisms and mediumship. These, he said, were not after all unrelated, but were all indications of a larger self, of which man's conscious self was but a fraction, no more indeed than the visible part of an iceberg. He coined a name, the subliminal (sub—beneath, limen—the threshold), for the submerged area of human personality, which Freud made famous as the unconscious. But Myers' view of it differed from Freud's. He called it "a gold mine as well as a rubbish heap". This submerged self, he thought, could only manifest itself through the conscious surface self to a very limited degree. Yet the threshold between

33

the two was a moveable one. There might be upheavals and alterations of personality of many kinds, so that what was once below the surface could for a time or permanently rise above it. In days when psychology was in its infancy, such views showed outstanding insight, particularly in a man whose training had been in the very different discipline of classical scholarship. They were put forward by Myers in a remarkable book *Human Personality*, which contains an account of his life work in search of *psi* and which would have attained far greater fame than it has, had it been written on a less unpopular subject.

But in the seventies such theorising was far ahead; they were still days of tentative and often discouraging groping. In 1874, however, Myers had an encouraging tonic. He met Stainton Moses, an Oxford graduate and a clergyman, who, on being introduced to spiritualism by friends, had found that he could himself produce apparent *psi* phenomena, including automatic writing. Here, for Myers, was the medium of his dreams, a man not out for financial gain and of obvious integrity in ordinary life, a man who resembled himself in standards and in outlook. Stainton Moses is typical of the psychic whose work it is hard to assess eighty years later with the personal factor lacking. For one thing much of his script referred to ostensible experiences in an environment not perceptible *via* the senses, so there was no means by which other people could check its objectivity. The script may all be subconscious fabrication— or it may not. For another, we cannot in theory be sure that the information he gave about 'this world' had not been obtained by normal means, whether conscious or subconscious, for the safeguards against this were not, by present day standards, watertight, and the standards of honesty of his Controls were at times elastic, though their professed morals were of the highest. But there seems no doubt that the conscious Stainton Moses was an upright man, and Myers' acquaintance with him was of real value in confirming that the actual phenomena of mediumship could be produced by persons of intelligence and integrity. It encouraged him to go on.

Here then was interest in *psi* as a subject for scientific study springing up independently in different places. Common sense made it obvious that the enquirers would do well to get together and pool their resources for further research. To this end Sir William Barrett convened a conference in January, 1882. At last *psi*, the elusive, the uncanny, the supernatural, the officially non-existent, was about to have turned on it the searchlight of co-ordinated, cold-blooded scientific research.

CHAPTER V

Foundation of the Society for Psychical Research

THE immediate stimulus which had encouraged Sir William Barrett to call a conference was his own apparent success with some 'thought-transference' experiments in Dublin. These also revived Sidgwick's interest, which had been damped by his dreary and disappointing study of mediumship, and he agreed to attend. At the conference it was decided to found a society, to be called the Society for Psychical Research (now commonly known as the S.P.R.). Its membership was to be broadly based, from scientists who were willing to admit there was something to investigate, to spiritualists who wished to purge their ranks of fraud. To found such a Society was essential if systematic research was to expand, for research even then was expensive and so was the publication of results, and both could obviously be carried on better by a group with a common fund.

The Society's first task was to elect a President. Sidgwick was the obvious choice. "His reputation for sanity, truthfulness and fairness", says Professor C. D. Broad, "was well known to everyone who mattered in England, and ... it was hardly possible to maintain without writing oneself down an ass, that a society over which Sidgwick presided ... consisted of knaves and fools, concealing superstition under a cloak of verbiage. Needless to say, this feat was not found to exceed the capacity of some critics, but with almost anyone else as President their numbers would have been far greater and their influence might have sufficed to kill the Society."[1]

Sidgwick's friends put great pressure on him to accept the

[1] C. D. Broad, Essay on Sidgwick in *Religion, Philosophy and Psychical Research* (Routledge & Kegan Paul, 1953).

presidency. Myers and Gurney said that they were only prepared to join the Society if he did so. But it was asking a lot of a busy man. Why, as Myers put it, should he devote time and energy to getting the moon for a child who had not even cried for it? Fortunately for the Society he finally agreed to undertake the task. And he was supremely fitted for it. He had studied *psi* longer than anyone else and he was no fly-away visionary but exceedingly matter of fact. Indeed, he kept the noses of S.P.R. members so firmly down to earth for so many years that they formed the habit and have dutifully remained there ever since.

Among the men who became Sidgwick's colleagues were Sir William Crookes, Lord Rayleigh and Gerald Balfour. His wife felt unable to join until two years later, in spite of her great interest, for she was playing a major rôle in the founding of Newnham College and dared not risk adding to the east winds of contempt it already had to endure. Not that England in the eighties was the world of Copernicus or Galileo or Roger Bacon. These eminent men and women did not risk torture or death. But they did risk—and suffer—the hostile scorn which the herd usually metes out to heretics. "We were told somewhat roughly", Sidgwick wrote, "that being just like all other fools who collected old women's stories and solemnly recorded the tricks of impostors, we only made ourselves the more ridiculous by assuming the aims of a scientific society and varnishing this wretched nonsense with technical jargon." Moreover, their task was the lonely one of pioneering into the blue. "Our methods, our canons", wrote Myers in later years, "were all to make. In those early days we were more devoid of precedence, of guidance, even of criticism that went beyond mere expressions of contempt than is now readily conceived."

Before setting to work on research, they had to define their subject. It was, they said, that large group of debatable phenomena designated by such terms as mesmeric, psychical and spiritualistic. It was in fact everything that was vaguely known at the time as supernatural; in other words everything that to scientists was non-existent, to the rest of the world beyond the realm of natural law. But from *belief* in the supernatural—from belief as such of any kind—they were at once careful to dissociate the society. "To prevent misconception", they wrote, "it is here expressly stated that Membership of this Society does not imply the acceptance of any particular explanation of the phenomena investigated, nor any belief as to the operation, in the physical world, of forces other than those recognised by Physical Science." This was matter-of-fact and uncompromising enough, but it did not prevent the misconceptions, in particular the unfortunate confusion of psychical research with spiritualism.

Their next step was to classify, with Victorian majesty of expression, the various forms of *psi* which they hoped to investigate. Among other projects, their list included:

(1) An examination of the nature and extent of any influence which may be exerted by one mind upon another, apart from any generally recognised mode of perception.

(2) The study of hypnotism, and the forms of so-called mesmeric trance, with its alleged insensibility to pain; clairvoyance, and other allied phenomena.

(3) A careful investigation of any reports, resting on strong testimony, regarding apparitions at the moment of death, or otherwise, or regarding disturbances in houses reputed to be haunted.

(4) An enquiry into the various physical phenomena commonly called spiritualistic; with an attempt to discover their causes and general laws.

(5) The collection and collation of existing materials bearing on the history of these subjects.

This was a formidable task, involving a very great deal of detailed work, as anyone who has tried to investigate even one case of apparent *psi* will know; and formidable too were the standards with which they expected the S.P.R. to undertake it. These were, they pronounced in the same rolling Victorian prose, "to approach these various problems without prejudice or prepossession of any kind, and in the same spirit of exact and unimpassioned enquiry which has enabled science to solve so many problems, once not less obscure nor less hotly debated." Exact and unimpassioned enquiry, without prejudice or prepossession of any kind. *Psi* had never before been faced with that, and even Sidgwick and his friends did not realise how hard to attain was the ideal they had set themselves—and their successors—in a subject which so easily stirs the depths in human nature. But they strove towards it so well that their work is still a model, even though our present knowledge of psychology—arrived at partly as the result of their work—has shown that some evidence which in their day seemed inexorably to point towards *psi*, can now be otherwise explained.

Their main question was simple: Does *psi* occur? To ask why and how came later. They soon reached the conclusion that the answer was an emphatic Yes. And this their successors have confirmed. But living as we do in a different mental climate, with a different approach to the eternal question of mind-body relationship, our interpretation of its nature and implications is more tentative than theirs. And we are only now learning to formulate such further and vital questions as: In what personal relationships does it occur? To what psychological needs does it minister? Is, for example, the urge to make contact with another human being, when this is impossible by more usual means, often or always behind it?

The methods of science when studying a new phenomenon are quite clear cut. First, observe it as often and as objectively as possible. Next, tentatively put forward a possible cause for it. And finally, learn to reproduce it in controlled conditions, as and when required. This procedure is comparatively easy in the physical sciences; less so in biology; less so again in psychology; and in psychical research immensely difficult.

So far evidence for *psi* has been found mainly in four ways. The most recent is by controlled experiments, which have been frequently repeated in laboratory conditions and assessed mathematically to estimate the number of coincidences which may have occurred by chance. It thus conforms to the accepted standards of the physical sciences. The other sources of evidence are automatic writing, the utterances of sensitives or mediums, and spontaneous cases reported by the public. This evidence differs in kind from that provided by controlled experiments. It is not exactly repeatable, but is rather of the type to be found in a court of law, and it involves in nearly every case an element of subjective judgment in the assessment of its value. To begin with, it was the only kind of evidence available to the researchers of the new Society.

Very early, however, they realised the vital importance of the first type of evidence, ESP to order, assessable as physical phenomena were assessable, and they set out with enormous energy to devise all kinds of experiments. Some of these were of a type which they hoped could be checked by statistics, and much care was devoted to working out suitable formulae. Others were attempts to 'transmit' such things as simple drawings, as they described it, 'from mind to mind'. Apart from a few tentative efforts by the London Dialectical Society, all this was breaking new ground. The experiments had to be invented from scratch. In one case very striking results were obtained. Two gentlemen in Liverpool, Malcolm Guthrie, J.P., and James Birchall, a Headmaster and Honorary Secretary of the Liverpool Literary and Philosophical Society, tried to convey drawings by telepathy to two percipients—both women—and their success was such that they appealed to students of science in Liverpool to take a hand. Among those who responded was the physicist, Sir Oliver Lodge, then a young man and an expert experimenter in physics. The result of one successful experiment is given in Fig. I, and a short extract from the original report of the series in S.P.R. *Proceedings* will indicate how they were done. "The originals of the following diagrams were for the most part drawn in another room from that in which the 'subject' was placed. The few executed in the same room were drawn while the 'subject' was blindfolded, at a distance from her, and in such a way that the process would have been wholly invisible to her or to anyone else, even had an attempt been made to observe it. During the process of transference, the agent looked steadily and in perfect silence at the original drawing which was placed upon an intervening wooden stand; the 'subject' sitting opposite him and behind the stand, blindfolded and quite still. The 'agent' ceased looking at the drawing, and the blindfold was removed, only when the 'subject' professed herself ready to make the

40

FIG. I

Originals

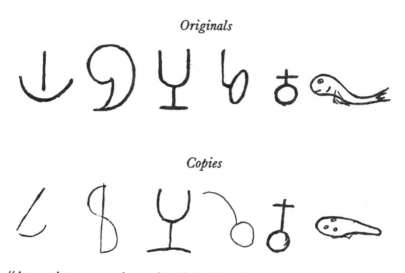

Copies

"A complete consecutive series of six drawings transmitted by telepathy from Mr. Guthrie to Miss E. without contact during the Liverpool experiment. . . . When No. 6 was being transmitted, Miss E. said almost directly, 'Are you thinking of the bottom of the sea, with shells and fishes?' and then, 'Is it a snail or a fish?'—then drew as above."

Proceedings S.P.R., Vol. II.

reproduction, which happened usually in times varying from half a minute to two or three minutes."[1]

Results of this kind were unexpected and startled the experimenters. Desperate attempts have since been made to explain them away, but this is not easy, for both Guthrie and Birchall were men of known integrity and Lodge not only controlled some of the experiments in their absence with the same care he gave to work in his own laboratory, but at times he also acted as agent himself. He introduced some interesting variations, including the use of two agents to look at the drawing, and these he described in a letter to *Nature* (Vol. XXX, 1884):

"One evening last week—after two thinkers, or agents, had been several times successful in instilling the idea of some object or drawing, at which they were looking, into the mind of the blindfold person, or percipient—I brought into the room a double opaque sheet of thick paper with a square drawn on one side and a St. Andrew's cross or X on the other, and silently arranged it between the two agents so that each looked on one side without any notion of what was on the other. The percipient was not informed in any way that a novel modification was being made; and, as usual, there was no contact of any sort or kind—a clear space of several feet existing between each of the three people. I thought that by this variation I should decide whether one of the two agents was more active than the other; or, supposing them about equal whether two ideas in two separate minds could be fused into one by the percipient.

In a very short time the percipient made the following remarks, every one else being silent: 'The thing won't keep still.' 'I seem to see things moving about.' 'First I see a thing up there, and then one down there.' 'I can't see either distinctly.' The object was then hidden, and the percipient was told to take off the bandage and to draw the impression in her mind on a sheet of paper. She drew a square and then said, 'There was the other thing as well,' and drew a cross inside the square from corner to corner, saying afterwards, 'I don't know what made me put it inside.' "

It will be noted that the drawings reproduced above are consecutive; it is not a matter of choosing the best hits among

[1] *Proceedings* S.P.R., Vol. II, pp. 24–42. See also Vol. II, pp. 189–200, and Vol. III, pp. 424–452.

many thousand misses. And, but for the last one, they are designs rather than representations of physical objects, so that to believe what is sometimes suggested—that the agent unconsciously whispered instructions as to what to draw and was heard by the percipient alone and by no-one else in the room—is something of a strain on one's credulity.

These experiments were the ancestors of others done at intervals throughout the years in England, France, Germany and the U.S.A. with comparable results; and when such parallels occur time and again, with different people in different places, they begin to acquire the evidential value of repeated experiments.

The early investigators, however, were mainly concerned with what may be called spontaneous *psi* or cases which seemed to occur without any pre-arrangement. A fair number of such cases had already been collected by Sidgwick, Myers and a few other enthusiasts before the formation of the S.P.R., but these were not nearly enough. The immediate—and enormous—task was to go out into the highways and byways and get hold of a great many more, checked, verified and corroborated to the greatest possible extent. Gurney and Myers threw themselves into it with their usual thoroughness, and they also enlisted the help of Frank Podmore, a competent worker from the Oxford group of enquirers. In 1883 alone they wrote ten thousand letters, which they followed up with innumerable interviews. These involved much travelling—and much tact. The investigation of spontaneous cases of *psi* is exceedingly delicate. The difficulty of getting, say, a motor car accident accurately reported, even on the spot, at the time, and by detached witnesses, is well-known. It is far greater when the incident is in the past and the personal emotions of the witnesses are involved; and emotions can be even more deeply involved in a case of *psi* than in a lawsuit. There is a very human desire for the marvellous and an equally human desire to feel important. Quite unconsciously, therefore, some people will twist evidence to sound watertight when there are tiny leaks in it. Others, again, may have a latent tendency to hysteria, resulting in hallucinations which seem to them to have an exterior origin when in fact they are self-created.

43

Fortunately Myers and Gurney were endowed with good judgment and great industry and they collected a large crop of raw material. Having no precedents to follow, they had to begin by establishing their own canons of evidence, and these were so high that after seventy years the dispassionate critic can find little to cavil at, except that as in their day less was known about the extraordinary vagaries of human memory, their attitude towards old cases was less cautious than ours. In their view much of the material they collected fell under the heading of the first item in their list, which Myers defined as "the communication of impressions of any kind from one mind to another independently of the recognised channels of sense" and which he labelled telepathy. In general the material was found to take roughly one of two patterns:

(1) a percipient, B, gets an impression of an event or of a state of mind occurring to an agent, A, or
(2) B feels aware of the presence of A when A in fact is physically elsewhere.

Numbers of such cases were reported to them, but it soon became obvious that few were ideally watertight, though many came close to it. For a case to be susceptible of *no* explanation but ESP several factors were necessary.

(1) B must write down or describe to somebody else his impression of A shortly after its occurrence and—most important—before knowledge of the event described could have reached him by normal means;
(2) there must be reliable evidence of what actually did occur to A at the approximate time of B's impression;
(3) one person at least must confirm that B told him of his impression before B could have heard of the event himself by normal means.

The three investigators were satisfied that many out of the thousands of cases they studied were at least not due to fraud and were most unlikely all to be chance coincidences, and they made a collection of these entitled *Phantasms of the Living*, which has become a classic.[1] These cases and the many others which have subsequently been collected by the S.P.R. range from the trivial to impressions of serious crisis. Here in summary are typical examples of each. Mrs. Atlay, the wife of the Bishop of Hereford, dreamed that after reading morning prayers in the hall of the palace she went into the dining room for breakfast and found an enormous pig standing between the sideboard and the table. She was so amused at this dream that she told it to the children and their governess before prayers began. After prayers she went into the dining room and there she found a pig standing where she had seen one in her dream. It had escaped from its sty while prayers were being read. It has been suggested—not by a farmer—that the true explanation of this case is that one of the children hastened to the sty, drove the pig up to the palace dining room and persuaded it to remain there alone in the right position until his mother arrived.

The next case, an impression of crisis, occurred when the percipient, a Mrs. Bettany, was a child of ten.[2] "I was reading geometry as I walked along [a country lane]," she reported, ". . . when in a moment I saw a bedroom known as the White Room in my home, and upon the floor lay my mother, to all appearance dead. The vision must have remained some minutes, during which time my real surroundings appeared to pale and die out; but as the vision faded, actual surroundings came back, at first dimly, and then clearly. I could not doubt that what I had seen was real, so instead of going home, I went at once to the house of our medical man and found him at home. He at once set out with me for my home, on the way putting questions I could not answer, as my mother was to all appearance well when I left home. I led the doctor straight to the White Room, where we found my mother actually lying as in my vision. This was true even to minute details. She had been seized suddenly by an attack of the heart, and would soon have breathed her last but for the doctor's timely advent. I shall get my father and mother to read and sign this."[3]

[1] Edmund Gurney, F. W. H. Myers and Frank Podmore, *Phantasms of the Living* (Trubner, 1886).   [2] *Ibid.*
[3] *Phantasms of the Living*, Vol. I, p. 194.

In answer to questions Mrs. Bettany added:

"I was in no anxiety about my mother at the time of the vision.

I found a handkerchief with a lace border beside her on the floor. This I had distinctly noticed in my vision.

This was the only occasion, I believe, on which I saw a scene transported apparently into the actual field of vision, to the exclusion of objects and surroundings actually present. I have had other visions in which I have seen events happening as they really were in another place, but I have been also conscious of real (i.e. immediate) surroundings."

When Myers and Gurney had a large number of cases collected together under their own eyes an interesting point emerged. Though few of them, taken alone, were evidentially perfect, they were seen to have factors in common to an extent which looked incredible had each case been separately 'invented'. The two investigators also found it incredible that hundreds of people who did not know each other should "draw the same arbitrary line between mistakes and exaggerations of which they will be guilty and those of which they will not." Neither could they believe that the hypothesis of chance was elastic enough to cover the lot, for that would involve a normal explanation for each one of these hundreds of cases; explanations which had been sought for by themselves at length and in vain.[1]

[1] In a number of cases, collected by Myers and Gurney and by others later, chance coincidence is rendered more improbable by the fact that the percipient's impression and the event which seems to have caused it correspond in several details. In the two following dreams, cited by G. N. M. Tyrrell in *The Personality of Man* (Pelican Books 1947), there are no less than seven items which correspond. "On the 7th October, 1938, Monsieur X (the real names are all known) attended a reception at the house of Madame Y in Brussels. He left at 10.30 p.m. The same night Madame Y had the following dream: She is at the railway station with a gentleman (unknown); several friends see her off, including Monsieur X. Suddenly the train starts and Madame Y leaves without having time to take all her luggage. She calls through the open window to Monsieur X: 'Please bring my luggage and don't forget the yellow suitcase.' Arrived at her destination, she goes upstairs to the luggage depôt and finds all her luggage except the yellow suitcase. Monsieur X is there, too, and the lady severely rebukes him for his negligence."

"The next morning, 8th October, 1938, Madame Y related her dream to a witness, Monsieur Z: and an hour or so afterwards, while Monsieur Z was still present, Monsieur X arrived and before anything was said to him about Madame Y's dream, he recounted his own dream of the previous

There were many cases recorded in *Phantasms of the Living* in which people believed themselves actually to have heard or seen friends or relatives who were not physically present at times when they were afterwards discovered to have been in danger or distress or, even more frequently, near the moment of death. These came to be known as crisis cases. Myers and Gurney analysed large numbers of them and came jointly to the conclusion that there was at least a connection between such experiences and the events occurring to the person seen or heard; that is, they seemed to be testimony to some kind of ESP. The actual nature of such apparitions was another problem and much more complicated.

Phantasms of the Living was published in 1886 and was the first authoritative study of *psi* made by members of the S.P.R. It is not, very naturally, without flaw. Some of the cases quoted are now thought to be too old. From the strictest point of view some of the experiments undertaken to test ESP had inadequate safeguards. But it cleared large areas of bush, it laid open new objectives, and for the first time it began to formulate scientific methods of pursuing *psi*. It still makes very instructive reading for, as Gurney said, the impact of such a large number of spontaneous cases is far greater than that of any one isolated case. It also does away with a criticism that particularly aroused Gurney's indignation. Some people, he said, say that such incidents cannot happen now because they did not happen in the past and that they could not have happened in the past because they do not happen now.

Two years after the publication of *Phantasms of the Living* Gurney died suddenly and unexpectedly. This was a blow, not for psychical research alone but for medical psychology in general, for he had also been doing pioneering work in hypnosis. "Gurney's experiments were received with incredulity," wrote the psychoanalyst Dr. T. W. Mitchell, "and few realised that he was laying the foundations on which the psychology of

night, which was as follows: He finds himself at a station and in charge of Madame Y's luggage. A yellow suitcase is specially recommended to his care. He transports all this with great pains, but the yellow suitcase is somehow lost. He mounts the stairs to the luggage depôt and there meets Madame Y. She gives him a severe scolding for his bad behaviour."

abnormal mental states during the next twenty years was to be based."

In spite of the severe loss which they had incurred through Gurney's death, by the end of the 1880's the founders of the S.P.R. felt that they had grounds for restrained optimism. In their view experimentation had already indicated that it was not impossible to evoke ESP deliberately, and one experimenter had even appeared to succeed in making an apparition of himself visible to a friend at a distance. In spontaneous cases too they had found a significant number of impressions and hallucinations which coincided with distant contemporary events, and these were beginning to show a pattern. Consequently, in 1889 Sidgwick felt able to report to the Society that the committee appointed to investigate telepathy (the Gurney–Myers group) had pronounced decisively in its favour and had produced 1200 pages of evidence to support their statement.

Sidgwick and his co-heretics believed their findings to be so impressive that in spite of the inherent improbability of *psi* the outer world would accept them or at least consider that a case had been made out for further investigation. But they were wrong: their case rebounded like a tennis ball off a wall and, except by a very few, their work was ignored. Among those few, however, were some who mattered. Oliver Lodge joined the S.P.R. and so did a clever Australian lawyer, Richard Hodgson, who had come to study philosophy at Cambridge. He was a man of remarkable character and under Sidgwick's guidance he became an outstanding investigator, with a flair for unmasking the tricks of fraudulent psychics. Like Myers and Gurney he ended by devoting his life to psychical research, but he worked mainly in America where, together with William James, who took a deep interest in the subject and wrote a good deal about it, and Proffessor J. H. Hyslop, another able worker, he laid the foundations of the American S.P.R. in the same basic fashion as their colleagues had done in England. It is tempting to describe their work in more detail but to do more than indicate the highlights in either country would make this sketch too long.

48

Mrs. Sidgwick was now actively working for the English S.P.R. and she had taken on a young biologist, Alice Johnson, as her secretary. This was a fortunate choice. Alice Johnson was a small, quiet, kindly woman of extreme integrity, but under her gentle exterior she possessed a mind as acute and critical, as little impressed with the marvellous, as that of Mrs. Sidgwick herself. Later on she became editor of the Society's *Proceedings* and finally, years later, its research officer. A nice story is told of a visit paid to Mrs. Sidgwick and Miss Johnson in their old age by the Irish authoress, Martin Ross, who was anxious to impress them with her remarkable discovery of a tiny slipper on an Irish hillside. It was no doubt, she explained, the work of a leprechaun. "Did they think your evidence watertight?" a friend asked her after the visit. "They did not!" she replied indignantly. "Those two white-headed old weevils would bore a hole in anything!"

One of the first investigations undertaken by these two rather formidable ladies was on a major scale. In 1889, undeterred by the lack of general interest in psychical research, Henry Sidgwick set on foot a large project to compile a Census of Hallucinations.[1] For his team he chose the two Myers brothers, Frank Podmore, Mrs. Sidgwick and Alice Johnson. The main object of the Census was to question a representative section of the public for evidence of telepathy, in particular telepathy which appeared to take the form of waking hallucinations. Dreams were excluded.

Hallucination is another of those words which, through much knocking around in popular speech, has acquired all sorts of unfortunate associations, so that it now conjures up visions of drugs, drink and disease, of pink elephants and snakes. But there is no suggestion of morbidity in its dictionary definition: "any supposed sensory perception which has no objective counterpart within the field of vision, hearing, etc." A hallucination, in other words, is a percept, though not one which has been aroused by an outside impact on a sense organ. It was

[1] *Proceedings* S.P.R., Vol. X, pp. 25–422. A detailed description of the Census' findings is contained in G. N. M. Tyrrell's *Apparitions* (Duckworth, 1953).

found through the Census that such harmless hallucinations occur not infrequently to perfectly normal people in perfectly good health. They might be called the equivalent of waking dreams.

Sidgwick's team—all volunteers—worked like beavers on the Census for five years. They collected 17,000 replies from members of the public to the question: had they ever, when awake, had the impression of seeing or hearing or of being touched by anything which, so far as they could discover, was not due to any external cause? Nearly ten per cent of the persons approached answered Yes. (A similar though smaller Census was taken in 1948, in which 14·3 per cent answered Yes). The ten per cent were then put through a friendly third degree, as a result of which it was found that a number of their hallucinations appeared to be veridical: that is, they tallied with distant, more or less contemporary situations, which were at the time unknown to the percipients. Of these, a large proportion were crisis cases, many of them connected with a death. It now struck the committee that here might be an opportunity for tackling the bogy of chance coincidence in a big way. They would take veridical waking hallucinations, occurring within twelve hours either way of the death of the person seen or heard—this was an arbitrary period but they had to impose some limit—as a basis for estimating such coincidences. The probability that any particular person in the British Isles would die on any particular day they worked out to be about one in 19,000. Thus, on that basis, if chance only were involved, no more than one in 19,000 hallucinations should be a death coincidence. They then went through their cases with a tooth comb and an outsize conscience, making almost exaggerated deductions for possible faulty reporting and other errors. But they were still left with a proportion of death coincidences to waking hallucinations that was not one in 19,000, but one in 43, or 440 times the number likely to be caused by chance alone. This, they felt, was satisfactory. And the improbability of chance coincidence was actually greater than they estimated, since the time correspondence was often much closer than twelve hours, and they deliberately took each

50

case as a simple one, whereas there were often a number of coincidences within a case.[1] In the view of Sidgwick's team these results were valuable testimony for ESP on the grounds that if unusual experiences frequently coincided with events unknown to the percipients, it was very likely that one was the cause of the other.

Gurney and Myers were the first serious students of apparitions to accept them as genuine phenomena. But what kind of phenomena? There was no evading the difficult question: What is an apparition? Gurney proposed an ingenious hypothesis to get over the embarrassing snag of having to postulate a non-physical vehicle for them. An apparition, he suggested, might be an hallucination constructed by the percipient himself to present his surface consciousness, in a form it would be willing to accept, with information which had been telepathically acquired by his subconscious self. To project such an hallucination might be a way to evade his own 'censor'. Gurney's is a psychologically plausible theory, but it is hard to fit to traditional haunting apparitions, some of which appear to have been seen by a number of people independently, each being ignorant that they had been seen before. Gurney also ran into trouble when he tried to fit his theory to collective cases, in which apparitions are reported to have been seen by several persons at the same time, each observing the correct aspect from their own angle, as if the figure had been a normal physical one. His solution here was that in the first place one person only had the experience and that his companions then 'caught' it telepathically from him. Myers allowed himself a little more latitude than Gurney. It was also possible, he thought, that at times and in some way not yet understood, the agent of an apparition did actually 'invade' the 'space' in which the percipient was placed, so that anyone else who was with him

[1] In 1922 a second collection of spontaneous cases of *psi* was made by Mrs. Sidgwick, which showed similar characteristics to those in the Census of Hallucinations, and in 1939 Sir Ernest Bennett, an ultra-cautious investigator, published a further volume. Much can be learnt by comparing collections made at different times. The first Census, for instance, showed that 32% of the hallucinations reported were of living persons, 14·3% of the dead, and 33·2% were unidentified. The 1948 survey gave 40·5%, 9·0% and 27·5%, a roughly similar proportion.

could also see it—though, as a matter of fact, they more often did not.

The immediate result of their study of apparitions was to bring the founders of the S.P.R. right up against that most knotty of all questions: Does man survive bodily death?

CHAPTER VI

Does Man Survive Death?

THE problem of man's survival of death was more vivid and immediate to the early researchers than it is to us, for survival had been an axiom all but universally accepted for thousands of years and the guns of modern science had only recently begun to submit it to heavy bombardment. They lived at a time when the irresistible force of modern science was beginning to crack up against the immoveable post of religious belief. Sidgwick's own words bring their predicament home to us. "When we took up seriously the obscure and perplexing investigation which we call psychical research, we were mainly moved to do so by the profound and painful division and conflict as regards the nature and destiny of the human soul, which we found in the thought of our age. On the one hand, under the influence of Christian teaching, still dominant over the minds of the majority of educated persons, and powerfully influencing many even of those who have discarded its dogmatic system, the soul is conceived as independent of the bodily system and destined to survive it. On the other hand, the preponderant tendency of modern physiology has been more and more to exclude this conception, and to treat the life and processes of any individual mind as inseparably connected with the life and processes of the short-lived body that it animates . . . Now our own position was this. We believed unreservedly in the methods of modern science, and were prepared to accept submissively her reasoned conclusions, when sustained by the agreement of experts; but we were not prepared to submit with equal docility to the mere prejudices of scientific men. And it appeared to us that there was an important body of evidence—tending prima facie to establish the independence of soul or spirit—which modern science had simply left on one side with ignorant contempt; and that in so leaving it she had been untrue to her professed method and had arrived prematurely at her negative conclusions. Observe that we did not affirm that these negative conclusions were scientifically erroneous. To have said that would have been to fall into the very error we were trying to avoid. We only said that they had been arrived at prematurely . . ."[1]

Myers devoted the first volume of *Human Personality* to the study of what he called "the actions and perceptions of spirits still in the flesh", and the second to an inquiry into "the actions of spirits no longer in the flesh, and into the forms of perception with which men . . . respond to the unfamilar agency". He did not accept the popular notion that an apparition was the whole of a deceased personality, but looked on it as merely a manifestation of persistent personal energy, continuing after the shock of death; a manifestation incomplete, probably telepathic in nature and profoundly difficult to achieve. "An apparition", he said, "is a function of two variables: the incarnate spirit's sensitivity and the discarnate spirit's capacity of self-manifestation."

But although they admitted that such manifestations might be faint and fragmentary, it will be noted that neither Myers nor those of his colleagues who with him became convinced of survival—there were some who did not—seemed to doubt the traditional assumption that the human spirit was a separate entity inhabiting a physical body, or that it was the whole of this entity which survived with all its idiosyncracies, loves and hates. Nowadays, when what is called personality seems to be so intimately connected with endocrine glands, even those who accept the possibility of some kind of survival find so complete a form of it a very tough nut to swallow. It must not be forgotten, of course, that the early pioneers were only beginning to realise the dramatic talents of the subconscious when ministering to the psychological needs of its 'owner', and that, in consequence, alternative explanations to survival for some of the phenomena they unearthed were less plausible for them than they are for us. Also it so happened that the hypothesis of telepathy fitted many

[1] Henry Sidgwick, *Presidential Address*, 1888. *Proceedings* S.P.R., Vol. V, p. 271.

of their cases of spontaneous *psi* like a glove and they did not think of looking for other explanations, although it is now apparent that many, if not all, could also be attributed to clairvoyance, thus transferring the initiative to the percipient. They also took for granted that precognition, if it occurred at all in human beings, only did so to the slightest degree and they therefore assumed that testimony for it implied the existence of discarnate beings with a wider sweep of vision. This assumption also blinded them to the fact that precognition or retrocognition plus telepathy or clairvoyance could provide an alternative explanation for further phenomena which otherwise had an overwhelmingly strong appearance of having come from the dead. In the end Lord Rayleigh, Crookes, Myers, Mrs. Sidgwick, Gurney, Lodge and William James all accepted survival. Sidgwick and Podmore were never convinced of it although they accepted ESP.

The evidence upon which the early workers formed their opinions was of two kinds: spontaneous phenomena apparently originating with the dead, and the utterances of certain mediums whom the most rigorous investigation and surveillance had shown to be honest.

Myers observed that in ESP between the living there were three main classes of 'messages': sensory hallucinations, emotional impulses and impulses to action, and definite intellectual messages. He found too that what appeared to be post-mortem communications could also be divided into the same three classes. His argument that this resemblance was evidence for survival takes over 600 large pages to expound and illustrate and cannot fairly be summarised in half a dozen. The spontaneous cases he studied divide roughly into six types. First, direct death coincidences. Gurney had pointed out that nearly three-quarters of the apparent *psi* experiences recorded in *Phantasms of the Living* either coincided with the agent's death or very shortly followed it. This might be indirect evidence of survival since it suggested that there was something within a man which was free enough of bodily activities to make contact with distant friends around his time of death.

But the situation was sometimes reversed. The dying person

seemed to be not the agent but the percipient, and cried out as if in welcome to persons already dead. There was one variant of this phenomenon which Myers and Gurney felt could not be entirely ignored. There have been times when a dying person has also greeted, with his friends known to be dead, another person whom both he and his living friends had believed to be alive and well, but who, unknown to them, had died. Sir William Barrett collected a number of such cases.[1]

Apparitions clustering round the moment of death of the apparent agent might be explained by assuming that they were all caused by telepathic impacts which originated while he was still alive and remained latent for a time in the percipient's subconscious mind. But this hypothesis is somewhat strained by a second class of apparitions which are seen months or even years after the agent's death. Myers records one such case concerning a Mr. Akhurst, who was deeply in love with a certain lady. She married another man, Mr. Clark, but that Akhurst remained in love with her was clear enough when he visited her and her husband about two years later. He left them to go to Yorkshire and Mrs. Clark did not hear from him again. Not quite three months later her baby was born, and shortly afterwards, very early one morning, he 'appeared' to her as she was feeding the baby. "I felt a cold waft of air through the room," she reported, "and a feeling as though somebody had touched my shoulder ... Raising my eyes to the door (which faced me) I saw Akhurst standing in his shirt and trousers looking at me, when he seemed to pass through the door."

Mr. Clark corroborated that his wife had told him of her vision later the same morning but that he had dismissed it as nonsense. She had, however, persisted and had said that Akhurst had been wearing only his shirt and trousers. On enquiry they learnt that ten weeks earlier Akhurst had been found dead clad in shirt and trousers, having taken an over-dose of chloral.[2] This is one of many independent cases when the

---

[1] Sir William Barrett, *Deathbed Visions* (Methuen, 1926).
[2] F. W. H. Myers, *Human Personality*, Vol. II, pp. 371–2 (Longmans, 1954).

person who has the experience, whatever it may be, also has an impression of physical cold. An element of frustrated attachment similar to Akhurst's has been noticed in cases of ESP between the living, particularly in those in which the ESP appears to crop up frequently between the same two persons. It is as if intense desire on one side or the other—or on both—can open channels of communication normally closed.

A Mrs. V, wife of a man who had held an important post in India, gave Myers four cases which illustrate some of the testimony for survival produced by apparitions and also the strength and weakness of such cases. (The concealment of names is tiresome but understandable, for sensitive persons are naturally reluctant to have their intimate and emotionally disturbing experiences discussed in public.) Myers knew Mr. and Mrs. V. well and recorded that she had had other similar experiences which were too intimate to make public. The first case she gave him was a death coincidence, but it could be explained away as the subjective result of her own anxiety. "In 1874", she reported, "I was in India at a hill station. On the 7th June between one and three o'clock in the morning, I woke with the sensation that half my life had been taken away from me (I can only describe the feeling in this vague way). I sat up and pressed my side in wonder at what was happening. I then saw most beautiful lights at the end of the room. These lights gave place to a cloud and after a few moments the face of a dear sister then living (as I believed) appeared in the cloud which remained a little while and then faded away. I became much alarmed and at once felt I should hear bad news of my sister who was living in London and had been very ill, though the last accounts we had received had been better. I told my husband what had happened and when a telegram was brought by a friend at eight o'clock in the morning I knew what the contents must be. The telegram contained news of my sister's death the previous night."[1]

The second case reported by Mrs. V. occurred eleven years later. It was an apparition of her dead sister, who still seemed to be concerned with the welfare of the living. It may thus

[1] *Human Personality*, Vol. II, pp. 332–3 (Longmans, 1954).

suggest survival but it could be dismissed as created subconsciously by Mrs. V. alone. "I was present in Church at the Confirmation of my sister's youngest boy", she told Myers. "I was in the left hand gallery of the Church, the boy in the body of the Church, on the right side. As I was kneeling, I looked at the opposite gallery which was of dark wood. I here saw the figure of my sister, the head and arms outstretched high above the boy as if blessing him. For the moment I thought it was impossible, and closed my eyes for a few seconds. Opening them again I saw the same beautiful form, which almost immediately vanished."

Mrs. V's. third case can again be dismissed as the result of her anxiety about a dying man. Or it can be explained as a telepathic impact from the man's wife, who was longing for her presence and who subconsciously conveyed to her the brother's name. Or it can be taken at its face value, which hints that the wife's deceased brother felt continuing concern for her welfare and was trying to persuade Mrs. V. to go to her aid. Here is Mrs. V's. account. "In India, in the winter of 1881, the husband of an acquaintance was lying dangerously ill at a hotel about five miles from us. Knowing this I went frequently to enquire for him. One particular evening I remained with his wife some time as the doctor thought his condition most critical. When I returned home about ten o'clock that night I ordered beef essence and jellies to be made to send early the next morning.

"The night was perfectly calm and sultry, not a leaf stirring. About twelve o'clock the venetians in my bedroom suddenly began to shake and knockings were heard, which seemed to proceed from a box under my writing table. The knocking and shaking of the venetians went on for half an hour or more, off and on. During this time I heard a name whispered, A— B—, of which the Christian name was unknown to me, the surname being the maiden name of the sick man's wife. I felt so certain I was wanted at the hotel that I wished to start at once, but I was advised not to do so that hour of the night. Early the next morning a messenger arrived with a note begging me to go at once to the hotel, as my friend's husband had died at one o'clock. When I reached the hotel she told me how she had wished to send for me during the night whilst his death was impending. I ... found that the Christian name I had heard whispered was the name of her brother who had died seven years previously."

The fourth case occurred when Mrs. V. was staying at a villa in the South of France, and at its face value it may suggest survival as the apparition was of a person Mrs. V. believed to be unknown to her. "One night", she told Myers, "soon after we arrived, I went from my room upstairs to fetch something in the drawing room (which was on the ground floor) and saw a slight figure going down the stairs before me in a white garb with a blue sash and long golden hair. She glided on into a room near the hall door. This startled and impressed me so much that I afterwards went to the house agent and asked if anyone had lately died in that house, with long golden hair. He replied that an American lady, young and slight, with golden hair, had died there a few months before—in the very room into which I had seen the figure gliding."

It is worth considering Mrs. V's. cases a little more closely for they are typical of many others and indicate the problems to be faced when assessing the testimony of spontaneous cases not only for survival but also for ESP. In their favour it can be said that the percipient, Mrs. V., was well-known to Myers, who had had much experience in sifting testimony and was only too well accustomed to embroidered exaggeration by mediums and others. She reported her cases with simplicity, and they 'ring true' to those who have had similar ones. Moreover, her cases resemble many others for which the testimony, at least for ESP, is so good that it needs real intellectual contortions to explain it away.

But there are other factors, some of which reduce their value as evidence. Of Case I Myers for example recorded that "Mr. V. remembers being told of Mrs. V's. vision, though at this distance of time he cannot state whether the telegram announcing the death had arrived before he was told." Of the other cases Myers said, "In Case II he (Mr. V.) was told at once of the incident. On Case III he has made and signed the following remarks: 'The noise resembled the shaking of the lid of the tin box. I got up and went to the box, which continued making the noise, to see if there were rats, but there were none. There were no rats in the house and there was nothing in the box. A night light was burning in the room. The rattling was continuous—not like that a rat could produce. It went on again after I had investigated it in vain. This incident was unique in my experience.' "

Myers further recorded that Mrs. V. added in conversation: " 'The Christian name whispered was Henry. The brother was not an Indian official and I had never heard of him.' Mrs. V's. acquaintance with the lady whose husband was dying was not an intimate one. In Case IV Mr. V. again informs me that he was at once told of the incident."

Myers' notes bring out the kind of evidential weakness that is almost inevitable in spontaneous cases. Case I may not even have been an hallucination, for if Mr. V. could not remember whether he was told about it before or after the arrival of the telegram, it could be said that Mrs. V. imagined the figure as a result of the telegram. In Case III Mrs. V. may have heard the brother's name casually and forgotten it, although her subconscious stored it up. But if this experience is to be dismissed as subjective Mr. V's. corroboration of the rattling box will have to be explained away, and that seems to entail that both Mr. and Mrs. V. were somewhat weak-minded or liars. It is possible that light may be thrown on the box incident by recent experiments in what is called psychokinesis; that is, the alleged power of affecting a distant physical object by mental means without any known transmission of energy (Chapter XVI). In Case IV it can again be said that Mrs. V. had heard of the young American and forgotten it.

Myers also found evidence for survival in the apparent display of active initiative by the dead. One of such cases he quoted was exhaustively investigated by Richard Hodgson.[1] An American farmer was found dead in an outhouse far from his home, and strangers prepared his body for burial in garments which included a pair of black satin slippers of a new

[1] *Proceedings* S.P.R., Vol. VIII, pp. 200–5.

pattern unknown in his home district. His own clothes, which were filthy, were thrown away outside the morgue. On hearing of her father's death, one of his daughters fainted and remained unconscious for a long period. On coming round she declared she had seen her father and correctly described his burial garments, including the slippers. She then asked for his old clothes, saying that he had told her that after leaving home he had sewn a large roll of dollar bills inside his grey shirt in a pocket he had made from a piece of her old red dress, and that the money was still there. To soothe the girl her brother made a journey to retrieve the clothes and in the presence of a number of people the money was found in the red pocket as she had said.[1]

[1] The arguments used to explain away even the most apparently water-tight spontaneous cases are usefully summarised in *Psychical Research Today*, by D. J. West (Duckworth, 1954).

CHAPTER VII

Mediumship—Mrs. Piper

THE early researchers also sought for evidence of survival in the utterances of mediums. The term medium, as Myers said, is a question-begging and barbarous one, since it assumes that the information which mediums acquire does not come from this world even by ESP, but is given them by the dead. Unfortunately, too, the term is used, not only for mental mediumship—trance utterance, automatic writing and so on—but for physical mediumship as well. Physical mediumship is the alleged power of producing physical phenomena by means of emanations from the human body or by other unknown methods. There is a little evidence in its favour, but not enough to include it in a short study of the trail leading to established facts. If possible it has been—and is—even more dishonestly faked than mental mediumship and one of the tasks which fell to the lot of the S.P.R. was to expose the activities of fake mediums who make a good living by representing lengths of butter muslin to sorrowing widows as their departed husbands, and other similar frauds. One of their activities is to produce what are known as apports, or small objects which they claim to bring from afar by psychic means. On one occasion the Hon. Everard Feilding, who was at the time research officer for the S.P.R., arranged a sitting with a reputed physical medium, of whom he had his doubts. She was unwise enough to leave him alone in her room beforehand and he took the opportunity to have a look behind the curtains. Attached to these he found a number of prawns, and round their necks he tied bows of pink ribbon with which he had had the foresight to come provided. Thus adorned the prawns duly appeared at his sitting, purporting to have been brought from the sea by psychic means.

Throughout the ages mediumship had been looked upon as a

supernatural power and often too as witchcraft. It was something outside nature. The first generation of S.P.R. workers put it on the map to be studied as a natural phenomenon. Myers, with his usual insight, realised that it was linked with dreams, genius, hypnosis and automatisms, and that all these phenomena were signs of the existence of a subconscious self with certain powers more extended than those of surface consciousness. It was less difficult for him and his co-workers than it is for us to envisage the possibility that mediumship was also a means of communicating with the dead, not only because of the widespread assumption in their day that the spirit of man was an entity separable from his body, but because they were inclined to look upon telepathy as a matter of comparatively straightforward transmission of conscious thought from 'mind to mind'. It thus seemed to them not unreasonable to suppose that the discarnate, if they existed, could transmit a message by telepathy to a person specially endowed to receive it, who could then pass it on to others.

As studies progressed, however, particularly after the death of Myers, it became apparent that mediumship, whatever its nature, was infinitely more complex than this. Take the problem of the form in which communication through trance mediums purports to come. Trance is not, as many people think, an uncanny affair. As a rule the medium merely sits down in a chair, gives some deep sighs and a groan or two and falls asleep, to awaken a few minutes later apparently as another person. This is the Spiritualists' Control, whom they believe to be a discarnate spirit, able temporarily to manipulate the medium's body. His functions, they claim, are to protect the medium from invasion by the many spirits who wish to communicate with the sitter or with others still alive. Occasionally, with the Control's permission, one of these communicators purports to take over from him for a time.

Investigation began to concentrate upon this curious phenomenon and it began to look as if the whole dramatic form of Control and communicator might in fact be play-acting on the part of the medium's subconscious. Even so, as Mrs. Sidgwick pointed out, it might still be a framework within which genuine information could be obtained. Mediums, of course, are of all types and grades, from the scarcely literate to a very few highly educated sensitives who would not care for the label medium and prefer to keep their gift a secret. The great medium is more rare than the great artist and we are lucky indeed if half a dozen crop up in a century. There have been no more than three available for lengthy study by the S.P.R. since it was founded in 1882.

The finest medium studied by the early workers was an American, Mrs. Piper, who was under expert observation from 1886 until 1911. She was constantly watched for fraud and even at times shadowed by detectives, but during that whole period she was never found to make the slightest conscious attempt to cheat. On the contrary, she gave every sign of being a person of integrity. Her gift of mediumship was discovered almost by chance. Discouraged by the failure of normal treatment to clear up the effects of an accident, she at last decided to consult a 'psychic healer'. At her second visit to him she herself went into a trance, and soon afterwards developed the power to do this at will. Her head would fall on to a cushion, her surface personality fade out, and a new personality would speak or write matter of which it was clear she had no knowledge when she awoke. Several of these new personalities, or Controls, turned up, but quite soon one of them ousted all the others. He claimed to have been a French doctor called Phinuit—this was a variant of the name of the healer's own Control—and to transmit messages from a number of communicators. Whatever the truth of this, when he was ostensibly in control of the entranced Mrs. Piper she would often display remarkable ESP.

William James and Richard Hodgson, who were active members of the American S.P.R., came to hear of Mrs. Piper at a time when they were both very sceptical of mediums in general and suspected them all of tricks. But Mrs. Piper did not indulge in tricks, and finally James and Hodgson were so impressed by her constant display of apparent ESP that they advised the S.P.R. to invite her to England, where she could

64

be closely studied in conditions which ensured her ignorance of the people who sat with her. She came in 1889 and worked for some months with the S.P.R. under the supervision of a committee consisting of Oliver Lodge, Myers and Walter Leaf, a member of its Council who, like James and Hodgson, was inclined to lean backwards on the side of scepticism.[1]

In those days Lodge, who held the Chair of Physics at Liverpool University, was also extremely sceptical, and he gave Mrs. Piper no chance to acquire information about those whom she would meet on the tests. He was awaiting her on the landing stage and he took her directly to his own house, where his precautions were worthy of the security police. All the servants were new, photographs and papers were locked up, Mrs. Piper's luggage was searched, and sitters were introduced under assumed names. But she continued to produce information out of the blue. How and whence did she get it? Lodge devised a test which he hoped might provide a clue. He wrote to an uncle Robert for some object belonging to the uncle's twin, Jerry, who had died twenty years before. Robert sent him a gold watch which he handed to Mrs. Piper while she was in trance. Phinuit said right away that it had belonged to an uncle, whose name with some difficulty he gave as Jerry. This name could have been got telepathically from Lodge, but when 'Jerry' was asked about his boyhood he recalled a number of incidents—killing a cat in a place called Smith's Field, owning a long skin like a snake skin, and being nearly drowned in a creek—of which Lodge knew nothing. On enquiry his Uncle Robert remembered the snake skin but denied killing the cat. But a third uncle, Frank, was found to remember both the cat and playing in Smith's Field. He also gave details of the creek incident. So Mrs. Piper had made three hits on somewhat unusual incidents and had given the name, Smith's Field, in conditions in which it was considered impossible that she could have sent sleuths to nose them out. Even had she done so the sleuths would have failed, for as a test Lodge himself sent an enquirer to his uncle's boyhood home to try and extract

---

[1] *Proceedings* S.P.R., Vol. VI, pp. 436–659.

the information given by Mrs. Piper from old men in the village. He had no success.[1]

After careful study the S.P.R. committee agreed that Mrs. Piper was honest and her trance genuine. They also agreed that she had a remarkable gift of ESP. But they did not believe Phinuit's claim to be a discarnate personality. He could give no satisfactory account of his life on earth and he knew no French, and, although at times he would diagnose with brilliance, his knowledge of medicine was amateurish. Also he had a habit, unworthy of the profession he claimed, of 'fishing' for information and padding with airy nothings when Mrs. Piper's ESP was not at its best. This is painfully true of most Controls.

Three years later, in 1892, Mrs. Piper developed a new Control who largely ousted Phinuit. He purported to be a young friend of Hodgson's, George Pelham (a pseudonym for Pellew) who had died very suddenly in New York. But there were times when the new Control—he was called G.P.—and Phinuit together performed a *tour de force*: Phinuit would talk on one subject while G.P. wrote simultaneously on another. Although Mrs. Piper did not know it, she had once met George Pelham when living. He had had one sitting with her under an assumed name, and it is possible that she may then have telepathically discovered his right name, tapped his store of memories and studied his personal characteristics without consciously knowing that she had done so.

The records of sittings in which G.P. took part are extremely long and their total effect is far more life-like than isolated summarised items. The question is, how could an ordinary woman have collected enough information to keep up what appears to have been a fantastic impersonation for years and remain in ignorance that she had done so? G.P., for instance, picked out 30 of George Pelham's personal friends from 150 strangers and made not one mistake. He also spoke to them of memories in common and reacted towards them as the living George Pelham would have done. If G.P. were not George

---

[1] It has been suggested that the two living uncles merely imagined that they remembered the three incidents. If so, this argument must be applied to numbers of similar hits made by Mrs. Piper during the next thirty years and many people must have done a great deal of apt imagining.

Pelham, asked Hodgson, how could he do this? In the end G.P.'s characterisation of George Pelham, added to an in-communicable sense of presence, broke down Hodgson's extreme scepticism. "I cannot profess", he wrote, "to have any doubt but that the chief communicators to whom I have referred ... are veritably the personalities that they claim to be, that they have survived the change we call death, and that they have directly communicated with us whom we call living through Mrs. Piper's entranced organism." William James and Mrs. Sidgwick, although they came to accept survival, in-clined to the view that Mrs. Piper's actual Controls were her own subconscious creations.

It often happens in psychical research that a run of positive evidence will suddenly be brought up short by an incident indicating that the problem is more subtle than it seems. A pendant to Hodgson's conversion did just this. He died in 1906 and at times thereafter purported to control Mrs. Piper. In 1909 a sitter, Dr. Hall, invented a dead niece for himself, whom he called Bessie Beals, and asked the communicating 'Hodgson' to produce her. This was duly done, and by her third appearance she was connecting specific memories with Dr. Hall. When 'Hodgson' was finally laughed at for producing a fictitious niece, he wriggled badly and said she had been related to another sitter. Finally he made the implausible excuse that he had been mistaken about the name and that the other sitter's friend was *Jessie* Beals. The trance consciousness is a great myth maker and to sift fact from fantasy in its pro-ductions is a tough job. It often seems indeed as if the medium were wandering in a dream world.

Ultimately G.P. was replaced as Mrs. Piper's main control by a band of purported V.I.P.s who unfortunately talked a lot of nonsense. One of them, for instance, who claimed to be George Eliot, said she had met Adam Bede. William James came to the conclusion that mediumship was unlikely to be the simple matter of either/or which we are inclined to demand. There may be, he said, outside 'wills to communicate' as well as the medium's own 'will to personate', and they may help each other out. Real flashes from an outside 'will' may be mixed up with the rubbish of trance talk, and it may be the outside 'will' which activates the medium's own 'will to personate'.

Of Mrs. Piper's mediumship it can be said that it was of great value to research in that, under strict supervision, she was the first to produce communications from purported spirits which were not only of a straight-forward mental type, un-mixed with suspect physical phenomena, but were in them-selves worthy of serious consideration. Their origin remained, however, a matter of opinion, because the limits of telepathy were—and are—not known. Mrs. Piper also made another valuable contribution to case material by taking part in a new phenomenon which first occurred soon after Myer's death. In this appeared what was claimed to be a new type of evidence for survival, which depended, not on super-normal knowledge by medium or automatist, but on evidence of design in the actual communications. It was the next highlight in the explorations of the S.P.R., and it was one of the greatest case histories in the whole progress of psychical research.

CHAPTER VIII

Cross Correspondences (1)

SIDGWICK died in 1900 and Myers in 1901. Gurney had already been dead ten years. The three main spearheads of psychical research had gone. Such a moment is always dangerous in any exploration, but the S.P.R. was fortunate, for other expert enthusiasts were able and willing to carry on. Fortunately too they were stimulated by some unexpected phenomena which began to occur shortly after the death of Myers.

Among his friends in Cambridge had been the classical scholar, Dr. A. W. Verrall, and his wife, who was a lecturer in classics at Newnham when Mrs. Sidgwick was Principal. (In her youth Mrs. Verrall had meant to read Political Science at the University but had been persuaded by her friend, Jane Harrison, the Greek scholar and anthropologist, to switch to Classics.) Mrs. Verrall, and to some extent her husband, had been infected by Myer's enthusiasm for psychical research, and after his death she decided to try and enable him to demonstrate his survival of death through automatic writing done by herself. This was an act of courage and devotion on her part. since she had been brought up in a rationalist ambience, she was no heretic by temperament, and for one in academic circles to indulge in such an activity was to label herself a prey to superstition for which she had a particular horror.

In view of the task she had undertaken it was fortunate that her integrity and her appetite for work were both ferocious, for it took about three months of abortive efforts before she began to write automatic scripts which showed some sort of meaning. They were mostly in a Latin and Greek far below her own standard of scholarship and were so mysteriously worded that it was arguable that their meaning was being intentionally concealed. They were signed 'Myers'.[1] Gradually they became more coherent and better expressed, though no less cryptic, and a year later a curious thing happened. Allusions to subjects referred to by Mrs. Verrall began to be made in America by Mrs. Piper, and these too claimed to come from Myers. In another year or so Mrs. Verrall's daughter, Miss Helen Verrall also began to write automatically, and it was found that before she had seen her mother's scripts she was alluding to the same subjects as her mother and Mrs. Piper. After this their scripts were all sent to Miss Alice Johnson, who had by now become secretary of the S.P.R.

The next person to come into the picture was Mrs. Fleming, who was a sister of Rudyard Kipling and lived in India. (She used a pseudonym, Mrs. Holland, as her husband and family strongly disapproved of psychic activities.) In 1903 she read Myers' book *Human Personality*, and this renewed her interest in her own gift of automatic writing. She too began to obtain scripts signed 'Myers', and in one of these she was instructed to send it to Mrs. Verrall at 5 Selwyn Gardens, Cambridge. She had read Mrs. Verrall's name in *Human Personality* as being interested in some experiments, but had never met her personally. Nor had she ever been to Cambridge or consciously heard of Selwyn Gardens. But Mrs. Verrall did in fact live at number five. Mrs. Holland was a gifted and educated woman and extremely sceptical of her own scripts. She did not therefore obey these instructions, but she did eventually send the scripts and subsequent ones to Miss Johnson at the S.P.R.[2] Miss Johnson peacefully filed them for it did not occur to her that Mrs. Holland in India could be making veiled references to the same subjects as the Verralls and Mrs. Piper, with whom she had no contact. It was not until 1905 that Miss Johnson realised what was happening, by which time the scripts themselves appeared to be making the extraordinary claim that Myers, Gurney and Sidgwick had devised them to demonstrate their

[1] Mrs. A. W. Verrall *On a Series of Automatic Writings, Proceedings* S.P.R., Vol. XX, pp. 1–432.
[2] Alice Johnson *Report on the Automatic Writing of Mrs. Holland, Proceedings* S.P.R., Vol. XXI, pp. 166–391.

continued existence and prove their identity. As G. N. M. Tyrrell put it, the material to be investigated was experimenting upon itself.

We have seen that the dramatic powers of the human subconscious would make it extremely difficult for the discarnate to prove their own identity, even should they exist. Investigators will dismiss the simple statement, "I am Myers, or Smith or Jones" almost without interest as the product of the automatist's subconscious imagination, and if facts about a purported communicator's past life are given as evidence of identity it will be assumed that, normal means excluded, the automatist has acquired them by telepathy from the mind of a living person. Before they died the first generation of psychical researchers had come to realise the snags in the way of identification and their successors had devised no way to get over them. The scripts now seemed to indicate that a new method had been worked out by the deceased Myers and his friends. This was to send fragmentary allusions to various subjects—usually classical—through separate automatists, some of whom never met each other. According to the scripts their intention was to make these fragments appear random and pointless to the individual automatists, in order to avoid giving clues to the train of thought behind them. They would only become meaningful and show evidence of design when pieced together by an independent investigator. Most, though not all, of the fragments were taken from the normal contents of the automatists' own minds. The interest lies in the question: Who selected them to convey a train of thought which could not be deduced from any one person's script? They were sometimes interspersed with more coherent passages of general advice or comment.

The investigators considered that the claim made in the scripts was justified to the extent that they appeared to show evidence of design by minds possessing more classical scholarship than nearly all the automatists involved, of whom only Mrs. Verrall and her daughter had any classical training. In their view, too, scripts displayed some of the characteristics and interests of their purported authors and made apt references to their past lives. They also stressed their continued efforts to serve humanity and avert disaster and contained a number of oblique warnings of the 1914 war before it was generally looked upon as a serious risk, as well as some other apparent predictions. In February and May 1914, for instance, the script of one automatist, Dame Edith Lyttelton, alluded to the sinking of the *Lusitania*, which took place a year later, and in 1915 she wrote warnings about 'the Munich bond' and Berchtesgaden which people took to be nonsense at the time. But this study must be confined to the attempts made in the scripts to prove the continued existence of Myers and his friends.

Needless to say, the discovery of these phenomena stirred the S.P.R. investigators to an intensive study of the scripts. This was undertaken mainly by Gerald Balfour (later the second Lord Balfour) who was an expert classical scholar, Sir Oliver Lodge, that sceptical couple, Mrs. Sidgwick and Alice Johnson, and Mr. J. E. Piddington, ex-Honorary Secretary of the S.P.R. He was a down-to-earth business man with a strong sense of humour and he too was familiar with the classics. The team had undertaken a tough job and it became tougher as time went on, for scripts by this group of automatists continued to appear for thirty years and in the end amounted to more than three thousand. (Some of the communications were written, some spoken, but it is convenient to refer to them all as scripts.) Ultimately over a dozen automatists became involved. In 1908 a Mrs. Willett (pseudonym for Mrs. Coombe-Tennant, who wished to remain anonymous until her death which occurred in 1957) was found to be producing fragments which fitted in with the others, and in 1913 Dame Edith Lyttelton began to do the same. From 1915 onwards a Mrs. Stuart Wilson came in and other automatists made sporadic contributions. Mrs. Piper was the only professional medium among them.

This series of scripts came to be known as the cross correspondences and they abounded in literary allusions and quotations in both classical and modern languages, many of them so abstruse that it needed a scholar of the quality of their alleged authors even to recognise them. The work of assessment was laborious and complicated. The first appearance of any allusion or quotation had to be noted and its reappearance or any complementary statement watched for thereafter. To do that was particularly important, for the essence of the plan as it grew more complicated appeared to be for the allusions and quotations not to repeat but to complement each other. Also, although their integrity was not in doubt, a careful search had to be made for any conceivable normal means by which the automatists might have obtained the information they recorded and remembered it subconsciously although their conscious selves had forgotten it. The second Lord Balfour and Mr. Piddington gave up much of the latter part of their lives to the study and interpretation of the scripts[1] and the scripts themselves took an active interest in this task. In one, for example, written by Mrs. Willett, appeared the question: "Write the word Selection. Who selects, my friend Piddington. I address this question to Piddington. Who selects?"

Only a small proportion of the cross correspondences have been published and they alone fill volumes. Without all three thousand original documents available for study no final assessment of their value can be made, but unfortunately the contents of some were so private that it was not considered possible to make them public until after a lapse of time. None the less, from the evidence already available it is hard for the dispassionate critic to avoid the conclusion that for thirty years in dozens of cases something was causing a number of automatists, not only to refer to the same topic—one often abstruse —but to make their references complementary, to create what have been called classical jigsaw puzzles. There were also a number of simpler cases—sometimes called cross references— which were more a repetition of motifs, either alluded to or directly quoted, in various languages and settings and taken from both classical and modern literature. Here are the bare

[1] H. F. Saltmarsh gives a useful short account of the Cross Correspondences and a full bibliography in *Evidence of Survival from Cross Correspondences* (Bell, 1938).

bones of one simple case. On April 17th, 1907, Mrs. Piper said what sounded like Sanatos, then she repeated it as Tanatos. A week later she said Thanatos (the Greek word for death) three times. Mrs. Piper knew no Greek. To repeat a word on different occasions out of the blue seemed to be a sign that a cross reference or correspondence was being attempted. On April 16th Mrs. Holland wrote an automatic script in India. It contained the words: "Maurice Morris Mors [Latin for death] And with that the shadow of death fell upon his limbs." Here again, the automatist seems to be feeling her way towards a word by the sound.

On April 29th Mrs. Verrall took a hand. In her script were the words: "Warmed both hands before the fire of life. It fades [sic] and I am ready to depart." She next drew a triangle, which is also the Greek letter delta and which she had always taken as a sign for death. (This letter also turned out to be significant in another connection.) Then she wrote: "Manibus date lilia plenis" (give lilies with full hands), which is a quotation from a speech in the Aeneid where an early death is foretold. This was followed by :"Come away, come away, Pallida mors," (Latin for pale death) and she finally wrote: "You have got the word plainly written all along in your writing. Look back."

Some of the more complicated cases contain these simple cross references as well as cross correspondences. Of these a well-known and not too complicated example is the "Hope, Star and Browning Case", where the words Star and Hope are repeatedly given, together with quotations from Browning which his friends said were characteristic of Myers. These are given by both Mrs. and Miss Verrall, but they are only pulled together when Mrs. Piper's 'Myers' in America indicates that he has completed a cross correspondence and gives the words Browning, Hope and Star as the clues. To those who are not classical scholars this cross correspondence is more easily intelligible than most, for the references are mainly to Browning's poetry instead of to some little-known legend of antiquity. The more detailed summary of it given below may therefore make the general nature of cross correspondences easier to visualise, but nothing less than the study of a large number of the originals can convey the apparent human element and intention in them. And even that cannot convey the vividness of characterisation which seems to have impressed the investigators who had known Myers and his friends.

The Hope, Star and Browning case started soon after January 16th, 1907.[1] On that date Mr. Piddington asked Mrs. Piper's 'Myers' if in future he could indicate that a cross correspondence was being attempted by drawing, say, a circle with a triangle inside. But he naturally did not mention this request to the other automatists. On January 23rd Mrs. Verrall's 'Myers' wrote in her script: "... an anagram would be better. Tell him that—rats, stars, tars and so on ... or again tears, stare." This was followed by another anagram which Mrs. Verrall afterwards remembered had also been devised during their lives by Myers, her husband and Sir Richard Jebb. Some time later, when Mr. Piddington was going through Richard Hodgson's papers—Hodgson died in 1905—he found that Hodgson and Myers had been exchanging anagrams for years and that both the star anagram and the other quoted were among the papers. (Another obvious use for anagrams in cross correspondences is to play down the key words and thus help to keep the automatist from understanding what is being written.)

On January 28th Mrs. Verrall's 'Myers' set about elaborating the Star idea. "*Aster*" (Latin = star), he wrote, "*Teras* [an anagram for *Aster*, occasionally used in Greek for a constellation and also meaning a wonder or a sign]. The world's wonder. And all a wonder and a wild desire. The very wings of her. A WINGED DESIRE. *Hupopteros eros* [Greek = winged love]. Then there is Blake. And mocked my loss of liberty. But it is all the same thing—the winged desire. *Eros potheinos* [Greek = love, the much desired] the hope that leaves the earth for the sky. That is what I want. On earth the broken sounds—threads—in the sky the perfect arc. The C major of this life. But your recollection is at fault."

[1] *Proceedings* S.P.R., Vol. XXII, p. 59 et seq.: and Vol. XXVII, p. 28 et seq.

After this was drawn:

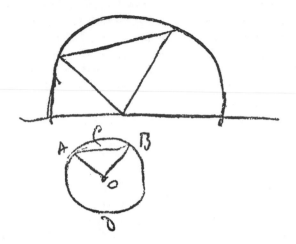

and the script concluded: "ADB is the part that completes the arc."

It is clear that only a fraction of the meaning in this script was apparent to its writer, Mrs. Verrall, for when she sent it to Miss Johnson she commented: "Is the enclosed an attempt at Bird? Winged *hupopteros* and Abt Vogler (*Vogel*) suggest it. The latter part is all quotations from R. B.'s *Abt Vogler*, and earlier from *The Ring and the Book* ..." The phrase "That is what I want" did not apparently attract her attention to the preceding sentence where "The passion that leaves the earth" is wrongly given as "The hope that leaves the earth." There are indications later that this may be a deliberate misquotation.

Miss Verrall had not seen these scripts of her mother's but on February 3rd she wrote "... where the song birds pipe their tune in the early morning", and followed this by "*Therapeutikos ek exoticon*" (a healer from aliens) which was a veiled hint of what was to come later. Next came a monogram, the drawing of a star and a crescent moon and the words: "A monogram, the crescent moon, remember that and the star." Finally she drew a bird.

On February 11th Mrs. Piper's 'Myers' asked Mr. Piddington if Mrs. Verrall had received the word Evangelical. He answered that he did not know, and 'Myers' went on: "I referred also to Browning again. I referred to Hope and Browning . . . I also said Star." Later on he said that the word Evangelical was wrong. He had meant to say Evelyn Hope (the title of a poem by Browning) but in transmission the words had been distorted into Evangelical. Next came a nice touch. Miss Verrall had so far done comparatively little automatic writing and to stimulate and encourage her she was told that she had taken part in a cross correspondence which included the words Planet Mars, Virtue and Keats. To avoid giving her information should she write more, these words were used to represent Hope, Star and Browning. But her subconscious self was not deceived, for on February 17th her script became more explicit. "That was the sign", said her 'Myers'. "She will understand when she sees it . . . No arts avail . . . and a star above it all rats everywhere in Hamelin town." Here the anagram begun in Mrs. Verrall's script is going strong,—arts, star, rats—and by the mention of "rats everywhere in Hamelin Town", the script is linked to the earlier phrase, "The healer from aliens", which is an apt description of Browning's *Pied Piper*.

On March 6th Mrs. Piper's 'Myers' told Mr. Piddington that he had given Mrs. Verrall a circle. He then tried to draw a triangle, but commented: "It did not appear." This is an interesting mistake, as Mrs. Verrall had in fact succeeded in drawing a triangle as well as a circle. He also said, correctly, that he had written something about Bird when he gave Mrs. Verrall the circle.

On March 13th Mrs. Piper's 'Myers' repeated that he had drawn a circle for Mrs. Verrall and he again drew a circle and a triangle. Afterwards he said: "But it suggested a poem to my mind, hence B H S". [i.e. Browning, Hope, Star].

Finally, on April 8th Mrs. Piper's 'Myers' once more repeated that he had drawn a circle for Mrs. Verrall and added that he had also drawn or had tried to draw a star and a crescent. That these two symbols had been drawn was correct, but it had been Miss Verrall, not her mother, who had drawn them.

This case is a typical example of a series of allusions, implications and direct cross references written by two automatists, Mrs. and Miss Verrall, which were made meaningful by key words given by a third, Mrs. Piper. It is far more complicated than it appears in summary for some of the allusions are meaningful in connection with other cross correspondences and are also links in coherent trains of thought which emerge elsewhere. For example, Mrs. Verrall's drawing of a circle and triangle not only carries out the request made to Mrs. Piper's 'Myers' for such a drawing; added to her reference to Abt Vogler it also ties up with the scripts' answer—an answer that makes sense—to a question which had been put to Mrs. Piper's 'Myers' in Latin, a language Mrs. Piper did not know. (But the question was put when she was giving sittings in England to S.P.R. members who did know both Latin and the message, and this proximity may have helped her to pick up its contents telepathically from them. Although on the one hand ESP seems to be more or less independent of time and space, physical proximity does at times appear to facilitate telepathy.)

After the cross correspondences had been going on for some years, Piddington and an American, G. B. Dorr, devised two ways of testing them. One was to try and check whether they could result from ordinary associations of ideas on the part of the automatists, the other to find out if their creators, whoever they were, would produce a cross correspondence to order. In the first test fourteen people were each sent quotations, twelve in all, from Shakespeare, Milton, Shelley, Rostand, Virgil, Wordsworth, Coleridge and Homer, and were asked to write down some words or phrases associated with them. The results were very different from the cross correspondences produced spontaneously by the automatists. Only momentary cross references occurred and there was no tendency to return again and again to one master theme. In fact there was no resemblance to a real cross correspondence.

The next test was to set the purported 'Myers' a subject for a cross correspondence which would give scope for classical knowledge beyond that of most of the automatists. He passed it with honours. The plan was that in America Dorr should ask Mrs. Piper's 'Myers' the question, "What does the word Lethe suggest to you?", Mrs. Piper herself being no classical scholar. He did so and at several sittings he obtained in response a number of classical allusions which meant nothing to him and also nothing at first to the scholars of the British S.P.R. The allusions included Myers-like references to the little-known story of Ceyx and Alcyone and to the sending of the Goddess Iris to the underworld as this is told in connection with the river Lethe in Ovid's Metamorphoses. Later on, Sir Oliver Lodge asked Mrs. Willett's 'Myers' the same question. He answered that it had already been asked elsewhere, and with great effort spelled out the word DORR in capitals. Then, over a period of weeks, Mrs. Willett's script made many allusions to references in Virgil's Aeneid to the river Lethe and these fitted Mr. Dorr's question from the point of view of such a man as Myers, who had known his Virgil inside out, but did not do so from that of people without his scholarship. Ultimately Mrs. Willett's 'Myers' wrote: "That I have different scribes means that I must show different aspects of thoughts underlying which Unity is to be found and I know what Lodge wants. He wants me to prove that I have access to knowledge shown elsewhere."

Unfortunately, even when read in full, the elaborate aptness of the classical and other allusions in such cases as these can only be appreciated by scholars of the same calibre as their author, whoever that was. But what is patent to all is the intensity of desire to get the plan carried out—not, of course, that this desire is evidence for it could be simulated. The instructions in the scripts are frequent and explicit. "Record the bits", writes Mrs. Verrall's 'Myers', "and when fitted they will make the whole." Again, "I will give the words between you neither alone can read but together they will give the clue he wants." In March, 1910 Mrs. Verrall wrote a series of scripts referring to the main events in the history of the City of Rome. On March 7th, five thousand miles away, Mrs. Holland wrote: "Ave Roma Immortalis. How could I make it clearer without giving her the clue?" Such remarks occur again and again.

The last of the apparently self-contained type of cross correspondence was the Master Builder case, which straggled on from 1913 to 1924, with a high spot in December and January, 1918–19.[1] That they should cease seems logical enough, for if the large number obtained by the end of the first World War was not enough to carry conviction of their authorship it could be argued that nothing would be gained by continuing indefinitely a type of evidence which was a strain on all involved. However that may be, the cross correspondences as such gradually merged into the wider pattern of scripts concerned largely with world affairs, in which the purported communicators had always professed the deepest interest. These had gone on concurrently with the cross correspondences from 1901 and they only faded out altogether in 1932.

[1] *Proceedings* S.P.R., Vol. XXXVI, p. 477.

CHAPTER IX

Cross Correspondences (2)

A NUMBER of automatists were engaged in the cross correspondences and their reactions and methods of producing scripts were varied. Mrs. Wilson 'saw' pictures and then described them. Others spoke of their interior impressions; others would both speak and write; others again, Mrs. Verrall for instance, would only write. She generally fell into the more or less dissociated state common to most automatists, getting very sleepy at times and occasionally for a moment losing consciousness altogether. "Whether I write in the light or in the dark", she said, "I do not look at the paper. I perceive a word or two but never understand whether it makes sense with what goes before ... When the script is finished I often cannot say till I read it what language has been used, as the recollection of the words passes away with extreme rapidity ..."

Her daughter, Miss Verrall, would speak more often than write, and afterwards she too could remember but little of what she had said. Both their scripts purported to come from Myers, but Mrs. Holland's were sometimes signed Gurney or Sidgwick. A fifth automatist, Mrs. Willett, also got scripts signed Verrall after Dr. Verrall had died.

Mrs. Holland said that she was always fully conscious when writing but that the pencil moved too quickly for her to grasp any meaning. To amuse herself she had written automatically for ten years before she read *Human Personality*. In it she came upon some experiences similar to her own, which she had been unable to understand, and this encouraged her to write about these to Alice Johnson, the Secretary of the S.P.R. Miss Johnson asked for details which Mrs. Holland sent. Her scripts, she said, had always come at great speed; she once wrote fourteen poems in an hour. On one occasion she had been surprised to find that she had written a letter beginning with a pet name and signed with another, both of which were unknown to her. "It was clearly impressed on me for whom the letter was intended," she told Miss Johnson, "but thinking it due to some unhealthy fancy of my own, I destroyed it . . . I was punished by an agonising headache and the letter was repeated, till in self-defence I sent it and the succeeding ones to their destination." The recipient told her that the handwriting resembled that of someone who had been dead some years and that the letters were signed with the name of that person and referred to matters known only to them. Beyond that he did not wish to discuss the matter. On three later occasions Mrs. Holland wrote similar letters and these all came as a surprise both to her and to the recipients, with whom she was never more than slightly acquainted.

Mrs. Holland's share in the cross correspondences began when she was about thirty-five. She told Miss Johnson that she was not a person with any morbid desire for wonders and she had no connection with spiritualism. "It puzzles me a little," she wrote, "that with no desire to consider myself exceptional I do sometimes see, hear, feel or otherwise become conscious of beings and influences that are not patent to all. Is this a frame of mind to be checked, or permitted or encouraged? I should like so much to know. My own people hate what they call 'uncanniness' and I am obliged to hide from them the keen interest I cannot help feeling in psychic matters."

In this somewhat lonely situation it seems natural enough that when she learnt for the first time from Myers' book that intelligent and balanced people did not consider *psi* to be necessarily morbid or hysterical, her scripts should claim to be inspired by Myers, even if they were in fact subjectively produced. On the other hand, if a discarnate Myers did exist, it is perhaps conceivable that Mrs. Holland's interest in his book might have singled her out for him, turned a searchlight upon her, in some telepathic fashion to us unknown. It was after doing some automatic writing in November 1903 that she first sent a 'Myers' script to Miss Johnson. Her hand had scrawled the letter F., which, although she did not know it, happened to be a habitual signature of Myers. She remarked: "My hand feels very shaky, shall I let it scrawl?" and the script answered: "Yes, let it go quite freely, just exactly as it likes!" F. then wrote that he wished to speak to some old friends, Miss J. and A. W. (Alice Johnson and Dr. A. W. Verrall) and added: "There is so much to say and yet so very little chance of saying it—communication is so tremendously difficult—the brain of the agent [the automatist is meant] though indispensable is so hampering."

After this came a pretty accurate description of Dr. Verrall, whom Mrs. Holland had never seen, and finally: "It is like entrusting a message on which infinite importance depends to a sleeping person—get a proof—try for a proof if you feel this is a waste of time without. Send this to Mrs. Verrall, 5 Selwyn Gardens, Cambridge."

As we have seen, Mrs. Holland, being sceptical, did not obey these instructions but sent the script to Miss Johnson. She wrote in a covering letter: ". . . I am glad to know that you agree with me as to the harmlessness of automatic writing for a person of average common sense. Its snare for me lies in the direction of boredom rather than of blind faith. However in September I experimented for one week . . . every morning . . . at 11 a.m. That is a good commonplace hour when one is not likely to be over-imaginative . . . Will you forgive me for troubling you with the writing? I do not like to suppress it as it gave me the impression of someone very anxious to establish communication, but with not much power to do it. . . ."

Two years later a previous 'Myers' script by Mrs. Holland was discovered to be a correct description of Mrs. Verrall's dining room, except that she had described a filter which stood in a dark corner as a bust. Such trivial incidents provoke a number of questions. If Mrs. Holland drew her information by telepathy from the obvious source, Mrs. Verrall, why did she mistake the filter for a bust? If it came by direct clairvoyance of the actual room, has clairvoyance limitations in common with physical vision? For the same mistake had been made by a Cambridge friend of Mrs. Verrall's, and when Mrs. Holland's script was read to him he exclaimed: "But there *is* a bust in your dining room." Could she have drawn her information from this total stranger? Or if, as the script claimed, it came from Myers, when did he make the mistake, in life or after?

Other Holland scripts could well have resulted from direct telepathy with Mrs. Verrall. Two contained good descriptions of her and in one was written "a new dress not a black one this time," at a time when Mrs. Verrall was being persuaded to order a new coloured dress instead of a black one as she had intended. Such cases, however, merge into others when the explanation of simple telepathy becomes more difficult. And it may always be that to seek such an either/or type of explanation for any of them is barking up the wrong tree.

In January, 1904, when Mrs. Holland had been getting scripts from her 'Myers' for thirteen months, he wrote: ". . . It is impossible for me to know how much of what I send reaches you and how much you are able to set down—I feel as if I had presented my credentials—reiterated the proofs of my identity in a wearisomely frequent manner—but yet I cannot feel as if I had made any true impression upon them. Surely you sent them what I strove so to transmit—Your pride, if you name nervous vanity pride was surely not strong enough to weigh against my appeals—Even here under present conditions I should know I should thrill responsive to any real belief on their part—Oh it is a dark road . . ."

Another script, signed Gurney, also showed signs of displeasure. ". . . Back again in the old despondency. Why don't you write daily? You seem to form habits only to break them. . ."

Mrs. Holland told Miss Johnson that when this script came she had in fact been steadily resisting any impulse to do automatic writing, for she was very busy and interruptions jarred on her painfully. One cannot escape a certain sympathy with the communicators, whatever they were, for this script too joined the others in Miss Johnson's file, since she had not yet noticed the links between the Holland and Verrall scripts. Both these scripts also lament another shortcoming, the fear felt by educated automatists of being led up the garden path. ". . . Do try to forget your abiding fear of being made a fool or a dupe. If we ever prompt you to fantastic follies you may leave us . . . It's a form of restless vanity to fear that your hand is imposing upon yourself as it were ... You should not be discouraged if what is written appears to you futile—Most of it is not meant for you ... I do wish you would not hamper us by trying to understand every word you write ..."

Mrs. Holland's 'Gurney' was quite tough with her. "... If you don't care enough to try every day for a short time, better drop it altogether. It's like making appointments and not keeping them. You endanger your own powers of sensitiveness and annoy us bitterly—G."

Her 'Myers', on the other hand, was gentle but sad. "The nearest simile I can find to express the difficulties of sending a message is that I appear to be standing behind a sheet of frosted glass—which blurs sight and deadens sound—dictating feebly—to a reluctant and somewhat obtuse secretary. A feeling of terrible impotence burdens me ..."

This sort of lament was repeated again and again. "Oh, if I could only get to them—could only leave you the proof positive that I remember—recall—know—continue."

"Yet another attempt to run the blockade—to strive to get a message through—How can I make your hand docile enough—how can I convince them? ... Oh, I am feeble with eagerness—How can I best be identified? ... Edmund's help is not here with me just now—I am trying alone amid unspeakable difficulties..."

At the time Mrs. Holland was writing this Mrs. Piper's 'Myers' wrote that he was "trying with all the forces to prove that I am Myers." All this, whatever its source, is characteristic enough of the living Myers, who with dedicated intensity had given his life to an effort to prove survival by the methods of science. The same intensity is often found in Mrs. Willett's scripts. Her 'Gurney' wrote: "... the passionate desire to return to drive into incarnate minds the conviction of one's own identity the partial successes and the blank failures. ... I know the burden of it the burden of it to the uttermost fraction ..." Mrs. Willett noted that in this script there was a terrible sense of struggle—almost of pain.

It is worth pausing again to imagine the problems facing such men, did they indeed survive death with the same basic consciousness as before. How, lacking a physical vehicle, could they communicate scientifically acceptable evidence of their identity to the living, whose attention is normally concentrated on physical impressions? Myers in life had believed the answer to lie in that mysterious form of linkage he labelled telepathy, by which the living seem able to dispense with physical methods of transmission between themselves. But even between the living, telepathic communications are sporadic, vague, disjointed and short. Few people can make lengthy contact with their subconscious 'receiving layer' and when they do they bring up very mixed bags culled from diverse sources which it is hard for the investigator to locate or disentangle. Moreover, items of genuine outside information are often distorted or overlaid by the sensitive's own associations which the outside item itself has stirred up as a falling stone stirs up mud in a pond. A typical example of this occurs in what is known as the Spirit Angel cross correspondence.[1] Mrs. Verrall's 'Myers' wrote: "But you keep going round the idea instead of giving three plain words, 'Lost Paradise Regained.'" These words were a direct allusion to the subject of the cross correspondence. Then followed the irrelevant phrase, "Of man's first disobedience . . ." and then, after a pause, "No, that is something else . . ." But such pauses and comments are exceptional. Only too often the cross correspondence sensitives, like all others, wander along a train of thought of their own which has been aroused by what may have been a genuine outside stimulus. Hence, even if the Myers group scripts do originate with their purported authors they are likely at best to be greatly coloured and modified by the personality of the automatist. The communicators themselves often complain that the automatists are very inefficient channels, and they add that on their side too they have their troubles. To approach the incarnate, they say, is like diving into a black fog.[2]

[1] *Proceedings* S.P.R., Vol. XXII, p. 220 et seq.
[2] A hypothetical communicator might also be faced with the problem of what to talk about. Even when a living person's brain is experimentally or pathologically modified, he finds the words and concepts of physical life unsuited to describe his resultant experiences and is driven to analogies and poetic images. This would presumably apply even more to discarnate conditions.

There are reasons enough, then, why sensitives wander up pointless byways and get involved with extraneous matter in a fashion exasperating to the clear cut mind and either/or outlook of the investigator trained in physical science. But if the scripts do not originate with Myers and his friends, what are the alternatives? Could chance coincidence account for the thirty years' linkage between dozens of scripts? To check this it is worth doing a simple test: with closed eyes place a finger at random on a number of passages in various books and try to create from them a cross correspondence with a controlling theme. The results have little in common with the recorded cross correspondences. Are these, then, due to conscious fraud on the part of all concerned? If so, we have to believe that men and women of the calibre of Balfour, Lodge, Mrs. Sidgwick and Dr. and Mrs. Verrall jointly indulged in this fraud for thirty years. Or if the automatists only were cheating, we must suppose that the austere and upright Mrs. Verrall trained a team of virtuous Edwardian ladies, such as Dame Edith Lyttelton and Mrs. Coombe-Tennant, year after year to palm off spurious scripts on the investigators, scripts too which were often written under their own eyes. The motive here would be far to seek, for in Cambridge society Mrs. Verrall's automatism was anything but a social asset. Moreover, long term hoaxes at cross correspondence level would involve a great deal of work. Mr. W. H. Salter, who has been Honorary Secretary of the S.P.R. for thirty years and who saw the cross correspondences at first hand, as he married Miss Helen Verrall, has pointed out that this too is easy to test. To construct an elementary cross correspondence, a topic or quotation from a particular author must be chosen and further quotations collected from his work which allude to this topic but do not mention it directly. Puns are allowed. Finally an independent investigator must find the clue which binds the quotations into a coherent whole. Anyone who tries to construct a cross correspondence of the quality of those which claimed to come from the Myers group will sympathise with the remark in Mrs. Willett's script which purported to be made by Dr. Verrall shortly after his death: "This sort of thing is more difficult to do than it looked."

But it is possible that the cross correspondences resulted from subconscious fraud on the part of the living, since subconsciously even the most upright can be shameless dramatists. If this is the answer the main suspect is obviously Mrs. Verrall, for she knew two of the purported communicators, Sidgwick and Myers, personally, she was interested in *psi* and she was a very good classical scholar. But in all there were seven communicators, three of whom she did not know, and she did not recognise the many references to them in her scripts. If she were indeed the designer of the cross correspondences the network of telepathy implied is still astounding. For years she must subconsciously have taught the subconscious selves of her scattered pupils their rôles in the long term hoax—which was of course perpetrated on her own surface self as well as on other people. But she died in 1916 and the interlinked scripts still went on, when there appeared to be no-one left who combined her personal knowledge of the Myers group with the classical scholarship and deep interest presumably needed to induce the subconscious to work out such elaborate patterns.

If subconscious deception by the living is still the answer it looks as if, unknown to himself, some other classical scholar was holding a subconscious class in deception, or as if the team of automatists were subconsciously pecking their scholarship from some sources and the personal memories of the Myers group from others.[1]

Although Piddington disliked the idea of survival, as the years went by both he and the other investigators were more and more driven towards the authorship claimed by the scripts as their most plausible explanation. But we have already seen that psychical research is like a treasure hunt in which some invisible humourist places wonderful clues, and then, when these appear almost conclusive, throws in just one more which may lead in the opposite direction. This is what happened in what is known as the Sevens case. Piddington decided to leave a sealed letter containing information about himself known to

[1] That this is conceivable is suggested by experiments conducted by Dr. S. B. Soal with a Mrs. Stewart many years later. These are recorded in Chapter XVI.

nobody else and he hoped to be able to communicate its contents through a sensitive after his death before the letter was opened. (This seemed a more watertight proof of survival then than it does since experimental evidence of clairvoyance through packs of cards has been obtained.) In the letter he described his habit, which he called a 'tic', of playing with the number seven, walking in groups of seven steps, counting objects in sevens, observing sevens in literature and so on. Of course he kept the letter a strict secret, but three years after he wrote it six of the cross correspondence automatists began to bespatter their scripts with allusions to seven. Mrs. Piper's preference was for 'We are Seven', and she also wrote about the clock on the stairs going 'tick, tick,'—a typical twist this of the kind that results from the medium's own associations. The existence of a cross correspondence shouted itself aloud to those who read the scripts, and at last Mr. Piddington was driven to confess that the allusions tallied with the contents of his intended posthumous letter.

What is the answer here? Did Piddington have a leaky mind? Did it leak to so many automatists because of their common interests? And was it unable to leak until he had ceased to give the letter much conscious thought? The scripts themselves proffered another explanation in some quite plausible detail. They said that Myers had observed Piddington's plan and had caused the leak. It is true that at the time when Piddington was writing his letter in London, Mrs. Verrall's 'Myers' wrote the cryptic sentence in Surrey: "Note the hour—in London half the message has come ... surely Piddington will see that this is enough and should be acted upon." In view of later events this can be interpreted as suggesting that Myers thought he would produce evidence of his own survival by broadcasting his knowledge of Piddington's message before the latter's death. Moreover, when the cross correspondence had been achieved, but before Mrs. Verrall knew that Piddington had written his letter, her 'Myers' also wrote: "Has Piddington found the bits of his sentence scattered among you all?" He had indeed. It is noteworthy that the Sevens case developed a secondary and meaningful cross correspondence not implicit in Piddington's letter and for which therefore it cannot be assumed that he was psychically responsible. This was a series of references to the meeting with Beatrice in the Earthly Paradise Cantos of Dante's *Purgatorio*.

So once more the explorers were left with plausible evidence for communication between the living and the surviving dead, but once more that evidence had a leak in it. In the end, however, it did bring conviction to Mr. Piddington, who had spent much of his life on the scripts, and it led even the ultra-cautious Mrs. Sidgwick to commit herself to the statement: "I myself think that the evidence is pointing towards the conclusion that our fellow workers are still working with us." And Lord Balfour's personal belief, arrived at, he said, after much study and reflection, leaned "strongly in favour of an affirmative answer." But they could only say: I believe. They could not say: I know.

CHAPTER X

The Willett Scripts

THE constant insistence in the cross correspondence scripts that Myers and his friends were striving to find some means to establish their own identity was rendered more impressive to contemporary investigators by the startling fact that their material did appear to be experimenting on itself. This it continued to do in another equally ingenious fashion in some scripts written by Mrs. Willett. They became known as the *Statius* and *Ear of Dionysius* cases and in the second it was claimed that instead of messages from one discarnate entity being sent through several automatists, joint messages from two together were being sent through one. The two senders purported to be Mrs. Verrall's husband, Dr. A. W. Verrall, and a friend, Henry Butcher, Professor of Greek at Edinburgh, both of whom had recently died, and the scripts certainly indicate the common interests and inter-relationship of these two personalities and also give apt references to their past careers. An American psychologist, Professor Gardner Murphy, has said that to devise a more adequate or a more beautiful instance of co-operative thinking on the problem of survival evidence would indeed be difficult.

Whatever their authorship, these scripts are an interesting contrast to Mrs. Willett's surface personality and they also seem to transcend her intellectual attainments. She was a cultivated woman, much interested in English literature but not at all in scientific evidence—in no way an academic or professional type. Nor was she a classical scholar. Yet both scripts are concerned with recondite classical subjects, known but to few even among scholars. The type of knowledge involved can be brought out in a summary of the *Ear of Dionysius* case —the full report takes forty pages—but unfortunately the characterisation and indications of joint authorship cannot.[1]

[1] *Proceedings* S.P.R., Vol. XXIX, p. 197 et seq.

The bare bones of the case are these. Between 1910 and 1915 Mrs. Willett's scripts constantly referred to the following subjects:

The Ear of Dionysius (this was the name of a grotto in Sicily)
The stone quarries of Syracuse
The story of Polyphemus and Ulysses
The story of Acis and Galatea
Jealousy
Music
Something to be found in Aristotle's Poetics
Satire

The investigators could find no common link between these subjects, and the scripts insisted that until the experiment by Dr. Verrall and Professor Butcher was over Mrs. Verrall must on no account hear anything about it. The final script, which was written in 1915, said that the subject had been chosen as giving evidence of identity, and was "a fine tangle for your unravelling." It also gave the clues to the tangle. These were the words Cyclopean, Cythera, Philox and Jealousy, and the phrase: "He laboured in the stone quarries and drew upon the earlier writer for material for his Satire."

Once the scripts said that the experiment was completed Mrs. Verrall was able to join in the search for a connecting link between them. Among her husband's books she found a little-known American textbook entitled *Greek Melic Poets*, which he had made use of in his work. This book contained an account of an equally little-known Greek poet, Philoxenus of Cythera, of whose writings only a few lines remain, and this is the only source so far discovered in which the story of Philoxenus is given in a form containing *all* the references contained in Mrs. Willett's scripts. Here then, once more, we have classical knowledge beyond that possessed by the automatist being woven into clues in a subtle manner characteristic of the purported authors. Mrs. Willett, who had not known Professor Butcher personally, also had a vision of him which was found to correspond with his personal appearance, but this is not evidential as she may have seen a photograph of him and forgotten it.

Lord Balfour was able to watch the development of Mrs. Willett's automatism at first hand and he made a detailed report on it.[1] Unfortunately, most of her scripts were considered too private for publication, so to form our judgments we have but a fraction of the testimony which finally led him to the belief that they were inspired by the Myers group. For this reason his published report is deliberately made from the psychological angle rather than offered as evidence for survival, even though Balfour himself was strongly inclined to accept the scripts as a whole as such. But he considered that the published scripts were quite enough to prove Mrs. Willett's gift of ESP.

Testimony for survival apart, Mrs. Willett's automatism is of psychological interest for two reasons. First, she never, as is usual with mediums, lost consciousness of her own personality or handed over to a Control. On the contrary, her consciousness appeared to be balanced on a knife edge so that she seemed to communicate alternately with the investigator and with a small group of discarnate entities. Secondly, these alleged entities put forward elaborate theories about the methods and processes of communication which were almost, but not quite, in accord with the views of the living Myers, and such theorising was in no way characteristic of Mrs. Willett's surface personality. Although she was well read and exceptionally intelligent, said Lord Balfour, the psychological aspects of psychical research had singularly little interest for her. Also, to judge from her casual remarks, her normal understanding of them appeared to him much below the level on which they were treated in her scripts. In his view these showed a power of thought on difficult and abstruse subjects which he would not have expected from her normal self.

The Balfour report makes use of three types of material: first-hand observations by the investigators, Mrs. Willett's own descriptions of her experiences and statements by the

[1] Gerald, Earl of Balfour. *A Study of the Psychological Aspects of Mrs. Willett's Mediumship*, Proceedings S.P.R., Vol. XLIII, pp. 41–318.

communicators. As a child, Mrs. Willett had already discovered her gift of automatic writing but she had dropped it owing to lack of guidance. In 1908 she again became interested in the subject and began to correspond about it with Mrs. Verrall. Later in the year she read a report by Alice Johnson on Mrs. Holland's scripts and this impelled her to try once more herself. In October she wrote of her own first scripts to Mrs. Verrall: "After a few feeble attempts the script seemed to come very rapidly, but it is *too definite* and therefore I distrust its being from an external source ... What worried me was that the words seemed to form in my brain before the pen set them down—a sort of hair's breadth beforeness. Most are signed Myers or F.W.H.M., but I can't say I think them of value ..."

From this time on, regular records of her scripts were kept. The process of obtaining them developed further than with the other cross correspondence automatists and took about three years to reach its final form. According to the scripts themselves it was guided by the Myers group, who claimed to be making use of Mrs. Willett to study new methods of communication with incarnate persons. Whatever their origin, whether they were dramatisations by Mrs. Willett's subconscious self, or came from other living minds or from their purported authors, they portray with dramatic intensity intelligent beings seeking to break through a barrier. Only direct quotations can convey their vivid quality and the extent to which the communicators took charge and for the sake of clarity these will be given as if they came from the source they claimed, but without prejudice as to their real origin.

The plan to experiment with Mrs. Willett as what they called a channel was first mentioned by her 'Myers' in scripts written when she was alone in late 1908 and early 1909. Here are a few statements he made at that time. "Experiments are necessary here as on earth, constant experiments with machines no two of which are alike ..."

"I am now going to begin fresh experiments you might tell Mrs. V. when opportunity occurs that the need for experiment on our side has not been sufficiently grasped on your side ..."

94

"Much is unknown to us even here and you are all far behind us in knowledge."

Soon after this written script came the first hint of a modification in Mrs. Willett's method of reception. At the end of January she wrote in her script handwriting, which differed from her normal one: "Gurney . . . I am always keeping in close touch with you try for a minute in your own hand to set down thought only . . ." She now wrote in her normal hand; "Try to set down thoughts can't you hear me speak it saves trouble I want to say something Gurney Yes . . ."

"Here", Mrs. Willett recorded, "I left off writing and held a sort of imaginary conversation with E. G. . . . I was perfectly normal." A fortnight later her 'Myers' wrote: "I am trying experiments with you to make you hear without writing therefore as it is I Myers who do this deliberately do not fear or wince when words enter your consciousness or subsequently when such words are in the scripts. On the contrary it will be the success of my purpose if you recognise in your script phrases you have found in your consciousness . . . and do not analyse whence these impressions which I shall in future refer to as Daylight Impressions come from, for they are parts of a psychic education framed by me for you . . ."

A few days later Mrs. Willett had a Daylight Impression of this type, about which she wrote to Mrs. Verrall:

"Last night . . . I was sitting idly wondering at it all . . . when I became aware so suddenly and strangely of F. W. H. M.'s presence that I said Oh! as if I had run into someone unexpectedly. During what followed I was absolutely normal. I heard nothing with my ears, but the words came from outside into my mind as they do when one is reading a book to oneself. I do not remember exact words but the first sentence was: 'Can you hear what I am saying?' I replied in my mind: 'Yes'."

"I get no impression of *appearance*," she wrote in a subsequent letter, "Only character, and in some way voice or pronunciations (though this doesn't mean that my *ears* hear, you know!) . . . I don't feel a sense of 'seeing' but an intense sense of personality, like a blind person perhaps might have—and of inflections, such as amusement or emotion on the part of the speaker. If you asked me *how* I know when E. G. [Gurney] is speaking and not F. W. H. M. [Myers] I can't exactly define, except that to me it would be impossible to be in doubt one instant, and with E. G. I sometimes know he is there a second or two before he speaks ... it is as 'minds' and 'characters' that they are to me, and yet not at all intangible or not-solid realities."

A few months later, in May 1909, came another advance in the process. This was a triangular conversation between Mrs. Verrall, Mrs. Willett and the communicators. Such conversations became known as Spoken D.I.'s (Daylight Impressions) and in them, of course, Mrs. Willett had to pass on the communicator's remarks to the investigator. The communicator appeared on the whole to be aware of his replies.

The day following the D.I. at which Mrs. Verrall was present, a written script signed 'Myers' said that he was satisfied with these first attempts at D.I.'s but did not intend to renew the experiment for some time. From the beginning he and the other communicators treated Mrs. Willett as a piece of extremely sensitive mechanism which could easily be thrown out of gear. Rest and peace were essential, they often insisted, if she was to attain the delicately poised condition they sought, in which she could communicate alternately with incarnate and discarnate experimenters without, so to speak, tipping over her own consciousness on either side. Her 'Gurney' once wrote, "I can't do much here today, she needs solitude and *rest*, and the life of confused and jarring elements in which she has been breathing is a bar. ...."

The training towards the poised consciousness necessary for this dual task of grasping and giving out could not apparently be pressed, for it was not until nine months after the first Spoken D.I. with Mrs. Verrall that the written script said the time had come for more. It also asked for Sir Oliver Lodge to be present. At the second D.I. with him, 'Gurney' said: "Tell Lodge I don't want this to develop into trance. You have got that, we are doing something new. Then he says telepathy." (The words "he says" are always, of course, interpolated by

Mrs. Willett.) The sitting ended: "You can tell Lodge that you are not unconscious or too dazed to know who you are, what you are, and, as each word comes, what you say. That's all. Goodbye." Then, after a moment's pause: "Pull yourself together and open your eyes and wake yourself up."

About this time a 'Myers' script said: "Are you clear we wish to avoid trance?" The communicators appeared to be trying to find the point of balance of consciousness. In May 1910 'Myers' wrote: "Try for a D.I. and come back to script if I tell you," and in May 1911, 'Gurney' wrote: "Tell Gerald [Lord Balfour] I want to experiment upon one point. I want to find the proper balance between Sc. and D.I. proper.... What amount of script facilitates the emerging into the secondary stage, viz. D.I. ...."

There was always the danger, apparently, that Mrs. Willett would tip over too far to be able to report back. In March 1912, her 'Gurney' warned the investigator of this. "Lodge ... did you notice just now that she was so completely over the border that though in those instants things swept into her consciousness, she couldn't pass them back? He says I want Gerald to be fully told of this because he says it throws light upon the methods ... She projected herself in a rush of sympathy ..."

Again in 1917, 'Gurney' said: "Today one touch would draw you so deeply within our influence that you would be unable to record or carry back ... I want them to understand that I purposefully hold you away ... so that you may record."

The communicators insisted that Mrs. Willett's 'self' was never out of the picture and that telepathy was the basic process by which their communications were made. This was said at least nineteen times in the scripts. In April 1911, 'Myers' wrote: "Let me again emphasize the difference that exists between Piper and Willett phenomena the former is possession the complete all but complete withdrawal of the spirit the other is the blending of incarnate and excarnate spirits ... it is a form of telepathy the point we have to study is to find the line where the incarnate spirit is sufficiently over the border to be in a state to receive and yet sufficiently controlling by its own power its own supraliminal and therefore able to transmit . . ."

A month later 'Gurney' asked urgently for a sitting with Lord Balfour, who had been great friends with the living Gurney, but Mrs. Willett was at first reluctant to sit with a stranger. Professional mediums are accustomed to a procession of unknown sitters and communicators, but Mrs. Willett's only sitters had been Mrs. Verrall and Lodge and her only communicators the Myers group and two other persons who purported to be co-operating with them. The names of these two she did not know. One of them she called the Dark Young Man—he was easily recognised by the investigators—and the other, the Young Lady in the Old-fashioned Dress. She too was recognised as someone who had died in youth fifty years earlier, but Lord Balfour says that her family name never appeared in the scripts and that the normal Mrs. Willett had probably never heard of her existence.

In spite of her reluctance to work with a stranger, Mrs. Willett finally agreed to try and sit with Lord Balfour, and this was the beginning of a fruitful partnership. In a script written shortly after their first sitting, when Mrs. Willett was alone, her 'Gurney' said: "I wish I could get you to understand why I wanted to speak to Gerald . . . You don't understand his point of view. But it is completely intelligible to me. He is interested in the process as distinct from the product. And it was about the process I wanted to speak. And the less you know of the process the better . . . because the recipient is best left in ignorance of the method. But it does not follow that the investigator need be . . ."

This interest in the technical side of the problem was quite foreign to Mrs. Willett's surface temperament and leads to the speculation whether, if the scripts were indeed the product of her own subconscious self, such analytically-minded experimenters lurk in the bosoms of other poetical women.

Although in the many comments on process scattered throughout the scripts it was always insisted that communication was basically telepathic, in 1911 the communicators went on to say that for certain kinds of scripts this might be supple-

98

mented by two other processes. One of these was direct extra-sensory perception by Mrs. Willett of discarnate conditions, including ideas in the minds of the communicators, and the other was the use made by the communicators of material already in her mind. They called this mutual selection, and it demanded, they said, of the sensitive "a capacity for excursus allied to a capacity for definite selection". (By excursus they meant the power of passing outside herself into their conditions.) The surface Mrs. Willett, apparently, was vague about the meaning of this word, for on coming to herself at the end of a sitting in 1930, she said to Lord Balfour: "Everybody gone! What is excursus?"

"Going out to meet someone else," he replied. "It's the opposite to invasion."

"Well," she said, "it's the way I do these things."

The theory of mutual selection is developed at length by 'Gurney' in a spoken D.I. of June, 1911, when Lord Balfour was the sitter. Here are a few extracts: "Oh, he says, well, then I look over the available factors—oh, and see what will serve . . . Oh, he says, it isn't only I who select. Oh, he says, now you've got it. There's another field for selection—and its such part of my mind, I, Gurney, as she can have access to. Oh, he says, what part? Why? Oh, I've missed a word—something something limited to—then I've skipped something, but I hear him say thoughts potentially.

"Oh, he says, put it another way. Having access to my mind her selection is chiefly limited to that which can naturally link on to human incarnate thought. Oh, he says, I wish I could get the word potential rightly used. I'm not saying it's limited [i.e. the material she has access to] to the actual but to the potential content . . . Oh, he says, does he see what I am driving at."

In this sitting, which was very long, Mrs. Willett was obviously trying hard to express ideas that were largely meaningless to her, and it is full of suggestive remarks. At one point she said rather pitifully: "And all things he says like that, he says I don't repeat. I thought I'd said it, I wonder where I am . . ."

This last comment is a reminder that, though not in trance in the Piper sense of having lost consciousness, her attention was not focussed in a normal way on her physical surroundings. She went on, as if Gurney were speaking; "That's where the gamble comes in. How will it be used, the knowledge supernormally gained? Now then you have present in the whole self the matter from which I selected plus the matter supernormally acquired from me. Now comes the weaving. Oh, he says, that's where subliminal activity comes in. Oh, he says, it's a dangerous weapon, yet we can't do without it." (This seems to be a reference to the tendency of the subconscious self to run away down any chain of associations and mingle them with the subject in hand.)

She went on: "Often there is a fairly long period of—don't get that word—it contains a g and an s and a t and an n." (Lord Balfour suggested gestation, but she did not notice this.) "Say incubation he says—and then comes the uprush. And then he says, now I must bring in telepathy as the guiding influence. He says this process is only one among a great variety. Oh, he says, we must experiment—he says, so much is unmapped.

"Oh, and he says, the waste of material when we keep on hammering at one point—approaching it from every—can't read that word—point of the compass—only to find that the point has been grasped and that we might have passed on to new matter.

"Oh, he says, I can't see your mind, Gerald, but I can feel you in some dim way through her. He says, it's a sort of lucky bag, her mind to me—when I'm not shut out from it.

"He says I think I got some things I wanted said about selection. It's the thought of its being as it were a mutual process that I want driven home.

"Oh, he says, now say this for me. He says you want to foster in sensitives a sort of dual attitude, belief in their capacity —Oh! say it slowly—Oh, I'm so tired, I'm so tired—Oh, I'm climbing. Oh, I'm climbing—belief, Oh, I will say it, I will say it—belief in their capacity to have access to the mind of the communicator, together with a wholesome sense of discrimination in regard to the expressions—not right—regard to something to which that access leads—productions.

"Oh, he says, you mayn't know it, there's a natural bent to extreme scepticism here . . ."

Her 'Gurney' apparently meant that the scepticism was in Mrs. Willett. Her scripts, like those of Mrs. Holland, insisted several times that acceptance and reciprocity are essential to real communication and that the automatist's belief in the personality of the communicators is an absolutely vital part of the conditions which make it easy for them to work. "The response", said her 'Myers', in June 1909, "to some extent —how large an extent I do not yet exactly know—the response conditions the power of transmission . . ."

In a D.I., with Sir Oliver Lodge present, in May 1910, 'Myers' lamented the confusion and mistakes and apparently negative result. "Yes," said Lodge. "But I think we also are aware of the difficulties."

"He says it is far worse for him", answered Mrs. Willett. "He is trying to make himself real to people who are not only conscious of their own reality, but are also among people who admit their reality." Then, speaking as if directly from Myers: "How much of your sense of reality is due to that? Think that over. There is a paralysing sense of isolation in the experience of coming back . . . one needs something reciprocal . . ."

In another D.I. a few days later, she said on behalf of her 'Myers' : "He says that . . . the study of new sensitives would never lose interest for him. There are so many varying conditions and so many self-induced difficulties. Many of these really come from self hallucination of individual minds, who would stereotype the phenomenon, but it's best to let it go its own way unhampered, free serene and calm; above all calm and free . . ."

The amount of attention the communicators expected Mrs. Willett to pay to her script varied, says Lord Balfour, with the "style and subject matter of the communication itself. Sometimes a concentrated effort of attention on her part is called for; at others she is instructed deliberately to relax and 'let the pen run free'. The minimum of effort is apparently required in scripts of an allusive and disjointed type which are not intended to convey any connected meaning to her ... In other scripts, and especially in spoken D.I.'s, the degree of effort required seems to depend very much on the difficulty of the subject matter and to reach a maximum when that is highly abstract and beyond the automatist's ordinary powers of comprehension."

Mrs. Willett's surface self was often frankly resistant to abstract subjects whose terms she did not understand. "Oh, Edmund!" she exclaimed when her 'Gurney' spoke of the transcendental self. "*You do bore me so!*" And again: "Oh! Edmund says powder first and jam afterwards. You see it seems a long time since I was here with them. [She means with the Myers group]—and I want to talk and enjoy myself [spoken querulously]. And I've all the time to keep on working, and seeing and listening to such boring old—Oh! Ugh!"

The subjects discussed by the communicators must certainly have been trying at times to Mrs. Willett's non-scientific and non-philosophical temperament. In May 1911, Gurney apparently referred to a passage in Hegel's *Phänomenologie des Geistes*. "He is trying to explain something that I don't understand," said Mrs. Willett. "What is the process necessary for self-realisation? It's a German word and I can't see it. *Welt* something or other". The context suggests that she was trying for *Weltgeist*.

In May 1912, after Lord Balfour had been giving a philosophical lecture at Cambridge, her 'Sidgwick' tried her high by discussing three conflicting theories of mind-body relationship, parallelism, epiphenomenalism, and interactionism, about which her normal self knew little and cared less. "Sounds to me very stupid," she said at one point. "What does it mean? It's only words [gesticulating with both hands]. ... There, just like that—is—then there's a word *that* long—consciousness. I've got it—oh, it's disappointing when my lips won't say it ... Epiphenomenal—that's the last of the three words."

She coped better with what the communicators called "the specious lure of the parallelistic phantasy", though later on, oddly enough, she had great trouble with the comparatively simple word 'interaction'. "I've got it", she cried at last, triumphantly. "Oh, but now I've got to give it out. Oh, I'm all buzzing. I can't think why people talk about such stupid things. Such long stupid words." Then she sighed and stretched herself. After further efforts, including at attempt to draw a symbol of interaction, 'Gurney' helped her with a joke, which Lord Balfour considered was characteristic of the living Gurney. "Edmund makes me laugh," she said. "He says, 'Well, think of Ur of the Chaldees.' He's making a joke and they're very angry with him, but the point of it is the terrible effect of disembodiment in one singularly sensitive to shades of sound. He says that Ur [for er] would make Fred shudder. I must try it you know, it's perfectly ridiculous." She then printed INT UR AC SHUN at the foot of her drawing.

Later in the D.I. she asked with great disgust: "What is the parallelistic theory? To have to come all the way to talk about these things." Finally, having lamented that the pressure in her head was full to painfulness, she achieved some verbal triumphs on 'Gurney's' behalf. "You can't make parallelism square he says with the conclusions to which recent research points. *Pauvres parallelistes!* They're like drowning men clinging to spars. But the epiphenomenalistic bosh [pronouncing with difficulty] that's simply blown away. It's one of the blind alleys of human thought. Oh! I don't want to hear any more. I'm tired."

In January, 1922, her 'Gurney' tried her yet higher by discussing the origin of the individual soul, which he attributed to the process of the Absolute on its way to self consciousness. "So far as I can recollect", says Lord Balfour, "nothing quite like this is to be found in *Human Personality*. [Mrs. Willett had read an abridged edition of this]. It seems to me to bear the mark of derivation from post-Kantian idealistic speculation, of which, curiously enough, a good many traces crop up in the scripts. Here again, if they are the work of the automatist's subliminal self, from what source were the ideas expressed in them obtained? The normal Mrs. Willett is unable to throw any light on this question."

The difficulty of transmitting subject matter which is above the head of an automatist seems to be increased when the actual words are meaningless to her, as in the case of Mrs. Piper's Tanatos, Sanatos, Thanatos. Proper names always seem to be particularly hard, perhaps because, unlike the names of objects, they are not automatically linked to an image. Mrs. Willett was seldom able to get a Greek or Latin word correctly and her communicators would sometimes try to help her. In a lone script of 1912 she had trouble in writing the name Deucalion, the Noah of Greek mythology, of whom she afterwards said she had never consciously heard.

"Now another thought
                 Docalon

No no try again

                 Dewacorn [this word ended in a scribble]
                 Dewacorn

NO DEUCALION
The sound is DEW

                 K
                 LION not Lion

Write it slowly

                 Deucalion

I want that said. It has a meaning. The stones of the earth shall praise thee that is what I want said. It is I who say it and the word is Deucalion That was well caught Good child That sort of thing makes one feel out of breath doesn't it on both sides—I am going Say too this word He set his bow in [illegible] in the clouds."

On all this Mrs. Willett commented: "This part of the script was very odd. Though there was a great deal of effort about it, it was extremely interesting in the same sort of way that it is interesting to get a Patience out. It was written rather like this, as near as words can describe it: After 'now I want another thought' there was a pause, the Doocalon written slowly and very deliberately, then No No written impatiently but good temperedly. This leads me to suppose that it was not Fred who was writing, because I get a sense of irritability and grumpiness when I am trying to catch a word in this sort of way and he is writing."

Mrs. Willett and the other automatists suffered from one difficulty which is similar to experiences under mescalin. This was a sense of too much flitting past. "I'm so confused," she said during a sitting in 1914 when she was trying to give fragments in the *Ear of Dionysius* case. "I'm all with things flitting past me. I don't seem to catch them . . . That one eye has got something to do with one ear. [This was one of the *Ear of Dionysius* allusions] . . . That's what they wanted me to say. There's such a mass of things you see running through my mind that I can't catch anything."

Her 'Myers' once confessed: "In my eagerness . . . the thoughts come so quickly they slip past you." At another time he said that he could not get through a series of questions because "they jostle each other and I stand speechless and impotent from the very force of my longing to utter." Of this her 'Gurney' commented: "Myers doesn't manage things as well as I do. He takes more out of her. He doesn't shield off from her sufficiently; he lets the whole blaze come out in his impatience."

Whatever the cause of Mrs. Willett's changes of focus of consciousness, they were clearly a great joy to her. "I must come back, you know," she said in 1913, as she finished a written script. "It's just like waking up in prison from a dream when one has been at home. Don't you ever walk out of yourself? It's so heavenly to be out of myself—when I'm everything, you know, and everything else is me."

On another occasion, when she had again been describing a visionary journey, she was disturbed by noise and wrote, "I've lost the thread, it's all gone. I was seeing visions and I did not ever want to leave. Fred [Myers] was with me F.W.H.M. I also saw Henry Sidgwick. He had a white beard. . . . How *nothing* time is. All human experience is one . . ."

The second Lord Balfour's study of the voluminous scripts from which these extracts are taken is a cautious document. He had been in the Cabinet as Chief Secretary for Ireland for five years and President of the Board of Trade for another five, he knew something about evidence and about human nature.

Also he was a Balfour, and inclined, like his brother, Arthur, and his sister, Mrs. Sidgwick, to be a little remote, detached and dispassionate. It took a long time, therefore, for him to accept the claim that Mrs. Willett's communicators were indeed the Myers and Gurney he had known in life, but in the end he was convinced of it, though he did not, of course, consider it proven. He makes an interesting point of the differences in thought between the living Myers and Mrs. Willett's. Not that he looked on the two as contradictory; the views of the Willett 'Myers' seemed to him a reasonable development of Myers' own. But from wherever Mrs. Willett drew these views, it does not seem to be from Balfour himself, since both her Myers and her Gurney differed from him about the essential nature of human beings. Balfour, for instance, thought that the surface and subconscious selves of one individual might communicate with each other by telepathy. The Willett 'Myers' would have none of this. Balfour, again, had a tidy mind and he wanted a plain yes or no to the questions: Are the various currents of consciousness below the threshold separate selves?—as he himself was inclined to think—or are they fragments of one unitary self? But the communicators would not be pinned down to a definite answer. 'Gurney' once said: "Yet they are not two but one—put in for G.'s [Balfour's] benefit this. He tried to get me on the horns of a duality which would almost amount to a conception of the selves as separated in such a way as to amount to two entities—but I was *not* to be *impaled*."

On another occasion, when Balfour once more suggested that the surface and subconscious selves were separate as two persons are separate, he was firmly put in his place. "BOSH!" replied 'Gurney' "Different aspects of the same thing." Yet the communicators obviously admitted some kind of separation. It is as if human nature as seen by them was not explicable in definite terms of either/or.

It is to be hoped that one day it will be possible to publish more of the Willett scripts, for the published part already contains material of a higher intellectual quality than scripts from other sources and yet it appears to have been the unpublished part which most impressed Lord Balfour.

CHAPTER XI

Patience Worth

WHATEVER the origin of Mrs. Willett's scripts, they were not what would have been expected from a person of her interests and intellectual attainments. In consequence, they opened the eyes of contemporary investigators yet further to the powers of the subconscious self, whether of dramatisation, ESP from the living, or communication with the discarnate. In 1913 more evidence of that self's remarkable capacities, at least for dramatisation, came from across the Atlantic in the shape of ouija board writing and automatic speech by a Mrs. John H. Curran, an American middle-class housewife who lived in St. Louis, Missouri. Her interests and surroundings and the scripts themselves were exhaustively studied by an American doctor, Walter Franklin Prince, who, in view of his skill as an investigator, was later invited to become President of the S.P.R. in London.[1]

Mrs. Curran's automatisms are of interest to students of psychical research, not because they contain evidence of ESP obtained in test conditions, but as dramatic examples of what the subconscious can do on its own. They resembled Mrs. Willett's in being apparently superior to the automatist's surface intellectual attainments and in seeming to draw upon knowledge beyond that which she normally possessed. As with Mrs. Willett, her normal consciousness was never actually displaced, although she fell into an abstracted state when producing scripts. But she did not, like Mrs. Piper, go into trance.

Mrs. Curran left school at fourteen, and when her automatism began at the age of thirty-one she had never travelled away from the Middle West. She was not interested in spiritualism—she said she found mediumship repulsive—and her

[1] Walter Franklin Prince *The Case of Patience Worth* (Boston S.P.R., 1927).

literary interests were limited. Her ambition had always been to become a singer. One day a friend asked her to put her hand on a ouija board. At first the results were dull and Mrs. Curran was bored. Then, suddenly, on July 8th 1913, an ostensible entity, called Patience Worth, turned up. Who or what Patience Worth could be was and still is a mystery, but she was certainly a 'character' with a gift of biting repartee and a temperament very unlike Mrs. Curran's. She claimed to have lived on a Dorset farm in England in the sixteen hundreds and to have gone thence to America, where she had been killed by Indians. Whoever she was, she had a talent for writing, and she would use archaic words to which so far as Dr. Prince could discover the normal Mrs. Curran had no access. At enormous speed she spelled out poetry, proverbs, prayers and conversation, and also novels of surprisingly high quality, all of which were written consistently in different idioms. Several of these have been published, but a large mass of material written in her later life has never been studied.

One novel, *The Sorry Tale*, was set in the time of Christ, and another, *Hope Trueblood*, in the nineteenth century. This, incidentally, was long after Patience Worth's purported life on earth. A third, *Telka*, was an idyll of mediaeval England. An American philologist analysed the language in this tale and found that no words were used which came into the language later than the seventeenth century and that ninety per cent of them were derived from Anglo-Saxon. Dr. Schiller, at one time President of the S.P.R., pointed out that this was a philological miracle, since such a proportion of words of Anglo-Saxon origin was not found in the language after the beginning of the thirteenth century. For comparison, the Authorised Version of the Bible contains only 77 per cent of Anglo-Saxon derivations. Patience Worth also performed the feat of writing more than one novel at a time, a few hundred words of one and then of another, and even after a lapse of weeks she never forgot where to go on. On one occasion a chapter was lost, but two months later she redictated it, and when the lost pages later came to light she was found to have repeated the identical words.

A major puzzle is the knowledge displayed in the scripts of

social conditions at different periods. Mrs. Curran did not live in a literary ambience and her knowledge of history was of the vaguest. She thought, for instance, that Henry VIII had been beheaded and her apparent knowledge of New Testament times was on the same level. Yet the author of *The Sorry Tale* seemed to be casually familiar with the social customs, clothing, commerce and weapons of those times, of the political relations between Romans and Jews, the topography and architecture of Jerusalem, and many other contemporary details. As an author Patience Worth won approval from a number of critics. *The New York Times* called *The Sorry Tale* a noble book, and *The Bookman* commented that it had a well-constructed plot and gave an excellent picture of the Roman world when the Empire was at its height. English reviewers did not realise that *Hope Trueblood* was written by an American, and *The Athenaeum*, unaware that it was praising a 'psychic' production, called it "a novel of decided promise . . . definite and clear-cut characterisation, good dialogue and arresting runs of expression, deep but restrained feeling . . ."

The identity of Patience Worth is anybody's guess. Contemporary psychologists would tend to look at her as a secondary personality of Mrs. Curran's. Two cases of such dual personality are well-known, for one, Sally Beauchamp, was exhaustively studied by Dr. Morton Prince (not to be confused with Franklin Prince) and the other, Doris Fischer, by Franklin Prince himself.[1] But Patience Worth differed from the Beauchamp and Fischer cases in that she did not replace Mrs. Curran's normal consciousness, she was co-conscious with it. An American psychologist, Professor Charles E. Long, studied her mentality for two years in the hope of discovering what degree of rationality could be attained by a subconscious centre.[2] He came to the conclusion that her mentality was of a very high order, original and creative, and

[1] Morton Prince, *The Dissociation of a Personality* (Longmans, 1906). W. Franklin Prince and Dr. Hyslop, *Multiple Personality*. Articles in *Proceedings* American S.P.R., Vols. IX, X and XI.

[2] Charles E. Long, article in *The Psychological Review*, September, 1919. Since this book was written a new case has been discussed by C. H. Thigpen and H. M. Cleckley in *The Three Faces of Eve* (Secker and Warburg, 1957).

he was also surprised and impressed by her high moral and spiritual standards. "Here is a subconscious self", he said, "far outstripping in power and range the primary consciousness."

We are not today in a position to make this comparison, but of the actual swiftness of Patience Worth's intelligence there is written evidence in the hundreds of snap definitions and short poems she wrote instantly on being given a subject. Define "flapper", she was asked in the days when this word was current slang for too-progressive maidens. "They dare what the past hoped for", was the immediate reply. As a subject for a poem she was once given "The Finite and the Infinite", and she wrote without hesitation:

> Behold Him! The pith of chaos,
> That certain God, who, with a sure hand,
> Creates the universes, swings suns and moons,
> And lets the stars drip from his fingertips.
> Behold Him, the hunger urge within the breast of every man,
> Seeking, seeking, seeking back to the certain spot.
> Behold this INFINITE love,
> The honey of which holds the atoms of the day together
> The honey of which holds the universes suspended
> In a beauteous harmony held fast;
> The honey of which is God.
> Man and matter, finite, are but thirst vessels—
> Man for knowledge and for wisdom, matter for quickening.

This may not be great poetry but it appears pretty certain that Mrs. Curran's surface personality could not have achieved it at once to order.

The verdict that she far outstripped the surface Mrs. Curran in intelligence was one in which Patience herself entirely concurred, for she treated both Mrs. Curran and her friends very much *de haut en bas*. Mrs. Curran looked up to her with profound respect and there can be no doubt that she greatly increased the scope and drama of her otherwise not very varied life, since, as time went on, Mrs. Curran felt herself to be directly aware of the scenes narrated by Patience. "When the stories come", she said, "the scenes become panoramic, the characters moving and acting their parts . . . If two people are seen talking on the corner of the street, I see, not only them, but the neighbouring part of the street, with the buildings, stones, dogs, people and all, just as they would be in a real scene. If people talk a foreign language . . . I hear the talk, but over and above is the voice of Patience either interpreting or giving me the part she wishes to use as story."

And Mrs. Curran felt she could do more than observe. "This tiny figure of myself", she said, "would boldly take part in the play . . . walking up to the bin-side of a market man and taking up the fruit and tasting it, or smelling the flower within a garden or feeling the cloth . . . And the experience was . . . as real to me as any personal experience, becoming physically mine, recorded by my sight, taste and smell as other experiences. Thus I have become familiar with many flowers of strange places which I never saw, but know when I see them again in pictures . . . It is like travelling in new and unknown regions . . ."

Here again, as with Mrs. Willett, Mrs. Curran's automatisms appear to have brought new and stimulating experiences into her life, without reducing her efficiency in ordinary affairs.

CHAPTER XII

Mediumship—Mrs. Leonard (1)

WE have seen that one factor in particular seems to encourage the emergence of *psi*. That is faith of some kind in something. Mrs. Curran implicitly believed that Patience Worth was the disembodied spirit she claimed to be. In both the Holland and Willett scripts the purported Myers and his friends insisted that the automatists' belief in their reality immensely increased their power to communicate. Conversely, hostility and doubt on the part of any one involved, including the investigator, is water to flame, even in the case of straightforward experimental ESP between the living.

The spiritualist medium has absolute faith that the controls and communicators are the discarnate entities they represent themselves to be. This has the dual advantage of freeing the medium from self-consciousness and of shelving responsibility for mistakes on to some discarnate and inaccessible entity. The friendly co-operation of one avowedly spiritualist medium, Mrs. Osborne Leonard, enabled members of the S.P.R. to study the ESP and psychology of a genuine trance medium for over forty years. She has also demonstrated that a medium can remain both honest and a person of normal common sense in daily life. And the world does not help honest mediums to remain normal. Believers regard them as the mouth-piece of heaven, some psychiatrists class them as hysterics and the public in general look on them as frauds or mad. "Good gracious", exclaimed a stranger on meeting Mrs. Leonard, "you look quite sensible."

This attitude, however natural, may lead to unfortunate results. A psychiatrist has told me that there are persons confined in mental hospitals today who in past ages would have been revered for their awareness of other states of being and who might have been saintly examples to the community. In any case, to ignore mediumship because it is classed as a hysterical symptom helps to conceal the fact that in such states of dissociation genuine ESP can occur. That, it must be repeated *ad nauseum*, is the point of interest for psychical research.

In Mrs. Leonard, fortunately, S.P.R. investigators were able to study mediumship in the least unattractive conditions, for her helpfulness made friends of the most hostile critics, and no detective ever caught her swerving one inch from the path of honesty. She herself attributes the initial impulse of her mediumship to a bad shock at the age of eight which deeply affected her attitude to death.[1] Her father was wont to take her every Sunday to visit one of his friends, a large, kind, cheerful man who made a great fuss of her. One Sunday they arrived to find the blinds of the house drawn down. Then the parlour-maid opened the door with a tear-stained face. "The Master's gone," she sobbed. This terrified the child, from whom all knowledge of death had been carefully hidden and later on she asked her father, "Where is Mr. Underwood?"

"He's gone, dear."

"Gone where?"

"Don't ask questions, dear."

Two days later she saw her father leave the house, clad in mournful black, and the housemaid told her, "They're burying Mr. Underwood ... deep under the earth ... *Of course* he can't get out ... Stop asking questions ..."

"Will my mother be buried?"

"Of course she will, and your father and you and me and everybody ..." After this further shock the child found and read the burial service—ashes to ashes, dust to dust.

This painful episode would have caused her yet greater suffering but for a private consolation. "Every morning," she says, "soon after waking, even while dressing or having my nursery breakfast, I saw visions of most beautiful places ... Walking about ... were people who seemed radiantly happy ... I remember thinking to myself, How different they are, how different from 'Down Here' people, how full of love and light and peace they are."

[1] Gladys Osborne Leonard, *My Life in Two Worlds* (Cassell, 1931).

She called this place the Happy Valley but took care never to mention it to other people. One day, however, she forgot and, pointing to the dining room wall, she cried to her father to look at "the specially beautiful place we are seeing this morning." Then trouble arose. She was making it up. She was a naughty girl. Finally she was sternly forbidden by her entire grown-up world ever to see or look for her Happy Valley again. And gradually it ceased to appear. A few years later—she was now in her teens—she saw the advertisement of a spiritualist meeting, and went in. Enraptured she rushed home to tell her mother the glorious news. The dead were not only living, but easily accessible! The result was not what she expected. "All that," said her mother with cold anger, "is vile and wicked. I forbid you ever to go to that place again."

So this wonderful new-found way of escape from the inevitable deep dark grave was abruptly cut off. Parallels to these childhood experiences can be found in the autobiographies of other sensitives. They too visited worlds like the Happy Valley, had visions of dead relatives and played games with non-physical playmates. And in their cases, too, such experiences met with ferocious disapproval from those in authority.

Mrs. Leonard's adolescence was a shadowed period in other ways. Her prosperous family lost all their money, and to earn her living she began to train as a singer. But diphtheria ruined her voice and she was driven to take humble parts in touring theatrical companies. All this time her leaning towards spiritualism, though concealed, had never died and it was stimulated once more a few years before the first world war, when she was twenty-two. She woke up one night at 2 a.m. to see her mother close to her in a circle of light, looking much younger and extremely well. She had known that her mother was ill but had not thought it serious. Next morning a telegram brought the news that she had died at 2 a.m. This vision was of a type very familiar to students of psychical research. The girl accepted it without question as being her mother herself and it confirmed her literal belief in the spiritualist teaching and decided her to try and develop her own gifts, in the hope of being able to help others who were sad and bereaved.

There was a tradition in her family that about 1800 an ancestor of hers had married an Indian girl, who died very young in childbirth. This girl soon purported to turn up as a communicator. She called herself Feda, and not long afterwards became Mrs. Leonard's permanent Control. What she actually was, a separate entity, a dramatisation by Mrs. Leonard's subconscious self, or a secondary personality on the lines of Morton Prince's famous Sally, is still an open question. One psychical researcher, Whately Carington, tried to throw light on her identity by means of the word association test devised by Jung.[1] He found that on the whole when Mrs. Leonard's conscious reactions were fast, Feda's were slow and *vice versa*, which suggested that they were two sides of the one personality. But he thought that the reaction patterns of certain long-term communicators differed to some extent from both. Furthermore, when one sitter, Mr. Drayton Thomas, sat with two other mediums, his usual two communicators purported to turn up, and similar tests were made on them by Whately Carington. In his view these also seemed to suggest the operation of some kind of external factor or influence. But more recent experiments indicate that such differing reactions can occur when a person merely imagines he is someone else.[2]

Who or whatever Feda was, it makes for clarity of description to refer to her as a separate person. She was very like Margaret, the secondary personality of the Doris Fischer studied by Dr. Franklin Prince in America. They were both gay, childish and entertaining. But Margaret bullied Doris, whereas Feda merely looked down on Mrs. Leonard, though she would sometimes tease her, by giving away, for example, a loved piece of her jewellery. All the same, the most sticky sitters could never help liking Feda who was most friendly and co-operative. She thought she had a mission to further psychical research and she appeared very conscientious about transmitting messages from purported

[1] In these tests the subject is asked to respond, with the first word that comes into his head, to a series of words which are read out to him. The more a word affects him emotionally the longer he takes to respond, hence to a string of words each person will have an individual reaction pattern.

[2] The tests remain valuable despite some error in Carington's figures.

communicators. Moreover, unlike many Controls, if she made a mistake she said so and did not indulge in guessing. She shared, in fact, Mrs. Leonard's transparent honesty.

In the spring of 1914, says Mrs. Leonard, Feda sent her repeated instructions—this is a curious phrase but it must be remembered that her surface mentality was unconscious when Feda was in action—to begin work at once as a professional medium. "Something big and terrible is going to happen to the world," Feda insisted. "Feda must help people through you."

Such an appeal was certain of its effect on a woman as warm-hearted as Mrs. Leonard, particularly after her own childhood shock about death, and she obediently took a room and gave daily sittings. In 1915 a French widow came anonymously to one of these because she was in desperate grief at the recent death of her two sons in action. She knew nothing of mediumship but she told Sir Oliver Lodge's wife the results of this sitting—correct names and so on which were strongly suggestive of ESP. Shortly afterwards, on September 15th, Lodge's own son, Raymond, was killed. A little later on Lady Lodge paid an anonymous visit to Mrs. Leonard. This was on the French widow's behalf, not her own, but she was given a message purporting to come from Raymond that he had met a friend of his father's whose name was Myers. Lodge himself now went to see Mrs. Leonard—again anonymously—and he too was told that Raymond was in contact with an old friend, M., and with other friends of his. "These people " said 'Raymond', "tell me that a little later they will explain why they are helping me."

At this sitting Feda also made an allusion to a message which had been given for Lodge by Mrs. Piper's 'Myers' in America on August 8th. "Now Lodge ..." Mrs. Piper had written. "Myers says you take the part of the poet and he will act as Faunus." Mrs. Piper had also said that Mrs. Verrall would unravel this cryptic message which meant nothing to Lodge. Mrs. Verrall did recognise it as referring to an Ode by Horace, in which he mentioned a tree on his country estate which had fallen down and would have destroyed him in its fall had not Faunus lightened the blow. Lodge had assumed this to be a warning but had thought little of it until Mrs. Leonard's reminder.

Lodge and his wife then visited another medium, separately and strictly anonymously. He too gave them both good descriptions of Raymond and spoke of F. W. M. and the group who, he said, were interested in operating through the partition. He also reported Raymond as saying "Don't think it (the help) was only for charity's sake, he has got an ulterior motive, and thinks that you will be able to ... make the society, *the* Society, he says, of some use to the world."

About five weeks later Lodge again saw Mrs. Leonard who by this time knew who he was. To identify Raymond her Control, Feda, described a group photograph, its setting, some details about numbers, Raymond's position in relation to the man behind him, and so on. This seems at the least to have been precognition, or ESP at second hand, for such a photograph was sent to Lodge independently after the sitting by the mother of one of Raymond's brother officers. Unknown to him it had been taken in France three weeks before Raymond's death. Six months later, Lodge sought to check the Faunus incident by asking a friend to enquire of an outside medium who knew no classics, whether Horace meant anything to Myers in connection with Lodge. The medium, in answer, referred to a Satire by Horace, which describes the charm of his country place compared with the worries of Rome. But he did not appear to have any idea what he was talking about. Two months later, Mrs. Piper again wrote a message for Lodge, referring to a third poem by Horace which linked the previous two by combining the topics of the falling tree and the worries of Rome. This was the end of Mrs. Piper's connection with the S.P.R. and it may be called a good finish, since she achieved classical references beyond her normal knowledge, a tidy little cross correspondence with an outside medium in another country and what looks like a warning of Raymond Lodge's death, put as plainly as tact and decency would allow.

The above is a bare factual summary of the kind of testimony which convinced Lodge of Raymond's survival and which Mrs. Leonard continued to produce for him and other people for many years. It inevitably lacks not only the verisimilitude felt by the sitters themselves but that mysterious sense of presence which seems to be the straw that finally tips such sceptics as Hodgson over the brink of acceptance. It is obvious that the psychological conditions for the appearance of a life-like Raymond, authentic or not, were very favourable. The holocaust of the 1914–18 war was at its height. Mrs. Leonard's ardent desire was to comfort the many bereaved around her. Lodge had a profoundly compassionate nature and he had just lost a much-loved son. The kind of link which appears on occasion to evoke ESP must have been very strong between them.

The pattern of Mrs. Leonard's mediumship changed little throughout the forty odd years it was studied. It became clear that her surface consciousness knew nothing of what transpired while she was in trance. She usually spoke rather than wrote and Feda was her only Control, though with one or two regular sitters she would occasionally hand over to their regular 'communicators' to speak directly. Their great desire was to identify themselves, and their talk was mainly on the simple human level and thus differed from the intellectual approach and metaphysical speculations of the Verrall, Holland and Willett 'Myers Group'. However she did it, her characterisation of these communicators could be brilliant. W. H. Salter has pointed out that it went much further than the most startling reproduction of tricks and manner of speech.[1] For years on end a communicator, who purported to be a person Mrs. Leonard had never met in life, would give message after message without once speaking out of character or putting the mental or emotional emphasis wrong. The question is, could this remarkable feat have been achieved by no more than sub-conscious inference and dramatisation on Mrs. Leonard's part, plus telepathy from the sitter or other living persons?

It is only by reading hundreds of sittings that the characterisation in them can make its full impact, but the account by a regular sitter, the Rev. C. Drayton Thomas, of his purported father's first attempt to take over from Feda may give some idea of it. Here again the conditions would seem favourable for the production of a life-like communicator, whether authentic or not, for Mr. Thomas, like Mrs. Leonard, was a

[1] *Trance Mediumship* S.P.R., Pamphlet by W. H. Salter.

compassionate idealist and shared her ardent faith in the possibility of communication with the discarnate. Feda had been giving messages from Mr. Thomas's purported father. Then she said, "There is something he wishes to try now, so Feda will keep quiet for a minute."

After a long pause, says Mr. Thomas, came a voice, deep slow, stately and entirely different from Feda's childish treble. It was not his father's earth voice, but his manner of speech. "Charlie, Charlie, it is extraordinary, who would have thought it possible. I can control the hands and head but apparently not the lower part of the body. I fear I could not stand. Each time I will try to do this a little. It will be good to be able to talk freely together."

The 'communicator' clasped Mr. Thomas's hand, slapped his knee and continued to repeat, "It is extraordinary!" Then he felt, smilingly, for his moustache and beard and spoke of some joke about his face which, he said, Mr. Thomas's mother would know of, though Mr. Thomas would not. He said he had forgotten it himself until back in a body again. Mr. Thomas's mother later confirmed this joke.

Five sittings later the father purported to try again. "I found," he said this time, "that I could remember and use my mind to a certain extent, although told I should not be able to do so. I am advised to get control of the voice before attempting too much. I think I may be able to reproduce my own voice later."

Six months later, Mr. Thomas's sister, Ella, also purported to speak to him but she found direct speech very difficult. "I cannot think or connect up ideas", she said. "Even now I have a strong consciousness of being with you often, but no detailed recollection of things we have done. I want to practise remembering . . . This controlling feels like having a mask over the face [While saying this the hands were feeling over face, neck, arms and shoulders.] I have difficulty in regulating the breathing and preventing a hissing on the s-sounds, like the word 'Yes'."

At various times the communicators described some of their difficulties in making contact. It was very complicated. They must watch the medium's breathing. They must choose ideas she was most likely to get through. They must avoid starting a misleading train of thought in her mind. At the same time, when controlling the medium directly they themselves felt far from clear-minded and forgot things they knew perfectly well. They said that the division of the mind into conscious and subconscious ceases at death but recurs when they take possession of a medium.

The Control, Feda, also had her own problems. She knew no more of the communicators than they told her. When she was in control the medium often appeared to be listening intently, as though being dictated to, but Feda would say of a communicator, "He's showing me this or that", more often than "He says". She sometimes mistook a word which was obvious to the sitter and she would occasionally, strangely enough, be corrected by the communicator's ostensible voice at some distance from the medium. She once said, for example, "It's like being put in charge of a department of boars? Do you mean *pigs?* Boars in an institution?" and the apparently independent voice made an emphatic correction '*Borstal*'. Mrs. Leonard had undertaken never to read any of the literature published by the S.P.R., yet many of the processes and difficulties described by her communicators are similar to those described in the Willett scripts. Mr. Thomas's 'father', for instance, drew the same distinction as Mrs. Willett's 'Gurney' between himself projecting an idea or image in to the mind of the medium, or the medium picking up some—perhaps irrelevant—idea from his mind. Professor C. D. Broad has pointed out the distinction they made between various forms of telepathy.[1] Suppose they wanted to convey a message about a horse. They could speak the word, or they could make Feda hear the word horse or the sound of a horse's movement by telepathy. Or they could make her see an image of a horse, or see the written word, again by telepathy. Or they could use a symbol, say, a jockey with a whip. Or they could just convey the idea alone, without use of either words or images. Such hints and clues may all be nonsense or they may one day help to clarify the nature of ESP.

[1] C. D. Broad, *The Phenomenology of Mrs. Leonard's Trance*, Journal of American S.P.R., April, 1955.

CHAPTER XIII

Mediumship—Mrs. Leonard (2)

Mrs. Leonard's ESP usually occurred during attempts by her Control, Feda, and other communicators, to convince sitters that they were genuine discarnate entities. At the time telepathy from the living seemed the most likely alternative source of the information by which they tried to identify themselves and Feda suggested a new type of test in which it was difficult for this to occur. She offered to report something written on a particular page of a particular book, which stood on a shelf in a house which not only Mrs. Leonard, but sometimes even the sitter had never visited. These became known as Book Tests, and, although most of them were inconclusive, even the cautious W. H. Salter found some of them so apt and definite as to give him a strong impression that some other factor than chance was at work.

At one time Feda developed the habit of giving sitters tests from the books in Mr. and Mrs. Salter's own house. From their point of view, this had its drawbacks. They would get telegrams, 'Touch no books in your house', and would then, after further instructions, have to undertake the task, sometimes long and tiresome, of verifying tests for other people. One good test was given with Mrs. Salter as sitter. Without telling anyone Mr. Salter put some test books on a shelf in an unoccupied room. Feda clearly indicated that shelf and a book on it—it was Henry James's *Daisy Miller*—and she said that some words a quarter of an inch above a line drawn halfway down page 15 would form a cross correspondence, also that three particular words, 'a long pole', were to be taken from that line. The communicator then purported to show the Control a long pole in his hand.

The passage at that spot in *Daisy Miller* was " 'I should like to know where you got that pole', she said. 'I bought it,' responded Randolf."

Feda's report was not quite accurate. The actual words 'A long pole' do not appear on page 15, though the pole carried by Randolf was an alpenstock and on page 12 this was described as long. Nor was the passage a direct cross correspondence, though it had an association with some earlier experiments in telepathy between Mrs. Salter and Mrs. Stuart Wilson in which cross correspondences had arisen. Mrs. Wilson had felt her own scripts to come from a superior intelligence, to whom she could no more live up than Randolf's family could live up to him and for this reason she had called the script intelligence Randolf. Mrs. Salter knew this but Mrs. Leonard did not.

One purported communicator, A. V. B., suggested to two regular sitters, Lady Troubridge and Miss Radcliffe Hall, that she could sense the meaning of passages in languages unknown to Mrs. Leonard, to the sitters, or to herself when living.

In response the two sitters obtained some books in Greek which they put on a shelf in an order known to themselves alone. A. V. B. then made a number of attempts at this exacting task. Out of one group of fourteen of these, Mrs. Sidgwick classified four as definite hits, a further four as right, with elements of doubt, four as very dubious, and one probably and one certainly wrong.[1] A typical good hit, made ten days before the 1918 armistice, was to locate the Greek word for armistice on the right line of the right page of the right book, with the comment that this was what A. V. B. was wishing for on the sitters' behalf. But the difficult question still remains: How often can such coincidences be accidental?

Mrs. Leonard occasionally pulled off the *tour de force* of giving information relevant to a deceased person which appeared at the time to be known to nobody living. This occurred in an anonymous sitting by Mrs. Hugh Talbot, in which Feda

[1] In all Mrs. Sidgwick analysed 532 book tests, and she classified about 17% as successful, 19% as approximately successful, 18% as doubtful, and the rest as failures or all but failures. This appeared to be away above chance, so the usual control experiment was undertaken. 1,800 sham book tests were analysed by another investigator, and these gave less than 2% as successful, and less than 3% as partially successful, instead of 17% and 19%. But their judgments were, of course, subjective.

Proceedings S.P.R., Vol. XXXI, 1921, pp. 241–400.

made immense efforts to convince her of the continued existence of her dead husband.[1] One of these was to describe on his behalf a small dark leather book, about 8 to 10 inches long. "It's not exactly a book", she said, "it is not printed . . . It has writing in."

Mrs. Talbot suggested that this might be a red log book of her husband's, but Feda said, no, it was *darker* and would she *please* find it and look for something written on page 12 or 13. Mrs. Talbot still thought the log book was meant, but Feda insisted. "There are two books, you will know the one he means by a diagram of languages in the front . . . Indo-European, Aryan, Semitic languages . . . A table of Arabian, Semitic languages . . . there are lines, not straight, going like this."

Mrs. Talbot had never heard of a diagram of languages and thought the medium was talking rubbish. On her return home, she casually mentioned Feda's insistence about the book but could hardly be persuaded to look for it. Finally, right at the back of the top book-shelf, she found a shabby black leather book of the shape described by Feda. To her great surprise it contained a 'Table of Semitic or Syro-Arabian Languages' and a 'General Table of the Aryan and Indo-European Languages.' She also found on page 13 a long extract from an old book, entitled *Post Mortem*, describing the blissful situation of the author after death.

But the fact remained that Mrs. Leonard could have got most of the things she said by unconscious telepathy from the sitter. To eliminate this, a new type of proxy sitting was tried, in which the sitter was represented by someone else. That would at least ensure that telepathy from the living was indirect, since the real sitter and medium were at one remove from each other. The less, obviously, that the proxy sitter knew about the real sitter and the dead person sought the better, and in 1936 Professor E. R. Dodds arranged a careful experiment at what might be called two removes. On behalf of a Mrs. Lewis, he asked Mr. Drayton Thomas to try for a communication from her father, a Mr. Macaulay, who had been a water engineer.[2]

[1] *Proceedings*, S.P.R., Vol. XXXI, pp. 253–60.
[2] *Proceedings* S.P.R., Vol. XLV, pp. 257–306.

Mr. Thomas and Mrs. Leonard knew nothing of Mrs. Lewis or Mr. Macaulay, but on the face of it Feda got in touch with him right away. As evidence of his identity, she described his working instruments, tool chest, mathematical formulae, drawing office, etc., as well as could be expected from a woman who knew nothing of such things. She also correctly recounted incidents in his past life, gave his pet name for his daughter—Puggy—, spoke of his damaged hand, said he specially wanted her to mention baths and gave the names of some persons who had shared a particularly happy time with him. One of these puzzled her and she said, "It might be Reece but it sounds like Riss."

All this was meaningless to Mr. Thomas and he sent it to Professor Dodds who sent it to Mrs. Lewis. She said that her father's anxiety about wasting bath water had been a family joke, also that during the halcyon period referred to by Feda her schoolboy brother had hero-worshipped an elder boy called Rees and had drawn attention to the fact that his name was spelt Rees, not Reece, so often that his young sisters used to sing "Not Reece, but Riss", to tease him. This was eventually stopped by Mr. Macaulay as it hurt the boy's feelings.

Another communicator claimed to be the first wife of Mrs. Lewis's husband, and referred to a conversation on a bridge during which he had proposed to her 25 years earlier.

To those personally linked with purported communicators this kind of trivial material is often stronger evidence of identity than more dramatic statements. Professor Dodds does not, himself, believe in survival, but he doubts if fraud, rational inference, or telepathy from the sitter can account for the number of hits made by Mrs. Leonard, particularly such items as Puggy, Reece-Riss, or the bridge proposal. And he finds it equally incredible that these were all lucky shots. In his view, then, we are left with an important either/or. Mrs. Leonard must have had extra-sensory access to the thoughts of living persons who had never had any communication with her or with the sitter, or she had somehow tapped the past of a person no longer living.

In the Macaulay case Mrs. Leonard had been given the

distant enquirer's bare name, Mrs. Lewis, as a starting point. But on one occasion she produced veridical material about a family of whom neither she nor the sitter had ever heard. On October 28th 1938, Mr. Thomas was told by his purported father and sister that a middle-aged man would be writing to him. This man, they said, had once lived near an old home of his at a place which sounded like Morton and he wanted to get into touch with his son, who had recently been killed in a motor car accident. A fortnight later a letter came from an unknown Mr. A. For the past month, he said, he had been meaning to write his appreciation of a lecture given by Mr. Thomas and he would also be glad of advice about trying to contact his own son, who had recently been killed in an aeroplane accident. It transpired later that the A. family had lived for twelve years at Norton, not far from a town where Mr. Thomas himself had lived. The son, young A., purported to communicate at two further sittings by Mr. Thomas with Mrs. Leonard. At these striking veridical material was given which was unknown even to his father, Mr. A., but was later confirmed by another son. Feda said, too, that young A. spoke of a friend who had died, whose name began with BR., and as a clue to his identity she described in detail a model ship. This meant nothing to Mr. A., but once more the living son confirmed that he and his dead brother had had a friend named Br. . . . who had worked for a firm making model ships and had been killed about a year later than young A.

But once again, as in the Sevens case, when one or two good mediums were producing clues which fitted the survival hypothesis, other clues pointed to the living as the source of information which purported to come from the dead. A Canon Douglas reported one such case in *The Unpopular Review* for January–March, 1919. His chauffeur, a Frenchman named Réallier, had joined the French Army in 1914 and had occasionally written to him thereafter. Then, at a sitting with a non-professional sensitive, Canon Douglas was told that a deceased communicator, named *Ravallier*, wished to speak to him. To prove his identity, *Ravallier* gave many convincing details from the past and reported a recent journey to Salonica and other recent events in his own life. Canon Douglas knew nothing of these, but later found them all to be correct for Réallier. In fact *Ravallier* made no mistakes—except the vital one that Réallier was not dead and had never even been seriously ill.

Similar incorrect statements were made to Dr. S. B. Soal, who afterwards became famous for his successful card-guessing experiments. After some impressive sittings with a medium, Mrs. Blanche Cooper, he devised a test. He invented an imaginary friend, John Ferguson, and immediately before each further sitting he visualised an incident in which this John took part. And time and again John turned up as a discarnate communicator and reminded him of these incidents.[1]

The situation still remains the same. No absolutely watertight method of establishing the source of statements made by sensitives has been discovered. But that they often obtain their information by some kind of ESP it is hard to doubt.

[1] Another difficulty in assessing mediumistic material is that many lives are not very dissimilar. We all love, hate, fail, succeed and die. So a hit for sitter A. may often be a hit for sitter B. as well. Not long ago a widow gave an S.P.R. investigator an impressive list of correct hits made by a medium about her deceased husband, and as a test she kindly allowed him to get it annotated by some other widows as if the sitting had been for themselves. One or two of them found even more correct hits than the lady for whom the sitting had been given.

CHAPTER XIV

Qualitative Experiments

THE snags inherent in the study of spontaneous *psi* and of mediumship are obvious enough. The phenomena crop up at their own sweet will, usually in circumstances which make the elimination of all but one explanation virtually impossible; and chance, in theory, can never be ruled out. The difficulty of trying to evoke *psi* in experimental conditions is just the opposite. The guinea-pig is a human being, and his *psi* faculty appears reluctant to function when he is pinned down and bored. The result is, paradoxically, that as a rule the more talented psychics do not shine in the latest card-guessing or quantitative type of experiment which is undramatic and drearily repetitive.

For many years quantitative experiments were preceded by a slightly less constricted type, which have been labelled qualitative. In principle, these were similar to the early Guthrie experiments and a number were carried out at intervals by members of the S.P.R. and also by other investigators in America, France, Sweden and elsewhere. G. N. M. Tyrrell lists eleven such groups, in which on inspection the results seemed positive, in some cases staggeringly so. But chance was still, in theory, the nigger in the wood pile.[1]

One dramatic, and, in their belief, watertight test was made by a committee of the S.P.R. on the apparent remarkable ESP of a Polish engineer, M. Stefan Ossowiecki.[2] In the committee's own view, it took every conceivable precaution. Mr. Theodore Besterman, then Research Officer of the S.P.R., drew—in England—an ink bottle on ruled paper and near it he wrote the words *Swan*, underlined in blue, and *Ink*, underlined in red. He then put the paper, folded, in a series of three

---

[1] G. N. M. Tyrrell *The Personality of Man* (Pelican Books, 1947).
[2] *Proceedings* S.P.R., Vol. XII, p. 345.

SWAN INK

Original Drawing by Theodore Besterman.

29. IX. 1933

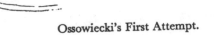

Ossowiecki's First Attempt.

Ossowiecki's Second Attempt.

Ossowiecki's Third Attempt.

opaque envelopes, marked these secretly, so that tampering could be recognised, and sealed them in a special way with surgical tape. In Warsaw, Mr. Ossowiecki, who knew no English, was allowed to handle the outer envelope in the presence of Lord Charles Hope and two other members of the S.P.R. Having done so, he made three drawings at intervals (Figures II, III and IV). Lord Charles watched the envelope carefully while it was handled by Ossowiecki and afterwards confirmed that the seal was untampered with. He then opened both it and the two inner envelopes. Ossowiecki had made one mistake. He had underlined the word Swan in red instead of blue. It has been argued that fraud is possible in this case since the S.P.R. committee's Polish co-investigators had for a time had charge of the letter, and could conceivably have opened and resealed it. But in the Committee's view to reseal the envelopes perfectly was impossible even had their Polish colleagues been prepared to cheat; and had they done so, Ossowiecki would presumably have used the right coloured ink—unless his mistake was a double bluff. Mr. Besterman devised the test in this form to give Ossowiecki the chance of picking up an idea either visually or symbolically—he might have drawn a swan. Moreover the drawing was deliberately folded to destroy the shape of the bottle and of one word, yet he still seemed to have got his impression as a visual image.

This test is reinforced by another carried out and vouched for by the anthropologist, Dr. E. J. Dingwall, who is famous for the basic thoroughness with which he carries out research.[1] When alone he wrote at the top of a sheet of paper the words: "*Les vignobles du Rhin, de la Moselle et de la Bourgogne donnent un vin excellent.*" On the lower half of the sheet he drew a very rough design meant to convey the idea of a bottle without actually being one (Fig. I).

The folded sheet he then placed in an opaque red envelope. This he put into an opaque black envelope and the black envelope into a brown paper one, which he sealed. Finally he pricked holes through them in four places. This packet, together with two white envelopes from other people, was

[1] *Journal* S.P.R., Vol. XXI, pp. 259–63.

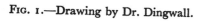

[Aug. 22. 1923]

Fig. 1.—Drawing by Dr. Dingwall.

Fig. 2.—Drawing by Monsieur Ossowiecki.

given to Ossowiecki in bright light in the presence of Dr. von Schrenk-Notzing and other trained observers, and he made comments on all three which were confirmed as correct. Some of his comments on Dr. Dingwall's envelope were as follows: "I do not know why I see a little bottle . . . There is a drawing made by a man who is not an artist . . . something red with this bottle . . . There is without doubt a second red envelope . . . There is a square drawn at the corner of the paper. The bottle is very badly drawn. I see it! I see it! [He draws Fig. II] I see it! I see it! At the corner on the other side. In the middle something also is written, on the back . . ."

Later on Dr. von Schrenck-Notzing asked in what language the words were written and Ossowiecki replied, "In French. The bottle is a little inclined to one side. It has no cork. It is made up of several fine lines. There is first a brown envelope outside; then a greenish envelope and then a red envelope. Inside a piece of white paper folded in two with the drawing inside. It is written on a single sheet."

Dr. Dingwall subsequently opened the packet in view of the other investigators and pointed out the precautions he had taken against it being tampered with, over and above the fact that no opportunity to do this had been given. His comment was that the supernormal character of the incident seemed quite decisive and that in his view coincidence could be wholly excluded.

Dr. Gilbert Murray has given us an enthralling account of a long and famous series of qualitative experiments undertaken by him at intervals from 1910 to 1929.[1] Yet even his many successes can always in theory be attributed to chance, though on inspection the idea seems ludicrous. "Let me say at once", he said himself, "that my experiments belong to the pre-statistical stage of psychical research when the experiments were treated as a parlour game. Still I do not see how there could

[1] The material for this summary of Dr. Gilbert Murray's experiments has been taken from: Dr. Gilbert Murray O.M., *Presidential Address*, *Proceedings* S.P.R., Vol. XXIX, p. 46 et seq.
Second *Presidential Address*, *Proceedings* S.P.R., Vol. XLIX, p. 155 et seq. and from two reports in *Proceedings* S.P.R., Vols. XXIX, pp. 46–110 and XXXIX, pp. 212–74.

have been any significant failure of control; nor did Mrs. Verrall or Mrs. Sidgwick."

"The method was always the same. I was sent out of the drawing room either to the dining room or to the end of the hall, the door or doors, of course, being shut. The others remained in the drawing room: someone chose a subject, which was hastily written down, word for word. Then I was called in, and my words written down. I may add that, out of the first 505 cases, Mrs. Verrall estimated the percentage as: Success, 33 per cent; Partial Success, 27·9 per cent; Failure, 39 per cent. But it may be remarked that as evidence for the presence of some degree of telepathy most of the partial successes are quite as convincing as the complete successes: this would produce something like 60 per cent evidential and 40 per cent non-evidential.

"First, two perfectly ordinary cases, where the emotional atmosphere is obvious and strong, and then is developed into something more definite.

October 26th 1924.
  "My wife gave a subject:

M. H. M. 'This is not a nice thing. What Nansen was describing the other day of the Church yard at Buzuluk, where there lay the great pile of corpses, numbers of children who had fallen dead in the night.'

  I was summoned and said:

G. M. 'This is perfectly horrible, It's the Russian Famine. It is the masses and masses of bodies carted up every night in the Church yard at . . .' (the scribe did not catch the name.)
M. H. M. 'Any particular bodies?'
G. M. 'Oh, yes, children. I associate it with Nansen's lecture here.'

"Here came memory in as a help. The subject was an incident that I remembered. In the next it was an obstacle: that is, a remembered incident thrust itself in and had to be rejected before I could get the real subject. I should explain that my mother had a story that when she was at a school in France she had been made to wear a placard labelled *impie*.

133

November 24th 1929.

Mrs. Davies (Agent) 'Jane Eyre at school standing on a stool, being called a liar by Mr. Brocklehurst. The school spread out below her and the Brocklehurst family 'a mass of shot purple silk pelisses and orange feathers'.

G. M. '. . . (I think of) my mother being at her French school, being labelled *impie* . . . I reject that. But a sense of obloquy. Girl standing up on a form in a school, and the school there, and people coming in, and she is being held up to obloquy in some way or other—A thing in a book certainly. I think they are calling her a liar. I get an impression of the one girl standing up and a group of people or a family coming in and denouncing her. I think it's English.'

Question: 'Colour of the people's dresses?'

G. M. 'I can't get the colour of the people's dresses.'

"I take another with a very marked but extremely different atmosphere.

January 22nd 1928.

Stephen Murray (Agent) 'George Hickey and me riding the motor-bike past the inhabitants of Moulsford Lunatic Asylum, and one cheery-looking man with gold spectacles on his forehead barking furiously at us, like a dog.'

G. M. 'A curiously confused and ridiculous scene. You and someone on a motor bicycle, and a scene of great confusion; . . . perhaps the bicycle is broken down. But there is a confused rabble and, I know it sounds ridiculous, but someone on all-fours barking like a dog.' (Then after a little encouragement). 'Are they lunatics by any chance?'

"Then two where the atmosphere is fainter and more subtle. The first came on a bad evening after two or three failures, and I was inclined to give up.

My daughter Rosalind. 'I think of dancing with the Head of the Dutch Foreign Office at a *café chantant* at the Hague.'

G. M. 'A faint impression of your journey abroad. I should say something official; sort of official *soirée* or dancing or something. Feel as if it was in Holland.'

"The second occurred on *May 14th* 1927.

R. M. 'I think of walking in the Park at Belgrade and meeting the English Governess."

G. M. 'I'm getting a different feeling. It's somebody who is in rather a state of mind. I should think escaped from Russia. You are meeting her in some curious country. Wait a bit! It's not anyone at Robert College or Constantinople College. It's some queer country where you seem to be alone, and you are meeting some sort of Englishwoman who has been driven out of Russia, and hates the place where she is ... Oh yes. I do remember. It's when you went out to Constantinople by the express alone, and met the English governess in the Park.'

"The history and state of mind of the English governess was correct, but had not been mentioned. I had some faint memory of the incident. The 'queer country' was Serbia.

"Next I will take two cases where I received a feeling or thought that had not been spoken, and was not in my memory at all.

November 17th 1929.
R. M. 'A scene in a book by Aksakoff, where the children are being taken to their grandparents, and the little boy sees his mother kneeling beside the sofa where his father is lying, lamenting at having to leave them.'
G. M. 'I should say this was Russian. I think it's a book I haven't read. Somebody's remembrance of childhood or something. A family travelling, the children, father and mother. I should think they are going across the Volga. I don't think I can get it more accurately. The children are watching their parents or seeing something about their parents ... I should think Aksakoff. They are going to see their grandmother.'

Dr. Murray here added a note: "They did just afterwards have to cross the Volga and Rosalind said she had been thinking of that, though she did not mention it.

"Much more curious is the next, though at first sight it is a mere failure.

May 15th 1927.
Edith Webster (Agent). 'I think of the Castalian spring at Delphi and how we drank the water there.'
G. M. I don't think I shall get it. But I've got a slight feeling of atmosphere, as if there was something terrible going to happen; as if it were the night before something ... an atmosphere of suspense.'

(*Note R. M.* commented). 'I had been thinking of saying goodbye
to someone who was going (to the war) to be killed, Hugo?
Rupert? I got the feeling of 'This is the end.'

"*R. M.* had not spoken. She had evidently intended or
expected to give the next subject, but *E. W.* was asked instead.
I add another failure which is, I think, equally significant.

November 24th 1929.
Margaret Davies. 'Medici chapel and tombs: sudden chill: absolute
stillness. Marble figures who seem to have been there all
night.'
G. M. 'I wonder if this is right . . . I've got a feeling of a scene in
my *Nefrekepta*, where the man goes in, passage after passage
to the inner chamber where Nefrekepta is lying dead with
the shadows of his wife and child sitting beside him . . . but
I think it's India.'

("My poem was translated from an Egyptian story; I
suppose I felt the subject was not Egyptian.) Sometimes the
subject was a bit of poetry. I was then apt to answer at once
without any groping or hesitation.

January 22nd 1928.
Margaret Cole (Agent). 'The man in Browning who is dying and
sees the row of bottles at the bed, and it reminds him of
where he met his girl when he was young.'
G. M. (Instantly on entrance). "How sad and mad and bad it
was, But oh, how it was sweet."
John Allen (Agent). 'I think of the priest walking by the shore of
the sea after he had been to Agamemnon and been refused.' "

In response to this Dr. Murray gave the actual quotation
from the Iliad in Greek as he entered the room.

It is strange, on reading literally hundreds of cases of this
quality, to realise our total ignorance of the process by which
this information came to Dr. Murray. Why too, should his
success be so complete in one case, while, in another similar,
he could get no impression?

There is a school of thought—very small—which puts down
Dr. Murray's many successes to collusion with his wife or
simply to the fact that he listened at the key-hole in the door.
'How do we *know* that he didn't?' it has been lamented. 'Did
anyone watch him all the time?' Then presumably the watcher

himself would need watching, in case he took part in the fraud and this argument can be extended *ad infinitum*. To those who knew Doctor Murray, of course, the 'listening at the key-hole' hypothesis is unthinkable, but in theory a hundred years hence it could stand. In the strict laboratory sense, we do not *know* that he did not cheat.

It has been suggested that some of these cases may be explained by hyperaesthesia, and at first Dr. Murray himself inclined to this explanation. Certainly very little is known of the extent if any to which the power of hearing can temporarily be heightened. It may possibly on occasion result from an effort to exercise ESP. In my own experience I have become agonisingly sensitive to sound—a light tap on the door felt like a crashing blow on my head—at a moment when I had apparently just succeeded in a conscious attempt to contact the thought of a distant person. But I would have heard the tap anyway and I did not hear the person who gave it approach the door. And the doors and walls in the house where the Murray experiments took place are of an Edwardian solidity. Since ESP has been demonstrated experimentally, to one who knows that house it is an easier explanation of Dr. Murray's successes than normal hearing so acute that speech in the drawing room could be heard in the dining room. However, the argument for ESP in these experiments does not depend on that kind of subjective judgment. It depends on cases where Dr. Murray could not have heard what he reported because it had never been spoken. Here are three examples:

Mrs. *Toynbee* (*Rosalind Murray*) (Agent).' Belgian Baron getting out of train at Savanarilla with us, and walking across the sandy track, and seeing the new train come in.'

G. *M.* 'Man getting out of a train and looking for something. I don't know if he's looking for another train to come. I think it is a sort of dry hot sort of place. I get him with a faint impression of waxed moustache—a sort of foreign person—but I can't get more.'

The Belgian Baron did have a waxed moustache, but Dr. Murray had never seen him and Mrs. Toynbee had never mentioned him.

August 24th 1913.

Mrs. Toynbee. 'I think of Mrs. F. sitting on the deck, and Grandfather opening the door for her.'

G. M. 'This is Grandfather. I think it is on a ship, and I think he is bowing and smiling to somebody—opening the door.'

Mrs. Toynbee. 'Can't you get the person?'

G. M. 'I first thought of the Captain, and afterwards a lady. I get a feeling of a pink head dress.'

Mrs. Toynbee. 'Yes, that is right.'

January 13*th* 1914.

Mrs. Toynbee. 'I think of that funny old Irishman called Dr. Hunt in the hotel at Jamaica. I'll think of the race where they wouldn't let him ride with his little grey mare.'

G. M. 'Tropics. It's—It must (have) something to do with Jamaica. I can't get it a bit clear. I feel as if it were a drunken Irish doctor talking with a brogue. I can't get it clear.'

The contemporary note records that Mrs. Toynbee did not mention that the doctor got drunk, but he did.

The comments on his own ESP by a man with such gifts of analysis and perception as Dr. Murray throw an interesting light on that of less articulate sensitives. "The conditions which suited me best", he says, "were in many ways much the same as those which professional mediums have sometimes insisted upon. This issuspicious, yet fraud, I think, is out of the question; however slippery the behaviour of my subconscious, too many respectable people would have had to be its accomplices. I liked the general atmosphere to be friendly and familiar; any feeling of ill-temper or hostility was apt to spoil an experiment. Noises or interruption had a bad effect. One question that arose was the degree to which the telepathy made use of real sights, sounds, smells, memories, to reach its goal. The general conclusion was curious. It seemed that I, or my subconscious, showed some anxiety to explain away the telepathy by seizing upon some such excuse. It said it had guessed Savonarola making the women burn their precious possessions because it smelt a coal which had fallen out of the fire; that it had guessed Sir A. Zimmern riding on a beach in Greece, because it said it had heard a horse on the road—when the rest of the company heard no horse. Memories, again, sometimes helped it, but more often hindered it in its search. At one time, indeed, I was inclined to attribute the whole thing to subconscious auditory hyperaesthesia. I got almost no successes if the subject was not spoken, but only written down. Two or three successes and at least one error could be explained by my having heard or misheard a proper name, e.g. by confusing Judge Davies and the prophet David. But, apart from other difficulties in this hypothesis, there were some clear cases where I got a point or even a whole subject which had only been thought and not spoken.

"Of course, the personal impression of the percipient himself is by no means conclusive evidence, but I do feel there is one almost universal quality in these guesses of mine which does suit telepathy and does not suit any other explanation. They always begin with a vague emotional quality or atmosphere: 'This is horrible, this is grotesque, this is full of anxiety'; or rarely, 'This is something delightful'; or sometimes, 'This is out of a book,' 'This is a Russian novel', or the like. That seems like a direct impression of some human mind. Even in the failures this feeling of atmosphere often gets through. That is, it was not so much an act of cognition, or a piece of information that was transferred to me, but rather a feeling or an emotion; and it is notable that I never had any success in guessing mere cards or numbers, or any subject that was not in some way interesting or amusing."

Dr Murray's own impression of what he describes as "this curious sensitivity which we call 'telepathy' " is very like those of other sensitives and throws light on the pleas for faith and understanding so often made by them. "As far as my own experience goes," he says, "it does not feel quite like cognition or detection; it is more like the original sense of the word sympathy (συμπάθεία) the sharing of a feeling, or 'co-sensitivity'. I seem to be passive and feel in a faint shadowy way the feeling or state of mind of someone else."

To father his Savanarola impression on to the smell of a burning coal was a typical example of Dr. Murray's instinctive desire to rationalise his ESP. Many sensitives—particularly the educated—share this desire. Mrs. Verrall said that her mind would grasp eagerly at any normal, solid, familiar fact to account for an impression which rose from below the threshold. It may be that the rational mind seeks to ignore phenomena outside the respectable laws of nature. And a censor too may discourage ESP for biological reasons. Dr. Murray's own inclination to put the whole thing down to hypersensitive hearing was in keeping with these motives. He clung to this explanation for a long time, but in the end was driven to change his views by cases in which he gave correct details not previously spoken of by the agent, and others in which he caught, not the thought expressed by the agent, but one, unmentioned, in the mind of another person present.

W. H. Salter, the Honorary Secretary of the S.P.R. and his wife, were among those who tested Dr. Murray's ESP. Mr. Salter points out that much could be learnt about the process from the incomplete successes, for Dr. Murray's mistakes often indicated whether his impression had taken the form of sight or sound (on occasion he even smelt) or of a general concept.[1] Some of his mistakes were such as might be due to mishearing—Cannan for Cameron, Mrs. Carr for Mrs. Carlyle. These are parallel to Mrs. Holland's visual mistake of a filter for a bust and also to apparent efforts to get words, such as *Sanatos—Tanatos—Thanatos*, or *Maurice—Morris—Mors*, by the sound.

Similar illuminating mistakes occurred in a series of experiments done in 1928 in America by the novelist, Upton Sinclair, and his wife.[2] Their interest was aroused by a young man's apparent feats of telepathy, but although he had no confederate they still felt 'the worm of doubt'. Finally Mrs. Sinclair said, "There is only one way to be certain. I am going to learn to do these things myself."

She soon achieved 'hits' on target drawings made by her brother-in-law forty miles away and on one occasion she appeared to pick up his mood as well. She drew a series of concentric circles with a black spot in the middle, and then she 'saw' a larger spot spreading over the paper. This made her

[1] W. H. Salter, *The S.P.R. An Outline of Its History* (pamphlet published by the S.P.R., 1948).
[2] Upton Sinclair, *Mental Radio* (Werner Laurie, 1930).

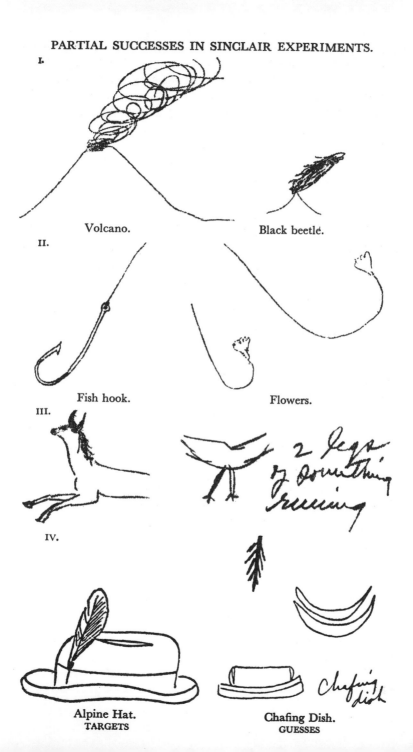

PARTIAL SUCCESSES IN SINCLAIR EXPERIMENTS.

I.

Volcano.

Black beetle.

II.

Fish hook.

Flowers.

III.

2 legs of something running

IV.

Alpine Hat.
TARGETS

Chafing Dish.

Chafing dish

Chafing Dish.
GUESSES

very depressed. She felt that the spot was blood and that her brother-in-law had had a haemorrhage. He had in fact drawn a circle with a compass, which had made a hole in its centre, just after he had been warned that he had an ailment which might result in a haemorrhage and was feeling very depressed about it.

After this Mr. and Mrs. Sinclair did many experiments together, but unfortunately, as they were convinced that her previous successes must have been due to telepathy, they no longer arranged for outside witnesses to confirm that she could not be getting her information by sensory means. On the hypothesis of ESP these partial successes give interesting hints as to process. In some the target picture was practically duplicated but a wrong name attached to it. In others the idea was right but differently expressed from the target. On one occasion Mrs. Sinclair failed to get a horse's head which her husband had copied from a newspaper, but her drawing apparently referred to an illustration on the page opposite which he had not consciously noticed. It appears not uncommon for an agent's subconscious, rather than his conscious, thoughts to reach a percipient.

Other investigators have reported similar experiments in which, on inspection, the proportion of hits seemed impressive, but they could neither be exactly assessed nor exactly repeated to order, and in consequence they made no appreciable impact on orthodox opinion.[1]

[1] Careful experiments are described in the following: Miles and Ramsden, *Experiments in Thought Transference, Proceedings* S.P.R., Vol. XVII; René Warcollier, *Experimental Telepathy* (Boston S.P.R., 1938); Carl Bruck, *Experimentelle Telepathie* (Stuttgart, 1925).

CHAPTER XV

Quantitative Experiments (1)

I<small>T</small> was more and more borne in upon investigators that the best available methods of confirming the existence of ESP lay in quantitative experiments of the card-guessing type, because statistics could be used to assess the proportion of correct hits which could be expected by chance. But we have seen that from the point of view of the guinea-pig these have great drawbacks. He is not after all a machine but a human being, and in such experiments he is not even being asked to exercise his reason, but his subconscious self, an element which clearly prefers drama to monotony. Yet experiments which are to be assessed by statistics cannot indulge in drama, and there is little emotional satisfaction in reciting a list of cards month in month out. I once heard Mr. Shackleton, a 'star' card-guesser, announce with passion, "I was bored! *bored!* BORED!"

The reader, too, is liable to be bored by accounts of these experiments. There is a sense of trailing along arid pavements, leading nowhere, after the dramatic and unpredictable jungles of the earlier days. Yet they are an essential part of the investigation, and for many people—particularly those who have had no *psi* experiences of their own—they supply the most interesting evidence for ESP.

They cannot, of course, be recorded here in sufficient detail for scientific assessment. That would need hundreds of pages of statistics and elaborate description of the set-up, and fortunately it has already been done by the experimenters themselves. But a short summary of one or two experiments, and some account of their results, may perhaps show that such apparently dry-as-dust work is very dramatic in its implications and has also thrown some startling gleams of light on the working of the human subconscious.

Sir Oliver Lodge was the first to propose that card-guessing might produce conclusive evidence for telepathy and as early as 1885 he worked out a mathematical formula for estimating the number of hits above those to be expected by chance. But it was not until 1917 that a fairly large experiment was undertaken on these lines. In it the odds against the hits achieved all being due to chance were about 160 to 1. But although odds of 100 to 1 are considered very significant in other subjects, the experimenter, Professor John E. Coover, reported with emphasis that his results gave no evidence of telepathy, and he is often quoted as having 'disproved' the existence of *psi*. It is interesting that Coover should have troubled to do the experiment, for he seems to have had no love for the idea of *psi*. When the French Nobel prize winner, Charles Richet, said that its phenomena ought to be accepted "on the grounds of the evidence for their occurrence, not because they are in any way understood", he answered: "Is the evidence for a phenomenon really sound if nothing concerning the phenomenon is understood?"

The next landmark was reported in 1921 by a group of psychologists at Gröningen in Holland.[1] The conditions resulting from their meticulous precautions against sensory clues must have been rather dreary for their percipients, of whom the best was a young dentist. They put him, blindfold, inside a kind of tent of black curtains. In front of this tent was a board marked out in 48 squares, with a raised series of 8 letters along one edge and 6 figures along another, at right angles to the first. Thus, by pushing his hands out from the tent and feeling his way across the board from a letter and a figure, the dentist could locate a particular square. The experimenters were in a room above. They had sound-proofed the floor and double-glazed a little window which had been made in it to enable them to look down on him. From two bags, one containing letters, the other figures, they would silently draw one of each, and the dentist's task was to find the square indicated by these two. The results were as dramatic as the procedure was dull. The test was done 187 times, and if chance only had deter-

[1] *Compte-Rendu du Premier Congrès International des Recherches Psychiques*, 1922.

mined the correct number of hits the most probable number would have been 3·9. But the dentist hit the mark 60 times. The odds against this happening by chance are no less astronomical than if red turned up at roulette 150 times running. There is no mathematical certainty that such a thing cannot happen, but it is safe to say that any mathematician would stake his life against it. Here then, at last, it seemed as if ESP had consented to appear to order in controlled conditions, and dull though they were it is worth noting that the young man was in a situation in which he could not be distracted by external events. Two criticisms have been made of this experiment: that through the double glazed window the experimenters could not see clearly which squares he chose and that he heard slight movements of pleasure on the part of observers as he approached the correct square.

The next card-guessing experiment to make history was reported by a member of the S.P.R., Miss Ina Jephson, in 1928. According to the statistical methods devised by Professor Sir Ronald Fisher, F.R.S., its results were significantly beyond chance. She did it to check an odd effect she had noticed earlier, that the proportion of hits declined as an experiment went on. She found this again and it has occurred in most subsequent experiments of this type. It may be the result of sheer boredom at endlessly repeated guesses. It does at least indicate that something other than chance is at work, particularly when at the end of an experiment the number of correct hits passes below the level of chance probability, for this suggests that percipients are unconsciously using ESP to express their boredom.

A little later members of the Universities of London and Columbia took part in further experiments, but they met with no success. The S.P.R. carried out a mass experiment via the B.B.C. The results were solidly negative. From 1927 to 1929 Dr. Soal, who had been encouraged by his sittings with the medium, Blanche Cooper, made thousands of careful tests. But his results, too, seemed obstinately negative. A few other experiments by well-known psychologists gave mildly positive, though not dramatic results, but these were ignored on the grounds that the degree of departure from chance considered significant in any other subject was not enough for the improbable *psi*.

Then, in 1934, a book appeared, entitled *Extra-Sensory Perception*. It was written by J. B. Rhine, a young associate Professor of Psychology in Duke University, North Carolina, and it caused a considerable flutter in the dovecots. Some years earlier Duke had had the courage to institute a department of parapsychology (psychical research) and to put Rhine in charge of it. He and his wife, Dr. Louisa Rhine, were the right people in the right place, for they combined the scientist's devotion to truth with enormous enthusiasm and the human touch and they fired their percipients to surprising achievements. The psychologist, William McDougall, was the first to put his finger on the importance of the human touch in this work. Rhine's spirit pervaded the group, he said, and was perhaps an indispensable condition of its striking success.

Like Miss Jephson, Rhine obtained his results by the simple process of guessing the order of cards at a distance. But he made it yet more simple by using, not ordinary playing cards, but a smaller pack which contained twenty-five cards of five patterns only, a circle, a square, a cross, three wavy lines (Waves) and a star. These five patterns were suggested to Rhine by a psychologist, as being quite simple, yet clearly different. Having five patterns only had two advantages. It made chance easier to assess and it set the percipient a far simpler task than in experiments of the Murray or Sinclair type, where the agent could choose anything in the world as a target. Rhine's percipients did not have to 'guess' *what* the agent was thinking of, but merely *which* of five known objects he had chosen. And in experiments designed to test no more than the mere existence of ESP this was a help, as a number of people seem to get flashes of it at this rudimentary level, whereas the triumphs of a Mrs. Willett or a Mrs. Leonard are far beyond them.

At first Rhine did mass experiments, mostly with students at Duke University who were within the orbit of his stimulating personality. Their overall success was well above chance but a few star performers stood out above the rest. Rhine seemed to excite some of them into a state of concentration so extreme that it may, paradoxically, have resembled the dissociated state of spontaneous automatists. One 'star' whom Dr. Rhine reports as having actually recited the whole twenty-five card pack correctly, said afterwards that he "wouldn't do that again for a million dollars." [1]

Dr. Rhine and a colleague, Dr. Pratt, had a long series of sittings in which they placed the agent and percipient, Herbert Pearce, in different buildings. The odds against the results obtained being due to chance were of the order of 10^{20} to 1. And there were other comparable experiments.

Rhine's unexpected successes had an unexpected result. The sceptics reversed their complaint, which had been that in previous experiments the odds against chance were too low to give evidence of the existence of ESP. They now said that in Rhine's experiments they were too high. Something must be wrong. There was a thunderstorm of criticism and every possible source of error was suggested. Some were found. The early Zener cards, for instance, were too thin, so that careful scrutiny of their backs could just give a hint of the symbols on their faces. But in response to criticism subsequent experiments were more and more tightened up, and those taking part in them were watched for fraud, conscious or unconscious, as if the talents of both cat burglars and conjurors were theirs. Yet their scores still remained at an astronomical level in conditions where the hostile critics could find nothing against the actual conduct of the experiments. But the sceptics still knew that *psi* was impossible. Therefore the only remaining source of error, Rhine's mathematics, must be wrong. To counter this, Rhine called in the American Institute of Mathematical Statistics. Their reply was unequivocal: "On the statistical side recent mathematical work has established the fact that, assuming that the experiments have been properly performed, the statistical analysis is essentially valid. If the Rhine investigation is to be fairly attacked, it must be on other than mathematical grounds."

Researchers in England were naturally most interested in Rhine's experiments. Dr. Thouless, Reader in Psychology at

[1] J. B. Rhine, *New Frontiers of the Mind* (Faber, 1938).

Cambridge University, commented on them: ". . . His methods are so simple and his results are so clear, that his experiments can be easily repeated, and it will be possible without difficulty to convince ourselves whether Rhine's conclusions are valid or whether they are due to some flaw in his experimental methods."

A new series of careful experiments on this side of the Atlantic did not repeat Rhine's successes. Did this mean that, after all, his conclusions had been invalid, or had our experimenters at some point thrown out the baby with the bathwater? If so, when had they done it? Nobody knew. However, a new figure now came to the fore who was able to suggest some reasons for success or failure. This was a radio engineer, G. N. M. Tyrrell, who quite early had thrown up a promising career to devote himself to psychical research, in spite of the fact that it meant a small income and comparative obscurity for the rest of his life. He had the rare combination of qualities needed both to evoke and to interpret *psi*: scientific training, the power to generalise from a number of apparently unrelated particulars, and an encouraging personality which never inhibited a timid percipient's ESP.

Tyrrell was vividly aware of a fact that most researchers, intent on making their experimental conditions as like as possible to those of the physical sciences, had tended to forget. This was that physical conditions are not the only ones operative in ESP. Psychological conditions, he told his fellow experimenters with some emphasis, were equally important. The reason they were surprised at being unable to duplicate Rhine's successes was their own *a priori* conception of ESP. They assumed it to be a fixed characteristic possessed by A., and not by B., and one which could always be revealed by a simple test with a pack of cards. But they were wrong. That so many per cent of Dr. Rhine's subjects scored high did not imply that the same percentage would do so anywhere, in any conditions. The experimenter's task, said Tyrrell, is to remove the percipient's inhibitions—to induce the faculty to work—to get the extra-sensory material externalised. This needs personal influence.

Tyrrell was able to study the subtle influences which affect ESP, or rather its exteriorisation, in his adopted daughter,

Miss Gertrude Johnson. She was an unusually gifted sensitive, and he and his gentle, unselfish wife created a calm and cheerful atmosphere in which her ESP could flourish unchecked. To the extraordinary serenity of this atmosphere I can bear witness, for Mr. and Mrs. Tyrrell and their daughter spent three years in my house after their own flat was destroyed by a bomb during the recent war. And I know Miss Johnson herself as no temperamental 'psychic', but a sensible, practical and equable woman who is also an unusually successful teacher of young children.

Tyrrell was thus able to watch the rise and fall of the ESP faculty in varying psychological conditions. It appeared to flicker, he said, like shadows in firelight. Friendly positive encouragement would stimulate it, chilly and repressive surroundings damp it out. The most subtle social and personal influences made all the difference between success and failure. He was the first to point out that to repeat Rhine's experiments the equivalent of Rhine's own influence must be included, and that the success of certain methods in physics did not imply their success in psychology. We cannot, he said, dictate to nature the conditions under which we will accept results. We must try and find out the conditions in which she will give them.

Tyrrell noticed early that Miss Johnson had a peculiar capacity for finding things with no apparent clues to guide her, and in 1921, when she was quite a young girl, he did a short experiment at 'guessing' cards with her, which seemed promising. Seven times she correctly gave him the denominations— but not the suits—of the top six to eight cards in an ordinary pack. But she found it a great strain. She seemed, said Tyrrell, to know the answer but be unable to say it—as if the knowledge was not related to brain-mechanism in the same way as normally acquired ideas.

He had no opportunity to experiment at length with G. J. (Miss Johnson) until 1934, thirteen years later. By then he had read Rhine's book and he also remembered observing that G. J. did best at finding lost objects when she was not consciously looking for them. "Why not," he thought, "convert this into an experiment on quantitative lines?"

With this idea in mind he made a peculiar machine, consisting of five little boxes, padded inside, which he fixed in a row with a screen above them.[1] He then sat one side of the screen, G. J. on the other. On her side the boxes had light-proof lids, on his they were open. The two then played hide and seek at great speed. Tyrrell would put the end of a wooden pointer silently into a box. G. J. would instantly open the lid of the box she thought he had chosen. In 30,000 trials, lasting five months, she made about the same enormous proportion of correct guesses over chance as Rhine's good performers, the odds against being billions of billions to one. He tested her next with six other agents instead of himself (8,500 trials) and the odds against the success she achieved were still significant, though less spectacular. He then tested himself as agent with twenty-nine other percipients. The odds against their successes being due to chance were only a hundred thousand to one and that mainly because of one percipient's high scores. The combination Tyrrell-Johnson stood out a mile. It must be remembered that although the monotonous 'guessing' could hardly fail to get dull in the end, conditions were as easy and pleasant as possible for G. J. She was working with a loved companion and was never asked to guess unless she felt in the mood, whereas the twenty-nine outside percipients naturally had to come by appointment, whether they were in the mood or not. The experiments, of course, were witnessed by outside observers, among them Professor C. D. Broad, Dame Edith Lyttelton, Mr. Gerald Heard and Mr. Kenneth Richmond, later Research Officer to the S.P.R.

After these good results, Tyrrell set about adding further refinements to his boxes. For, of course—and rightly—every alternative to ESP had been put forward to explain G. J.'s high scores. Some people suggested, as they had done in the case of Gilbert Murray, that her hearing was abnormally acute and that, through the screen, she could thus locate which box the pointer went into, although Tyrrell inserted it very gently and touched nothing. To counter this charge he

[1] These experiments are reported by G. N. M. Tyrrell in *Science and Psychical Phenomena* (Methuen, 1938).

made a new set of boxes, shut this time both on his side and on G. J.'s, and he took almost exaggerated care to make them light-tight, relining them with red velvet and revetting the lids. In each box he put a tiny electric pea-lamp which he could light by a silent key instead of using the pointer. To dispose of another proffered explanation for G. J.'s successes with him, that they both had a preference for the same boxes, he also devised a commutator which, on a button being pressed, would transpose the wires between the keys and the lamps. In this way he could light a lamp without knowing which it was. It also enabled him to test whether G. J.'s ESP was functioning as clairvoyance or telepathy, since it could not be telepathy when nobody knew which lamp was being lit.

The next criticism was that to get positive results Tyrrell had unconsciously falsified the entries of trials. To cope with this he made a mechanical recorder of each hit. And he finished by devising a mechanical means of choosing which lamp-lighting key to press.

The human element was now well and truly eliminated from the physical set-up. But Tyrrell's encouraging presence was still there. And G. J. still continued to score as before. He now tried an even more difficult test. Without telling G. J., he adjusted the machine so that the experimenter could press the key enabling a lamp to light, but it would delay to do so until the lid of the right box had been opened. That is, the experimenter's action chose the box but the percipient's action caused its light to go on. But G. J.'s remarkable scoring still continued. "It did not seem to matter", said Tyrrell, "whether the lamp was lit before the box was opened or afterwards." [1]

[1] It was interesting to see G. J.'s apparent ESP cropping up in the trivialities of daily life. In one case, a slightly unusual element reduces the likelihood of chance as an explanation. G. J. and the Tyrrells came to stay with me when I was equipping a small house in London during the war. Domestic utensils were as rare as diamonds and neither G. J. nor I could lay hands on a kitchen pail or a sink basket. One late afternoon she tried Peter Jones in vain but that evening she said, "I must go back to Peter Jones first thing in the morning. I know they will have a green pail and a green sink basket."

We doubted this, particularly as we had never seen *green* sink baskets, but undeterred she hastened early to Peter Jones and asked for a green pail and sink basket. "However did you know we had them?" said the assistant, "They've only just come in."

This was not the first time that apparent precognition had occurred in routine experiments. Rhine, too, had noticed it, and critics had gone to extreme lengths to propound alternative explanations. Some even suggested that the experimenter had mentally influenced the machine-shuffling of a pack of cards. That this would be *psi* of a high order did not seem to worry them. To cope with their objections Rhine had then cut the pack in a manner determined by the day's temperature record in the paper, which was unquestionably an unpredictable chance factor. The precognition scores still continued.

During the thirties the remarkable achievements of Tyrrell and G. J. were not matched by equal successes elsewhere in England. Between 1934 and 1939, Dr. Soal organised 160 persons to make 28,350 guesses on Zener cards. What this means in routine work—to be got through in the spare time of a busy University lecturer and with none of the excitement of work in the field—it is hard to realise for those who have not done it. Forms have to be printed and distributed, watertight conditions planned and arranged, percipients found and instructed, reliable observers brought in to guarantee absence of fraud. And all this before setting out on the monotonous, repetitive experiments themselves and the interminable labour of assessing results. And after it all Dr. Soal's results were once more exactly nil. It all appeared to be intensely discouraging. Why, if Rhine could succeed in South Carolina, could not others do so in London? The faith of some began to waver. Had Rhine really done it after all? Was there not some elusive normal explanation for his results? Some researchers began to doubt Tyrrell's successes with G. J. Why could he get high scores with his machine when others could not with cards? As a result, in spite of his repeated successes before witnesses, in spite of the meticulous care with which he had guarded against all possibility of normal perception on G. J.'s part, it was suggested that G. J. had cheated and offers were made to show Tyrrell just how she had led him up the garden path. Experimental research in England had indeed reached the doldrums when even enthusiasts remained unmoved by their co-worker's success.

CHAPTER XVI

Quantitative Experiments (2)

IT was not until the early forties that anotner advance was made in quantitative experiments, once more as the result of work by a lone enthusiast. This time it was Whately Caringston, who had earlier had the fruitful idea of applying word-association tests to mediums and their Controls. Science had been Carington's first love while he was still at Eton and he was happily continuing its study at Cambridge when the first World War disrupted normal life. He left to join the Royal Flying Corps, and during his service he learnt, to his boyish delight, to pilot twenty-nine different types of aircraft. But eventually a disastrous forced landing permanently damaged his health and he had to give up flying. About that time he heard from friends of some remarkable incidents with mediums and he at once booked some sittings with Mrs. Leonard. These gave results so striking that he set about studying psychical research from A. to Z.

After the war and on behalf of the Air Ministry and War Office, he returned to Cambridge to do research in acoustics with special reference to psychological problems, and in connection with this work he wrote a book, *The Measurement of Emotion*, in which he described some highly original methods of mathematical assessment devised by himself. These served him in good stead later on in psychical research.

Carington came early to the conclusion that witness box methods, as he called them, in other words the study of spontaneous cases and of 'hits' in statements by mediums, would never put *psi* on the map. Hence his methodical attempts to study the nature of a medium's Control by means of word association tests. He worked on these from 1934 to 1939 and they entailed all the disappointments and strain usual in pioneering. He had to start by teaching himself statistics which in itself was no mean task. Indeed, he worked so many calculations on a little hand-operated machine that he damaged his elbow and would have been unable to carry on, had not the S.P.R. come to his rescue with the gift of an electrically driven machine, which gave him immense pleasure.

Carington gave up all other work for psychical research and this left him nothing to live on but his private income of £120 a year. After spending some years in great poverty in a remote village in Holland, he was invited to apply for an important University post in England, which carried with it financial security and distinction. But he refused. "What", he said, pointing to a pile of work on psychical research, "would happen to all this?" In 1938 he did desert his work for a short time to go to Germany and rescue a lady who had suffered much at the hands of the Gestapo. Later on the two were married, and for nine years, as his health gradually failed, she nursed him—most of the time in a remote cottage in Cornwall —and most helpfully collaborated in his experiments. He died in 1947 at the early age of fifty-four, owing partly to the legacy of ill-health left him by the first World War, partly to continued overwork. "Time is so short", he said, "I must work". His was another life, like those of Myers, Gurney, Hodgson and Tyrrell, dedicated to the unpopular search for *psi*.

By the end of the thirties Carington had grown tired of bare experiments of the card-guessing type which seemed to him able to demonstrate little more than the mere fact of ESP. So he devised a more revealing pattern.[1] This was to combine the old qualitative experiments with drawings with statistical methods of assessment. His procedure was simple enough. At 7 p.m. on ten successive evenings he would hang up one of a series of ten drawings in his study. Each drawing depicted a single target object which had been chosen at random. They remained there with the door locked until 9.30 the next morning. Between those hours his percipients—he collected 251 of them, all living at a distance—had to draw what they imagined to be the target object on a form prepared by himself. This series of ten constituted one experiment. After a gap in

[1] Whately Carington, *Telepathy* (Methuen, 1945).

time the procedure was repeated. When a group of experiments was over the shuffled drawings from the whole group were sent to an outside judge for matching up with the shuffled originals.

Carington did eleven experiments and collected 20,000 drawings. Such experiments sound fairly straight-forward to organise. In fact the job is enormous. There is first the problem of choosing the objects. One criticism of Mrs. Sinclair's and G. J.'s successes had been that both agent and percipient had similar preferences. The answer to that was to ensure that the target object was chosen at random. Carington devised a watertight method of doing this. He opened a set of mathematical tables at random, having decided that, say, the fifth number in the sixth column of the page he happened upon would indicate the page in a dictionary on which he would find his target object. He then drew the first drawable word on that page. But assessment of hits was a far worse headache and involved an immense amount of labour. How much were percipients influenced by outside events, for instance? If the word boat came up as a target on the night of the Boat Race, how spurious would be a correct hit upon it? Again, was visual similarity, such as the Sinclair volcano and blackbeetle, a hit, or must the percipient interpret his image correctly? Carington was stern about this. He would not accept incorrect interpretations, however marked the resemblance to the target. A year or two later I was acting as his agent in a small sub-experiment and one target was a peach, which I drew on a twig with two leaves. My best percipient, who made an encouraging number of correctly named hits from twenty miles away, drew a similar circular fruit, also with twig and leaves. But she labelled it orange, because, she wrote, "I know it is not an apple as the skin is rough". So it was not classed as a hit. She also, incidentally, drew a corkscrew when the target was a double-headed axe, and a fluted rectangle, which she said might be either a radiator or a concertina, when it was a concertina.

Carington's sternness, of course, was essential in experiments undertaken to find out whether ESP was occurring, and, as he said, it did not prevent the separate study of drawings for hints as to how the object reached surface consciousness. Often the percipient himself has no idea. Sometimes there is a sense of 'knowing behind a veil' what the object is, but not being able to bring it to the surface. On one occasion, when acting as a percipient in drawing experiments, I 'felt' the target object to be a bird. "Perched or flying?" I asked myself. "Neither," I felt. "Don't be silly", I said, "It must be one or the other." So, although feeling sure I was mistaken, I drew it flying. It turned out to be an eagle hovering in a crouched position over her nest.

Another snag in assessment—in a way this was the worst of all—was that, if *psi* were not operating, percipients would clearly be more inclined to draw everyday objects, such as a house or a dog or a motorcar, than, say, a duck-billed platypus. In other words, every hit was not of the same value and some, of course, would just be lucky coincidences. Carington's solution here was to make a list of ten thousand objects which had been drawn by percipients in his earliest experiments and note how often each had been drawn, irrespective of targets. He then valued hits on targets in reverse order to their popularity in this list, giving most points to the object which had been least often drawn and vice versa.

Carington's brilliant gifts would surely have brought large material rewards if put to more mundane uses, but, like Tyrrell, he achieved the reward he wanted. His experiments with drawings were a marked success, for the hits were significantly more than one would expect from the effects of chance alone. The degree of significance in the different experiments varied from odds of a few hundreds to several thousands to one against. Moreover, the experiments gave some clues as to the process of ESP. Carington found, for instance, that percipients seemed to pick up ideas more often than visual forms, also that it did not seem to matter whether or not the target was actually drawn, so long as the agent had thought of it. But the great value of the experiments was to lay bare a quite unexpected effect. This was that hits on a particular target were not only most frequent on the night it was drawn—a bull's eye—but they were more frequent one night earlier or later than two nights earlier or later. In other words if a target pyramid was drawn on a Monday, percipients were more liable to draw pyramids on the Sunday before and the Tuesday after than on the Saturday before and the Wednesday after, and so on. The remarkable thing was that the rate of this decline was more or less the same both forward and backward in time, a rough analogy to the scatter round a bull's eye in space.

Carington's patience in collecting facts was monumental, but he was not satisfied. "Facts by themselves", he said, "are like curios in an ill-arranged museum. They do little or nothing of themselves to increase our understanding." His aim was to relate them by a theory and test that theory by further experiment.

The results of Carington's work led him to think that our individual minds are less isolated from one another than we assume. In fact he came to a conception which resembled Jung's of a common subconscious. But if it is by virtue of a common subconscious that telepathy occurs, how, he asked, does the percipient know which plum to pick out of the pudding? Why draw a pyramid in response to the target pyramid, rather than any other of a myriad images? His answer was to extend the well-known principle of the associa- tion of ideas. We all know how in a single mind one idea leads to another, how the sight of a pair of skis can evoke visions of snowy slopes, or broken ankles, or chance meetings on the journey home. But if, said Carington, A. and a distant B. both look at a pair of skis and they share a common subconscious, some of the resultant associations in A.'s conscious mind may also surface in B.'s. So for both agent and percipient to think *consciously* of the experiment they are doing may set up a kind of canalised subconscious linkage between them. Such linkage, he thought, can perhaps be deliberately reinforced, and in an attempt to do so he gave percipients, many of whom did not know him personally, a photograph of the study where he hung the target drawings. Any such links, whether of ideas or objects, he called 'K.' ideas or 'K.' objects.

If hits on a target drawing could occur both before and after that drawing was made, Carington wondered whether the same kind of displacement might not also take place in card-guessing experiments. With this possibility in mind he suggested to Dr. Soal that it might be worth while to reassess his many past experiments. Soal, who was thoroughly discouraged, felt little inclined to analyse thousands of columns of squares, crosses, waves, stars and circles all over again. But at last he decided to do so and was rewarded by the surprising discovery that two of his percipients had all the time been making magnificent scores. But not directly on the target card. One, a Mr. Shackleton, had been scoring on the card immediately after it—precognitively. The other, a Mrs. Stewart, had been doing the same thing on the cards both before and after.

Immensely cheered Dr. Soal, in collaboration with an equally meticulous worker, Mrs. K. M. Goldney, now set out on a new series of card-guessing experiments with Shackleton as percipient. They took even more extreme precautions than before to guard against any conceivable alternative explanations to ESP. Agent and percipient were strictly supervised by two experimenters. Unless all four were in collusion, the system adopted ruled out fraud. These experiments are described in Soal's recent important book, *Modern Experiments in Telepathy*, in which the statistical evidence for ESP is given in detail.[1] All we need to note here is that they were a marked success and provided conclusive evidence of ESP in test conditions. Rhine's triumphs had been repeated.

Unexpected and intriguing hints and clues as to subconscious relationships and preferences can be gleaned from the apparently arid material of card-guessing and several nice points emerged from Soal's new tests. If the agent did not look at a card but put it aside face downward to be checked with the guesses later, Shackleton's scoring at once fell to chance level—even when he did not consciously know that the procedure had been changed to a clairvoyance test. Soal tried him with about a dozen agents, but he could only succeed with three. He seemed to prefer a particular distance ahead in time, since when the rate of card-calling was doubled he scored on

[1] S. G. Soal and F. Bateman, *Modern Experiments in Telepathy* (Faber, 1954).

two cards ahead, not one. Although he failed in the clairvoyance tests, whereas in theory he might have 'looked' further ahead to the time when targets and guesses were compared, to some extent he could aim his scoring at will, since when Dr. Soal asked him to make a special effort to score on the contemporary target card the odds in 200 trials against his correct hits occurring by chance were more than ten million to one.

In 1945 Dr. Soal was able to experiment again with Mrs. Stewart, the second star performer in the early tests, who had scored high on cards both before and after the targets. He now made a number of variations in procedure which throw an interesting light on her ESP. He had already replaced the dull Zener cards by five somewhat more interesting pictures of animals—zebra, pelican, giraffe, elephant and lion—and on these Mrs. Stewart again scored magnificently. But she had changed her habits. She now scored her hits on the bull's eye direct, while on the card ahead they fell to significantly *below* chance. What, one wonders, was the motive behind this? Subconscious jealousy of Shackleton's precognitive triumphs has been suggested. It is interesting that both Shackleton and Mrs. Stewart scored positively in telepathy tests, but failed in clairvoyance tests, whereas Rhine's best percipients and Tyrrell's G. J. had managed both. Was this because Soal's own attitude was more receptive to the idea of telepathy? Shackleton himself did not prefer it, for he was very self-confident and believed that he could score equally well by both methods. Nevertheless the percipient's conscious attitude can be a vital factor. One of Rhine's star performers believed that he could use clairvoyance but not telepathy and he failed to score when he knew the conditions were set for telepathy only, although he did so quite happily in such conditions if he thought he was using clairvoyance. Such idiosyncracies, apparently, are not confined to percipients in modern scientific experiments. Ching Yu Wang, Director of Research in the Wah Chang Corporation of New York, relates that in the eleventh century a Chinese observer, Ch'en Kuah, noted that a *wu* or medium seemed to know the thoughts arising in others.[1] He was present

[1] Ching Yu Wang. Article in *Tomorrow*, Vol. IV, No. 1.

when some guests asked the *wu* to tell them how many draughts-men they held in their closed hands and she did so successfully when they themselves knew the numbers but not when they had picked up a handful without counting them.

At one time Soal used two agents with Mrs. Stewart. Half the information she needed to make a hit was known to one of them and half to the other. She still did nearly as well as when all the necessary information was known to one person. The experiment with two agents was then repeated for 200 trials, but Mrs. Stewart was deliberately told that there was only one. This false information reduced her score to slightly below chance expectation. For the next 200 trials she was told, correctly, that there were the two agents, and her score at once leapt up again to positive significance. In a further test she was told that the two agents would be working jointly, whereas they were in fact in opposition, that is, one might be looking at an elephant and the other at a penguin. Down went her score with both of them to near chance. She was then told that one only was acting as agent, whereas in fact the two were still in opposition, and she at once scored high on the one towards whom she was consciously orientated. All these tests indicate that she needed consciously to direct her ESP. They may also, possibly, throw light on the Cross Correspondences.

Soal's final triumph with Mrs. Stewart was to get her hitting a target in England as brilliantly from Antwerp as she had done from the next room. Calling and guessing were synchronised by the chimes of Big Ben on the wireless. But gradually, as time went on, her scores, like Shackleton's and those of Rhine's percipients, dropped to chance level. There seems to be a point in all quantitative experiments at which enthusiasm and pertinacity are defeated by the intolerable boredom of endless repetition. They are none the less invaluable, not only for having produced conclusive evidence of ESP, but for the flickers of light they throw on its behaviour.

Other experiments have demonstrated the importance of intention, expectation and general attitude in both experimenter and percipient. An American psychologist, Dr. Gertrude Schmeidler, found that her percipients who believed in

ESP scored significantly above chance and those who did not significantly below. She labelled them sheep and goats. This does not mean that the goats were not exercising ESP. On the contrary they were apparently doing so more than the sheep, for more cards are likely to be called wrong than right by chance, so a larger proportion have to be called wrong than right to get the same deviation on misses as on hits. Dr. Schmeidler also found by means of a psychological test (the Rorschach) that her percipients fell into four groups. What she called socially well adjusted sheep scored slightly higher than poorly adjusted sheep, and well adjusted goats slightly lower than poorly adjusted goats. It looked as if the well adjusted were more able to do what they wanted than the ill adjusted.

If only percipients knew how they make hits or why, experiments would be easier to devise. Professor Gardner Murphy tells a sad little story of a Miss Lillian Levine, a student who came to his laboratory to act as guinea-pig in a mass telepathy test. It was the usual card-guessing set-up, agents in one room and percipients far away in another. Miss Levine started by getting 15 correct hits straight off. The odds against this are about thirty thousand million to one, and Doctors and Professors hastened to her room to ask if she had any idea how she did it. She had looked across the room, she said, and had seen the crosses, and waves and the rest in the radiator. The experts retired as ignorant as they arrived and her subsequent scores were all at chance level. Why and how she suddenly got an apparent telepathic linkage with the experimenter, why and how she lost it, is anybody's guess.

An experimenter who has recently achieved excitingly positive results is Mr. G. W. Fisk, a member of the S.P.R. Council, who, like Tyrrell, combines a scientific approach with endless patience and a very encouraging personality.

In one experiment Fisk made a neat variation which seems to demonstrate the extent to which some personal idiosyncracy or relationship may inhibit ESP. His usual procedure was to send his percipients randomised packs of cards in opaque sealed envelopes. These were to be returned unopened, with a record of what the percipients believed the order of the cards inside to be. Normally he prepared the cards and envelopes himself, but on one occasion, unknown to the percipients, half the packs of cards sent out were prepared by Dr. D. J. West, who had conducted many experiments but had never achieved positive results. With the exception of Fisk's star performer, Miss Symonds, who scored well both for him and West, the other percipients scored positively for Fisk but only at chance level for West.

In 1956 a Mr. Downey scored significantly in a mass television test for ESP, in which Mr. Fisk acted as agent. In a further series of individual tests, with Fisk and West as alternate agents, he too continued to score positively for Fisk but at chance level for West. In the end, however, he got thoroughly bored with monotonous guessing over long periods and his scores dropped to chance level all round.

Recently some attention has been paid to another apparent manifestation of *psi*, which has been labelled psycho-kinesis or PK. PK is the apparent power of mind to influence matter directly at a distance, without any transfer of physical energy. Research into PK is only just beginning, by Mr. Fisk among others, and although the evidence for it is less in quality and in quantity than it is for ESP, in another subject it would be enough to be taken very seriously. G. N. M. Tyrrell once pointed out that there was more such evidence available than there was at the time he wrote for the accepted deflection of light in an eclipse.

J. B. Rhine was the first to report the apparent existence of PK. He tested it by throwing dice with the target face 'willed' to come uppermost, and he obtained what seemed to be positive results. Under more strict conditions as to possibly biassed dice and so on, Dr. R. A. McConnell at Pittsburg University, Dr. R. H. Thouless at Cambridge, and Mr. Fisk himself have done the same. Fisk's test was the most dramatic. He chose the target dice faces daily in Surrey by a random process. His co-experimenter, Dr. Blundun, threw the dice daily in Devon, willing as she did so that the target faces chosen by Fisk for that day would come up. But Fisk gave her a dual task. He did not tell her what the target faces were until after he had received

162

her scores by post. So she had first to find out target faces by telepathy from him and then cause them to come up on the dice by PK. Five main experiments were made covering a period of six years. All gave positive results and the odds against her repeated successes being due to chance were about 50,000 to 1. This was a satisfactory statistical confirmation of a PK effect which was associated over the years with one particular individual. Mr. Nigel Richmond did one PK experiment with paramecia in 1952, which showed a rate of scoring higher than any so far recorded with dice, but this experiment has not been repeated.[1] If PK is further confirmed it will make certain reported phenomena appear less inherently improbable than they do today.

[1] *Journal*, S.P.R., Vol. XXXVI, March 1952.

CHAPTER XVII

The Impact of *Psi*

How does the world of science today react to the challenge of *psi* and what new vistas does its discovery open up? These two questions are interlinked in a somewhat vicious circle. On the one hand established views are not overthrown simply because some new facts are discovered, but only when these are organised into a better system than its predecessor. On the other, it is not easy to propound new systems based on facts whose natural habitat seems to be through the looking glass.

Nevertheless there are signs of change in the general attitude to *psi* since the days of Sidgwick and Myers. Some Universities and learned bodies are gradually ceasing to look upon it as an unmentionable heresy. The Universities of Oxford, Cambridge and London, of Duke in America and Munich in Germany have all given doctorates for theses upon it. The Aristotelian Society of Great Britain has held three symposia to discuss it— the last in 1954—and, as a result of Professor Hardy's courageous insistence in 1949 to the British Association that telepathy was a fact, in 1950 the Society of Experimental Biologists met to consider the evidence for it. Hardy himself was chairman and C. D. Broad, Soal and J. B. S. Haldane were among the speakers. In the same year both the Royal Society of Medicine and the Royal Institution chose ESP as a subject for discussion, and in May 1955 the Ciba Foundation—an independent educational and scientific organisation—arranged an international symposium in London. In America the academic world has been less enterprising, though Rhine's work at Duke University and McConnell's at Pittsburg have respectively been supported by two great and conservative bodies, the Rockefeller and Mellon Trusts.

A few psychologists, too, are beginning to accept the fact

164

of ESP. In his latest book Dr. H. J. Eysenck says: "Unless there is a gigantic conspiracy involving some thirty University departments all over the world, and several hundred highly respectable scientists in various fields, many of them originally hostile to the claims of the psychical researchers, the only conclusion the unbiassed observer can come to must be that there does exist a small number of people who obtain knowledge existing either in other people's minds, or in the outer world, by means as yet unknown to science" [1]

All this implies an advance towards respectability which even if slow was unthinkable twenty-five years ago, and it is a tribute, not only to the tiny band of heretics who continued to seek their quarry undeterred by enormous difficulties, but also to the open-mindedness of some in academic high places. The most difficult mental act of all is to escape from prevailing doctrine. But, from the point of view of the heretic, progress towards recognition has seemed discouragingly slow and he has been driven to console himself with Whitehead's saying that all really new ideas have a certain aspect of foolishness when they are first produced.

If *psi* is a fact, its recognition will force renewed scrutiny of the axioms on which scientific work is based and particularly of that most knotty of all problems, the ultimate relation of mind to matter. Professor H. H. Price has put the situation in a nutshell. "Telepathy," he says, "is something which ought not to happen if the Materialistic theory were true. But it does happen. So there must be something seriously wrong with the Materialistic theory, however numerous and imposing the normal facts which support it may be." [2]

Most scientists prefer to avert their eyes from such a dilemma. Aldous Huxley recalls a solution to another not unlike it which was put forward a hundred years ago by the distinguished naturalist, Philip Gosse. "The geologists could prove that life had existed upon the earth for millions of years and that every existing plant and animal species had undergone far-reaching

[1] H. J. Eysenck, *Sense and Nonsense in Psychology*, p. 131 (Pelican Books, 1957).
[2] H. H. Price, *Psychical Research and Human Personality*. Article in the *Hibbert Journal*, January, 1949.

changes in the course of its evolution. But to Gosse, as to millions of other intelligent people, Genesis was literally true and the instantaneous creation of the world in 4004 B.C. was an unassailable fact. The evidence of geology had to be ignored or explained away. Gosse chose the latter course. The earth, he still maintained, had been created in a single instant, but it had been created in its present form, with all the appearance of having slowly evolved. In other words, 'God hid the fossils in the rocks in order to tempt geologists into infidelity.' Today, it would seem, God is hiding Mind in the ESP cards to tempt psychologists into infidelity towards another brand of fundamentalism—the faith in Universal Matter."[1]

The *psi* dilemma is reflected in the fair but almost embarrassed comments made recently by two well-known scientists, Dr. Grey Walter and Sir George Thomson, F.R.S. They are both considering the nature of the physical brain. Many people, says Grey Walter, assume that the impressive power of brain over body extends to another category altogether, the influence of mind over matter. But we must confess that as yet no study of brain activity has thrown any light on ESP or PK. It is useless to explain these phenomena by suggesting, as some do, that information could be transmitted from brain to brain by means of electrical activity, for the electrical disturbances created by the brain are too small; also if the largest rhythms of the brain were considered as radio signals they would fall below noise level a few millimetres from the head. And psychical researchers claim further that signals can be received before they are sent. "If", he concludes, "we accept these observations [of ESP and PK] for what they are said to be, we cannot fit them into the physical laws of the universe as we define them today. We may reject the claims of transcendental communication on the grounds of experimental error, or statistical fallacy, or we may withhold judgment, or we may accept them gladly as evidence of spiritual life; but it does not seem easy to explain them in terms of biological mechanism." [2]

In a discussion by Sir George Thomson of the brain as an

---

[1] Article in *Life*, Vol. XXXVI, No.2, p. 96 (1954).
[2] W. Grey Walter, *The Living Brain*, p. 176 (Duckworth, 1953).

electrical instrument this attitude of almost apologetic friend-liness is again apparent. He tacitly assumes, he says, a one—one correlation between brain and mind, although he points out that the evidence for this is very partial and rather indirect, certainly far less strong than the evidence for determination in the world of physics before 1900. But in his view the only facts, if they are facts, which do not fit in with it at all well are those of extra-sensory perception. He thinks the evidence for these facts is quite good, "good enough to produce acceptance if what is claimed were not such a fundamental upsetting of systems of thought adopted by most moderns and especially by scientists." He adds, moreover, that "the importance of the sub-ject is enormous and much too little work is being done on it. If true it will produce a revolution in thought." He does not think that ESP would necessarily disprove that brain and mind have a one—one connection, but it "would follow that thought is free to influence brains directly, not *only* but *including* the thinker's; it would show mind as a force acting more directly than we now suppose, and one might be inclined to regard the brain as merely the shell that holds the oyster, limiting it in some respects but not in all . . ." [1]

This generous attitude no doubt owes something to the advances made in physics in the last fifty years as well as to the impressive evidence for ESP. We are nowadays living in a mental world far removed from Kelvin's with its solid little atoms and all-pervading aether. Two mysteries, the quantum theory and Heisenberg's principle of indeterminacy, have undermined that orthodoxy. In the place of solid atoms we now have a group of elusive entities, electrons, protons, neutrons and the like which cannot be observed directly and whose behaviour can only be assessed by statistics. The new picture of basic matter as indeterminate is of great importance for psychical research. Sir George Thomson points out that the working parts of the physical brain are known to be exceedingly small and that they may be within the range at which the principle of indeterminacy can be effective. And the relation

[1] Sir George Thomson, F.R.S., *The Foreseeable Future*, pp. 157-9 (Cam-bridge University Press, 1955).

between an undetermined brain and a mind, he says, "may well be other than would be possible if the behaviour of the brain were determined in the same way as the motions of the planets are." [1]

It may be, then, that recent developments in physics are reducing the widespread hostility towards phenomena which cannot be explained in terms of the one-one correlation of mind and matter. But that hostility is still very strong. Some scientists, for instance, concede the fact of *psi*, but reject any explanation for it until they can find one which will harmonise with the apparently outdated mechanistic description of the universe. Their attitude still seems to be conditioned by the view of matter current half a century ago. Others openly deny the facts on prejudice alone. "Why," asks Dr. D. O. Hebb, Professor of Psychology at McGill University, "do we not accept ESP as a psychological fact? Rhine has offered enough evidence to have convinced us on almost any other issue, where one could make some guess as to the mechanics of the process . . . We are still trying to find a way out of the magic wood of animism, where psychology began historically, and we cannot give up the talisman of a knowledge of material processes. Personally I do not accept ESP for a moment, because it does not make sense. My external criteria, both of physics and physiology, say that ESP is not a fact, despite the behavioral evidence that has been reported. I cannot see what other basis my colleagues have for rejecting it . . . Rhine may still turn out to be right, improbable as I think that is, and my own rejection of his view is—in the literal sense—prejudice."

In 1952 an American Professor of Biology, Dr. Lucien Warner, surveyed the attitude of American psychologists to psychical research.[2] Most of those who replied at all considered it a legitimate scientific undertaking, but some frankly dismissed it on the grounds that psychical researchers themselves must be round the bend. Here are a few samples.

"What are the quirks of personality that lead an otherwise

[1] Op. cit. p. 160.
[2] *Journal of Parapsychology*, December, 1952, p. 284 et seq. (Duke University Press).

sensible psychologist to continue to waste his time on so unrewarding a field of enquiry?"

"One is forced to the conclusion that there is something about this problem that leads the people who are attracted to it to come to false positive conclusions."

"I feel that most of the investigations are designed to 'prove' something the antithesis of science. It is so improbable that the principal relevant topic for research is explanation of the present extent of interest in the question."

"It is a legitimate scientific undertaking in the sense that one can study anything. No, in the sense that the study is likely to be barren and futile."

"It will become a part of academic psychology if and when we have an adequate theory to explain the phenomena."

Dr. George H. Price, a research associate in the Department of Medicine, University of Minnesota, has recently put the sceptic's attitude in no uncertain terms. "Not 1,000 experiments with 10 million trials and by 100 separate investigators giving total odds against chance of 10^{1000} to 1",[1] he said, could make him accept ESP. He must have "one fraud-proof experiment, conducted before a committee of twelve prominent men, who were all strongly hostile towards parapsychology and had an adamantine faith that ESP was impossible!" [1] Parapsychologists must prove their case to the most "hostile, pig-headed and sceptical of critics." [1] The solution Dr. George Price thinks more probable—and he admits that there are no other alternatives—is that all concerned in all ESP experiments must have cheated.

In 1953 a vigorous stand against the quantitative evidence for ESP was made by Mr. G. Spencer Brown.[2] He did not criticise the integrity or technique of the experimenters, but in an article which appeared in *Nature* he suggested that the distributions in certain well-known tables of supposedly random numbers do not always behave in practice exactly as they should according to accepted mathematical theory.

[1] George H. Price. Article in *Science*, August 1955.
[2] Spencer Brown has since published a book on these lines, entitled *Probability and Scientific Inference* (Longmans, 1957).

In other words, statistics itself is not always a totally reliable instrument. So technical a claim can only be discussed by experts for experts, but as it is believed by some that Mr. Spencer Brown's statements have invalidated all quantitative experiments it is worth giving some reasons why this is not so. To take Dr. Soal's. Large numbers of the scores obtained by his percipients have been cross-checked with targets at which they were not aimed. He himself cross-checked a set of nearly four thousand guesses by Shackleton with non-target cards. In both cases the results, which had been highly significant on the right targets, tallied with chance. A statistician, Mr. Greenwood, made the enormous effort of matching half a million guesses from successful experiments against non-target cards, and the results were again at chance level.

Further reasons why Soal's experiments are unaffected are that changes in the experimental conditions made *meaningful* changes in the rate of success. Shackleton did well with only three agents out of twelve. When the rate of calling was doubled, he made a significant number of hits, not on one but on two cards ahead. Again, both he and Mrs. Stewart made high scores under telepathic conditions only, and, in similar experiments to Soal's, Dr. Schmeidler and others have found that different temperaments scored differently. And finally, G. J., Tyrrell's percipient (who also scored better with him as agent than with others), as well as Rhine's Hubert Pearce and Soal's Shackleton and Mrs. Stewart, went on producing high scores for very long periods.

Although it is still true to say that the majority among contemporary thinkers cannot bring themselves to accept the existence of *psi*, there seems little doubt that the majority is decreasing. And some of the best minds of the day go farther than mere acceptance. They are seeking to integrate *psi* into the pattern of nature. This task is beset with difficulties. "However broadly we use the words", Sir Mortimer Wheeler has said in a recent book, "man is in some sense the casket of a soul as well as five shillings' worth of chemicals. And the soul or sensibility or mind—whatever we like to call it—is beyond the reach of finite intelligence since the mind obviously cannot encompass itself." [1] *Psi* phenomena have a way of leading back to the scientific heresy of a soul in the casket and to guess at their nature seems like an attempt to encompass the mind itself. Moreover, if a would-be interpreter clings too closely to the rudimentary fact of ESP as disclosed by the latest experiments and ignores even PK, he may get nowhere. If, on the contrary, he spreads his net wider to include phenomena for which the evidence can be questioned, his hypotheses may be based on sand. But in every form of research hypothesis is a vital tool. It suggests questions to ask. It indicates new forms of experiment. It can help investigators to see significance in tiny clues which might otherwise escape them. And even mistaken hypotheses have led to new discoveries.

The few adventurous thinkers who in spite of the difficulties have sought to probe into the nature of *psi* always insist that hypotheses formulated at the outset of enquiry into such elusive phenomena are certain to be inadequate and are likely to be mistaken. But they are very stimulating and for this reason a few of those which have recently been put forward are summarised in an appendix to this record.

[1] Mortimer Wheeler, *Archaeology from the Earth*, p.229 (Pelican Books, 1954).

CHAPTER XVIII

The Future

THIS sketch could not be comprehensive and remain a sketch. The choice seemed to lie between trying to cover the whole ground very briefly or describing a number of highlights in more detail. The second course appeared to give the reader new to psychical research a better opportunity to form his own judgment. At the same time it has left gaps. It has also rendered the sketch parochial, for, apart from the Gröningen experiment, only research done in England and the U.S.A. has been described. But *psi* has not been entirely ignored elsewhere. Among others, Baron von Schrenck-Notzing and Dr. Hans Driesch in Germany, Professor Bozzano in Italy and the Nobel Prize winner, Dr. Charles Richet, Dr. Osty and Monsieur René Warcollier in France have devoted much time and energy to its pursuit. But along the central trail we have been following their work does not differ in kind from the examples given in this book.

We have now followed that trail to the conclusive demonstration of ESP. We have seen that a slowly increasing number of scientists and other contemporary thinkers are willing to concede that psychical research is not a form of lunacy. And we are left with the obvious question: What of the future? Where do we go from here?

Here, of course, is still very near the starting point. Little more than the preliminary task set themselves by the first pioneers—to establish the existence of *psi*—has been accomplished. Like Thales we are still rubbing our stick of amber, in the hope of discovering why, for no apparent reason, it will attract its wisp of fluff on Monday but not on Tuesday. One day, perhaps, psychic phenomena will be as obedient to control as electrical phenomena are today. Meanwhile the confirmation of *psi* has raised a number of immediate questions. First of all, was Walter de la Mare right when he said to Sir Russell Brain: "I believe that telepathy is almost continuous. If you and I were not in telepathic communication now we couldn't carry on our conversation." [1] Are there any clues to the nature of the *psi* process? What conditions favour its appearance? To what extent, if any, is it limited by physical factors? Can *psi* ability be developed? What type of personality makes the best percipient? Or agent? Is it a matter of personal relationship between two individuals? What are the respective roles of agent and percipient? What is the most favourable psychological condition for either or both to be in? Does, for example, a percipient's state of frustration *vis-a-vis* an agent tend to evoke his ESP? Is the agent really an agent, or, on the contrary, are telepathic phenomena caused by the percipient's clairvoyance of the agent's mental state? Can A.'s feelings or thoughts about B., even if unexpressed, even if repressed into his own subconscious, still affect B. at a distance for good or ill? Are emotions infectious? Can thoughts go out to war? Is a powerful intellect in a hermitage more potent than a squadron of tanks? Can love and hate be boomerangs? Is it in a literal sense impossible to harm another without harming oneself? Is it stark fact that all men, or even all living creatures, are members one of another? Is it true that "so long as one man is in prison, I am not free; so long as one community is enslaved I belong to it," in the sense that if a man jumps into the sea he will get wet?

Among such questions as these are some which have been dealt with hitherto only by religion and metaphysics. Research into them from the scientific angle demands prolonged work by the best brains, in conditions in which *psi* can flower. What in fact is being done? In America Dr. J. B. Rhine and Dr. Louisa Rhine are running a small Parapsychology Laboratory at Duke University, and a few experimenters have been given limited grants to do quantitative work at one or two other Universities. There is also the American Society for Psychical Research, a small but devoted body which does what research it can with the workers and funds available. In England the

[1] Russell Brain, *Tea with Walter de la Mare*, p. 34 (Faber, 1957).

parent Society and its daughter groups at Oxford and Cambridge are in a similar position. And they, like all interested in psychical research, are faced with a dual task. As well as research itself, the public has to be informed and educated, since the research will be less effective in a climate of opinion which regards *psi* as a fantasy. Yet to create a climate in which it can flower, but superstition does not run rampant, is no easy task.

The lack of funds for research mattered less in the days when most of it was done by enthusiasts at their own expense. Today this is scarcely feasible, for experimental work has become more complicated, some of it needs expensive equipment, and enthusiasts no longer have the leisure, private income and domestic help which would enable them to travel about investigating spontaneous cases with the thoroughness they demand. The early death in 1957 of one devoted and talented worker, Edward Osborn, was largely due to the strain of continued research over and above a responsible full time job. I once asked him how long it had taken him to get to the bottom of a curious visual hallucination which appeared to originate from outside the percipient but which he ultimately traced to a repressed psychological conflict of her own. He laughed as if in apology. "I'm afraid it took about two hundred hours to do properly", he said.

But a bright spot has recently appeared in this somewhat frustrating picture, created once more by the dedicated enthusiasm of one individual. Early in this century a girl, now Mrs. Eileen Garrett, was born in Ireland of Irish and Basque parentage. In childhood she had many experiences resembling those of Mrs. Leonard—hallucinations of relatives at moments of crisis, beautiful visionary surroundings, unseen playmates, and so on. Like Mrs. Leonard, too, she was bitterly condemned for mentioning such disgraceful happenings and in consequence grew up lonely and distressed at her own abnormality. Eventually she met a Mr. Hewatt Mackenzie, who was kind and sensible and did not treat her as a freak. But he was a spiritualist and he set about training her as a trance medium. In this she acquiesced, but in the end she found herself unable to accept without question the spiritualist interpretation of her ESP and decided that her task was not to be a spiritualist medium but to devote her life to a search for the real nature of *psi*. In 1952, in New York, after much hard work, she was able to set up the Parapsychology Foundation. This body has four main lines of activity. It gives grants to *bona fide* researchers of any nationality. It publishes original work on *psi* and encourages republication of important books, such as Myers' *Human Personality*, which are out of print. And it finances international conferences, which enable investigators from different countries to pool their findings and level up standards of work.

But even so enterprising a body as the Parapsychology Foundation is like a mouse nibbling at a mountain in face of the problems which need investigation. These demand, not only experimentation, but research in the field to provide clues for the framing of future experiments. And this is urgent. All over the world teams of investigators trained in both psychical research and anthropology are needed to seek for evidence of *psi* in traditional and primitive societies before these are disintegrated by the Western way of life. And the investigators must have more than training, they must outdo Myers and Gurney in discretion and tact. Not long ago I heard of an African student whom a friend asked quite casually to call through a pack of cards. He did so, I was told, with staggering correctness and then enquired what there was of interest in so simple a task. I could learn no more, but this seemed a clue. So I wrote to a farming friend in Africa who has excellent relations with his employees, to ask whether he would care to do some quantitative experiments with them on my behalf. His reply was, "Do you want me to be labelled a black magician by the whole district?"

A report has recently come out on one such field project, which was financed by the Parapsychology Foundation.[1] This was a search for traces of *psi* among Australian aborigines and it was made by an Australian anthropologist, Dr. Ronald Rose, and his wife. They achieved significant results in a number of card-guessing experiments and they noted one interesting point. An aborigine's apparent spontaneous ESP seems on occasion

[1] Ronald Rose, *Living Magic* (Chatto and Windus, 1957).

to be mediated to his surface consciousness by dreams or waking hallucinations of tribal totems. In one case a man and his wife reported that they saw a plover circling over their hut. They recognised this as a 'mind' bird, and as they had an uncle living two hundred miles away whose totem was a plover, they took its appearance to indicate that he had just died. This turned out to be the case. Crisis cases resembling those recorded in this book were related to other anthropologists as well as the Roses by aborigines who were not witch doctors. They looked on such experiences as perfectly normal for themselves but were much surprised to learn that white people had them too.

In most countries there is little time to be lost before embarking on this type of research. Sir Arthur Grimble recorded cases of apparent *psi* in the Gilbert Islands, but it will be far harder to track down there in its traditional setting since the violent impact on native society of the recent war in the Pacific. Two years ago a Sorbonne-trained Haitian doctor told me that there was still a fruitful field in his country, but that there too the *psi*-inhibiting tide of Western scepticism was rising fast. The same is true of India, Indonesia and Africa, whence travellers' tales of apparent *psi* have often come. Long distance telepathy has also been reported among the Esquimaux and the Scolt Lapps, peoples who, like the Africans, are liable to be separated by great distances and to whom in the past no postal or telegraph service, no telephone or radio, have been available. But today even the silent world of the Arctic looks like becoming an unquiet highway between Russia and the United States. It will be unfortunate if we fail to seek for *psi* in vanishing climates of opinion which encourage its appearance, even if coupled with superstition, before we have created such a climate, divorced from superstition, in the West.

As we have seen, there are also difficulties within the field of research. Quantitative experiments provide no more than crumbs of information about the nature of *psi* and even spontaneous cases will tell us little until we know better what questions to ask. Freud made the interesting observation that for psychological reasons a percipient's ESP of another person's desire and phantasies, which surfaces perhaps in a dream, can

176

be so censored and distorted as to be unrecognisable without skilled interpretation. And Professor Broad has pointed out that such perceptions are no more than the effect of distant events on the percipient and need not therefore resemble those events at all. (See Appendices C and D). Again, testimony for ESP is sometimes only communicable to those who have had similar experiences. Some investigators are in the position of the inhabitants of the Country of the Blind who found the description of a sunset perfectly meaningless.

In the early days of my interest in psychical research I felt I should report what appeared to be a case of ESP in my own life. A woman whom I had met a few times at parties and liked, was killed in an aeroplane accident. Two days later I seemed acutely aware of her presence, and she implored me to stop a course of action which was being taken by a close relative for her sake. The relative was little more than a name to me, and I thought the action most improbable, but so great was her insistance that I rang up my husband for advice. "Better be a fool than a knave," he said. So I went to the relative, very reluctantly as my husband was at the British Embassy and I knew the town would talk. The situation was as I had been told and I was able to put it right.

"Did you see the woman?" asked the investigator when I reported this experience. "No." "Did you hear what she said?" "No." "Then how did you know she was there?" "I didn't *know*. But it felt like her—her personality." "I see. And if you didn't hear what she said, how did you know what it was?" "I can't explain. She seemed to communicate it inside me. We seemed [I had a brilliant idea] We seemed to be in—in communion." The investigator looked pained. I could see that he was wondering why I did not wear green, and amber beads. "You realise," he said, "that there is no evidence here at all." "No, of course not," I said meekly, thinking of the intensity of the experience. "I suppose," he said, "that you are firmly convinced of survival?" "No," I replied, "I've never been able to envisage it."

But my sympathy is with the investigator. We are so made that it is hard to avoid interpreting all facts of experience in terms of sensory perceptions, and on the woolliest of evidence such cases as the above appear to suggest continued personal identity beyond the grave. It is very tempting to dismiss them as spurious because their assumed interpretation seems improbable. Nevertheless they remain facts of experience.

It is hard to doubt that in time answers will be found to the questions raised in this book. In the main these are focussed on extra-sensory perception of mundane events, which can be checked and corroborated. But a number of persons who appeared able to acquire such knowledge have also claimed to share a very different type of experience, in common with artists, poets and religiously gifted persons throughout the ages and throughout the world. This experience is of another order of being, whose phenomena, vivid and transcendant as they are, do not fall within the categories of sensory perception and cannot as yet be checked by any available tools. Nor can they even be indicated in our language, except by analogies, symbols and poetic images. T. S. Eliot has stated the problem in *Four Quartets*.

I can only say, there we have been; but I cannot say where,
And I cannot say how long, for that is to place it in time.

It is an interesting mental exercise to read statements made by visionaries about 'unknown modes of being' in a condition, as Eliot put it, "of complete simplicity which costs not less than everything". In other words, as a child might read a guide book. Take these:

The light of sense goes out,
But with a flash that has revealed the invisible world.

Oh, there is life that breathes not; Powers there are
That touch each other to the quick in modes
Which the gross world no sense hath to perceive . . .

Oh, world invisible, we view thee.

Then dawns the invisible: the Unseen its truth reveals . . .

Emily Brontë wrote with passion of the despair that is felt

by sensitives like Mrs. Willett, as well as by poets and mystics, on returning from conditions of greater freedom and more vivid awareness to the narrow limitations of the sensory world with its "estranged faces that miss the many splendour'd thing."

> O dreadful is the check—intense the agony—
> When the ear begins to hear, and the eye begins to see;
> When the pulse begins to throb—the brain to think again—
> The soul to feel the flesh, and the flesh to feel the chain.

Ouspensky once said that he was at times projected into a world of complicated mathematical relationships where the relation we know between subject and object was broken. In *Four Quartets*, again, Eliot has spoken of conditions where relationships differ from those obtaining in the world of sense.

> Neither flesh nor fleshless: neither from nor towards;
> At the still point, there the dance is
> But neither arrest nor movement. And do not call it fixity.

Has all this any meaning? Are those transcendent surroundings merely 'subjective', whatever that may mean, or no more perhaps than a distortion of remembered sensory perceptions resulting from derangement of the physical brain? Or is such an order of being actual? Does it exist in its own right, and is the function of the brain, as Bergson and others have suggested, to protect us from its too great glory or too intolerable horror? How are we to find out?

It is just possible that there may be a fresh clue from a new direction in the experiences of certain guinea-pigs who have taken one of the hallucinogenic drugs which are now being studied in the hope of finding a physical cure for schizophrenia. A few of these guinea-pigs have been transported into conditions far beyond the reach of language, and in a recent experiment two educated persons are reported on one occasion to have made more or less sustained telepathic contact when under the influence of a new hallucinogen. A report on hallucinogens by Dr. Humphrey Osmond, one of the pioneers in this research, was issued in March 1957 by the New York Academy of Sciences. In it he says: "Most subjects find the experience valuable, some find it frightening, and many say it is uniquely lovely. All, from ... unsophisticated Indians to men of great learning, agree that much of it is beyond verbal description. Our subjects, who include ... authors, artists, a junior cabinet minister, scientists, a hero, philosophers and business men, are nearly all in agreement in this respect. For myself, my experiences with these substances have been the most strange, most awesome and among the most beautiful things in a fortunate and varied life. These are not escapes but enlargements, burgeonings of reality. In so far as I can judge, they occur ... because the brain, although its functioning is impaired, acts more subtly and complexly than when it is normal. Yet surely, when poisoned, the brain's actions should be less complex, rather than more so? I cannot argue about this because one must undergo the experience oneself. Those who have had these experiences know, and those who have not had them cannot know, and, what is more, the latter are in no position to offer a useful explanation".

Is it possible that here again is a hint that the brain is an organ of limitation? But in such work researchers are only lining up for the start, and all that can be said as yet is that it may possibly converge with other lines of psychical research to cast fresh light upon the hidden side of human nature. And we should perhaps remind ourselves that increased *psi* awareness does not mean increased spirituality, even though in the saints the two have sometimes appeared to develop together. Through knowledge of *psi* we may learn more about our nature; by means of *psi* some of us may experience the unity of mankind and eventually escape into a wider world. Even so they will only perceive what it is in them to perceive and they will still be in a world of form and phenomena. Spirituality is something different in kind from these, something that shines through forms and can do so in Belsen as well as in Paradise. It is not the automatic reward of taking drugs or guessing through packs of cards.

But it would be unfair and misleading to end a record of careful, down-to-earth research on a note of wild surmise. The task of the psychical researcher is to explore his subject with the patient devotion of the scientist who is not blind to the unexpected and does not reject the new, but will nevertheless subject them to long and relentless scrutiny. And if we do not cease from exploration, if we follow humbly wherever nature leads, it may be that

> ... the end of all our exploring
> Will be to arrive where we started
> And know the place for the first time.[1]

[1] T. S. Eliot, *Four Quartets* (Faber and Faber Ltd., 1944).

APPENDIX I

Some Explanations and Hypotheses

G. N. M. Tyrrell and Whately Carington

IT was from a background of the physical sciences that the two lone enthusiasts, G. N. M. Tyrrell and Whately Carington, conducted their research into *psi* and formulated their hypotheses about it. In the forties, after his long years of practical experiment, Tyrrell turned to the theoretical study of apparitions, of which many more records had accumulated since Myers' day. These he thought might help to throw light on the subconscious methods of perception of which his work with G. J. had given him fleeting glimpses.

The early pioneers, it will be remembered, came to the conclusion that, contrary to traditional belief, an apparition was not something actually 'out there' in a physical sense, but was an hallucination. But although hallucinations are not brought to our notice by means of the physical senses, they are none the less as genuinely perceived as cats or tables. Some, of course, seem to originate within the percipient but what are labelled telepathic hallucinations correspond with the situation of another person who may be a hundred miles away. Tyrrell came to the conclusion that previous theories had not fully accounted for the apparent behaviour of apparitions and he analysed and compared every available well-authenticated report of them. From these he produced a clear picture of genuinely experienced apparitions in contrast to those of fiction.[1]

Apparitions do very remarkable things. In many crisis cases the apparition of a person in distress has adapted itself to the percipient's exact surroundings. But very often the distressed person did not know where the percipient was and certainly not exactly where he was sitting or standing at the moment of the apparition's appearance. An apparition can be reflected

[1] G. N. M. Tyrrell, *Apparitions* (Duckworth, 1953).

in a looking glass or cast a shadow, and it can avoid the furniture as it walks about. Moreover, it will look exactly like the ostensible agent from any angle, even faithfully reproducing the back of his neck. And the most extraordinary thing about the best quality apparition is that the person who sees it does not at first realise it is not a living person. To him it is quite normal. How, then, is it created?

Tyrrell finally came to think that an apparition is not a dramatic representation of the agent created by the percipient alone, but something produced jointly by agent and percipient at some mid-level between mind and body—rather perhaps as a dream is dramatised. (A reminder of George du Maurier's novel *Peter Ibbetson*.) In Tyrrell's view the agent supplies what he called the theme. But this is not 'sent' across space on the analogy of a wireless message. Much study drove him to the conclusion that agent and percipient can work together far more intimately than that, and he came to think that at those mid-levels human beings are in a sense non-separate. Agent and percipient are not two, but one. If that is so, why do we not all see apparitions all the time? Because, said Tyrrell, our main job is to be efficient in the physical world and therefore our attention is normally concentrated on physical impacts.

Tyrrell's conception of apparitions as joint dramatic representations gets rid of certain difficulties. He thought that what he called the subconscious mid-level 'producers' of the agent and percipient would naturally combine to include such assessories as clothes or horses, when appropriate, and that they would also make the apparition behave as in real life, though less skilled 'producers' might make mistakes such as walking it through a wall. (But there are reports of haunting apparitions which are seen to walk through a wall at a spot where the percipient afterwards discovers that there has previously been a door.) In Tyrrell's view his theory also explained collective apparitions. If the agent, he said, was subconsciously picturing himself in the company of the percipient, then it was dramatically natural that the agent should be seen from the appropriate angle by others present besides the percipient. (The most famous case of what may have been such an apparition is that of Christ at Emmaus.) On the other hand, if some 'producers' were less efficient than others, an apparition might well be seen—or a sound heard—by some members of a group and not by others. On occasion, indeed, it appears to have been the dog or the cat whose 'producer' was really efficient.

Although Tyrrell's theory of apparitions gets rid of some conundrums, it raises others. The vital rôle he attributes to the agent seems to separate telepathy from clairvoyance which needs no agent; yet both may be manifestations of a single *psi* faculty. And a very recent suggestion by Dr. Louisa Rhine is that in such cases the active agent is the percipient himself. She thinks that he probably becomes aware both of distant events and of the mental state of others by means of his own clairvoyance without any activity on the part of the so-called agent.[1] Perhaps such problems will one day be cleared up by experiment. And some of them may be found to arise only from our form of language and our conceptions of time and space. Meanwhile the point of interest is that Tyrrell's research work, like Carington's, drove him to postulate some kind of immediate linkage between human beings at a subconscious level. This hypothesis tallies with the conceptions of Hindu philosophy and also with those developed by Jung, partly as a result of his discovery that similar symbols people the human subconscious the world over and have done so throughout the ages.

Whately Carington went further than Tyrrell and postulated 'group minds' within the common subconscious.[2] He did so on the grounds that he found it impossibly difficult to conceive that such elaborate instinctive behaviour as, say, a spider's power to spin webs could be due to an inherited pattern of nerve paths in the brain. Behaviour of this high order, he thought, may come about through the individual's telepathic linkage with some larger system in which all spider web-spinning experience is stored up—the Spider Mind. He further suggested

[1] Louisa E. Rhine, *Hallucinatory Psi Experiences II—The Initiative of the Percipient in Hallucinations of the Living, the Dying and the Dead. Journal of Parapsychology*, March, 1957.

[2] Whately Carington, *Telepathy* (Methuen, 1945).

that basic mental units were not, as commonly supposed, whole 'minds' but individual mental images, which he labelled psychons, held together by common associations. Unfortunately, before he could develop this original suggestion, he died, but we shall see later that it does not quarrel with equally original hypotheses as to the nature of 'mind' put forward by Professor H. H. Price.

B. BY A BIOLOGIST

Professor Sir Alister Hardy

IN the view of Professor Hardy, the fact that individual organisms are in psychical connection with one another across space is one of the most revolutionary biological discoveries ever made. It has led him to put forward a hypothesis of group minds to illuminate certain biological facts which have hitherto defied explanation. He looks on such psychical connection as a property almost as fundamental as that of gravity between physical bodies, since he does not think it can be limited to a few individuals of one species, man. It is more likely that those few individuals happen to be conscious of what is really a general unconscious property of all organisms. If that is so, he says, psychical research is of immense importance: it could revolutionise the outlook of biologists in a matter of twenty years or less and with it that of the world at large.

Professor Hardy discussed the implications of telepathy for biological theory in two articles written for the S.P.R. in 1950 and 1953.[1] He emphasised that these were over-condensed and over-simplified, but they are nevertheless very stimulating.

The first article surveys the history of biological theory since Darwin and outlines the current view on the mechanism of evolution, according to which evolution proceeds by Darwinian selection exercised by the exterior environment on living creatures. Hardy cites phenomena which this view does not cover and suggests that the course of evolution may be affected, not only by external influences—predators, climate, etc.—but also by patterns of behaviour which influence the 'selection' of gene combinations within an animal. Evolutionary trends, he says, may thus be affected from within a species as well as

[1] A. C. Hardy, *Telepathy and Evolutionary Theory. Journal* S.P.R., May, 1950. *Biology and Psychical Research. Proceedings* S.P.R., Vol. L, 1953, pp. 96–134.

from without. And if telepathy is a property of all living things it may be that the patterns of behaviour which influence gene selection are partially moulded by telepathy between the members of a species. There may be a "sort of species memory governing to some extent the pattern of behaviour of the individuals of a race."[1]

By 1953 Hardy had reached the further conclusion that telepathy may turn out to be a vital factor in evolution. After quoting the Gilbert Murray and Guthrie experiments to emphasise the point that ideas, designs and figures appear to have been transmitted by telepathy from one person to another, he states the most vital task facing biologists today: to settle the mind-body relationship, to answer the question: Is there or is there not some vital non-material element in living things?

In his opinion there are certain biological phenomena, homologues for instance, which cannot be explained without supposing a non-material element. A homologue is defined as the same organ in different animals under every variety of form and function. A man's arm, a bird's wing, a porpoise's flipper, are homologues, for though they serve quite different purposes, they have the same basic structure of bones and they all probably derive from one single structure in a common ancestry. For instance, the humerus bones of all terrestrial vertebrates seem to be modifications of the primitive limb-like fins of the first fish-like amphibia which changed their habitat from water to land.

This concept of homology is fundamental to the current theory of evolution according to which selection by the environment suffices to account for the varying forms taken by living creatures. But Hardy points out the strange paradox that homology itself cannot be explained by that theory. Moreover, if exterior influences alone were at work, the basic structure of such different creatures as a porpoise, a sparrow, an elephant or a man must surely have become less similar than they are in the profoundly differing conditions in which they have evolved

[1] Hardy pays tribute to Samuel Butler's original ideas on this subject, but his own hypothesis is not open to certain objections which hold against Butler's.

over millions of years. Hardy suggests that there must also be a conservative factor causing them to adhere to some sort of general 'specification' or plan and that evidence for such a factor does exist. If biology takes such phenomena as memory, hypnosis and telepathy into account—as it must—it is faced with the conscious telepathic transfer of design, form and experience as in the Guthrie and Murray experiments. This suggests an illuminating question to Hardy. May not *subconscious* impressions also be transmitted on a far more universal scale, he asks. May there not be a general subconscious sharing of a form and behaviour design—a sort of psychic blueprint—between members of a species? In such a telepathic 'plan' he sees a racial experience of habit, form and development open subconsciously to all members of a species, as in Carington's group mind. It would also itself act by the Darwinian principle of selection, for those animals whose gene complexes allowed a better incarnation of the 'plan' of their species would tend to survive rather than those whose genes produced a faulty version.

Hardy suggests that the idea of the members of a species being linked by telepathy in a group mind would explain other phenomena which biologists have so far failed to fit into current mechanistic theory. One of these is the recent discovery that in two related types of, say, fish, the form of one kind can be transformed into that of the other by its relatively simple *mathematical* transformation. A similar principle can be seen in the mathematically harmonious transformation from human foetus to adult. Take two outline drawings, one of a five months old human foetus, the other of an adult human being, both in a standing position. If horizontal lines are ruled across the foetus at equal intervals from head to toe and similar lines at the same anatomical levels across the adult, the interesting fact emerges that the lines on the adult occur further and further apart in a regular progression from head to toe.

Hardy finds it impossible to imagine how such a mathematical plan of growth could have been evolved entirely under the selective influence of the very heterogeneous environment. To him, he says, it has all the appearance of a definite mental conception like that of an artist or designer—a pattern outside the physical world—which in some way has served as a template or gauge for selective action. It suggests "a species plan mirrored in each individual: a plan in which evolution may be stretched or warped in various ways, but always as a whole plan is stretched or warped, and usually according to a relatively simple mathematical formula."

There is a third problem which Hardy thinks might be explained on the hypothesis of a group mind acting as a selective agent. The study of fossils has suggested that evolutionary trends acquire momentum as they proceed. In his view this tendency also suggests some unit of life beyond the transient individual, which builds itself up from the unconsciously shared experience of all the members of the race.

(i) Sigmund Freud and Professor C. J. Jung

PSYCHOLOGY is another discipline on which *psi* is beginning to make an impact. The story of Freud's gradual acceptance of telepathy can to some extent be found in his biography by Ernest Jones, and this, together with some further information, has been usefully summarised in a recent article by an Italian psychoanalyst, Emilio Servadio.[1]

Ernest Jones was a resolute sceptic and looked on Freud's inclination to accept telepathy as an unfortunate lapse into superstition, to be combated at all costs. But it seems clear that in fact Freud changed from scepticism to acceptance after studying evidence that he found coercive. He knew of a number of cases in which the evidence for telepathy between analyst and patient seemed strong enough to remove any doubt about its reality. He was a member of both the S.P.R. and the American S.P.R. and in 1924 he wrote to Jones about the Gilbert Murray experiments: "I confess that the impression made by these reports was so strong that I am ready to give up my opposition to the existence of thought-transference. ... I should even be prepared to lend the support of psychoanalysis to the matter of telepathy."

Jones, however, considered that the acceptance of telepathy would be fatal to psychoanalysis and he prevented Freud from taking such drastic action by writing a circular letter describing its dangers. He also took similar measures at other times. For example, he prevented Freud from reading an essay on *Psychoanalysis and Telepathy* which he had prepared for the International Psychoanalytic Congress in 1922. It was not published until after Freud's death in 1941.

Freud suggested that telepathy may be the original archaic method by which individuals understood each other, but that

[1] *Tomorrow*, Vol. VI, No. 1.

it has been pushed into the background by methods of communication via the senses, which are more efficient. The older methods may still manifest themselves under certain conditions. He also came to think that some people might become aware by telepathy of the conscious or unconscious phantasies of others and express these in a distorted fashion. The distortion might take the form of displacing a past event into the future or of transferring one person's experience to someone else, and it would serve to hide undesirable aspects of the actual phantasies.

Servadio quotes a memorable observation made almost casually by Freud who did not seem to realise its importance. This was that psychoanalysis might sometimes reveal telepathic impressions which had been 'censored' and distorted before reaching the percipient's consciousness. Where that had occurred, of course, the impressions would go unrecognised unless they were properly interpreted. In Servadio's view Freud's observation opens up a new path in psychical research, for it shows that when searching for ESP we should not confine ourselves to the manifest content of, say, a dream which tallies only vaguely with an exterior event, but should look for psychological factors which mask a greater resemblance between the two.[1]

The most famous of living psychologists, C. J. Jung, has meditated on *psi* for twenty years in the light of previous thought from the Tao to Schopenhauer, and has based the whole argument of his latest book upon its existence.[2] The question he asks is: How is it that *psi* phenomena *can* occur, even though they do not fall within the framework of causality? And his answer is that there is nothing for it but to postulate a new category, which he calls Synchronicity as a Principle of A-Causal Relationships, or *meaningful* coincidence in time. He himself calls such an idea, *undenkbar*, unthinkable, and the arguments by which he supports it are too revolutionary and

---

[1] A number of psychoanalysts have recorded cases in which telepathy seems to have occurred in a psychoanalytic situation, in a book edited by George Devereux and entitled *Psychoanalysis and the Occult* (International Universities Press, New York, 1953).

[2] *Naturerklärung und Psyche*, by C. J. Jung (Rascher Verlag, Zurich, 1952).

intricate to be discussed except by experts for other experts. Even they seem to be finding them somewhat indigestible, and it will take time before the influence of Jung's new concept can be assessed.

(ii) Professor Gardner Murphy

An American psychologist, Professor Gardner Murphy, has tried to explain ESP in terms of what is known as field theory.[1]

The idea of field theory in physics began to take shape near the end of the nineteenth century, when pioneer work by Clerk-Maxwell made it possible to envisage electromagnetic activity as a distribution of energy in time and space. An area of such energy became known as a field. Until then classical physics had concentrated on the study of basic particles— Kelvin's billiard ball atoms—and had not considered big events as 'wholes', but solely as the sum of little events, in other words as the sum of the activities of these particles.

Einstein pointed out that the analytical method of working from parts to wholes often broke down. The remarkable fact came to be realised that to know what particles A., B., and C. were each doing individually did not make it possible to predict the results of their interaction. A structural whole is not the sum of its parts, and cannot be understood if considered only in terms of those parts. It was field theory which enabled physicists to approach structural wholes directly, as forms of organisation of energy distribution.

It came to be realised that this manner of thinking might bear fruits beyond the study of physics. Its laws appeared to have much in common with the laws of biology. When Hardy suggested that organisms as a whole seem to be provided with a blueprint of their future forms, he cited in support the fact that the embryo of some species of frog can grow an eye even

[1] *Field Theory and Survival*, by Gardner Murphy, *Journal* A.S.P.R., XXXIX, 1945, p. 181.

when the optic cup has been removed. Murphy approached the same situation in terms of field theory. He quoted Paul Weiss as showing by experiment that the same kind of cell, grafted at the same time from one part of one embryo to a different part of another, can become, as required by its new environment, a skin cell, a muscle cell, or a nerve cell. This suggests that growth is the expression of a field. Moreover, the action of living matter on living matter is never a case of single cell acting only on single cell. The structural whole or field is always involved. He gave as an example the biologist Spemann's demonstration that a mother's body and an embryo are physiologically a single unit. A prenatal environment—an egg or a uterus—is not separate from the embryo whose environment it is. They form a single energy field.

The field manner of thinking then spread to psychology and it was accepted that individual human beings formed highly complex organised units which also defied the method of description from parts to wholes.

Murphy argues that anthropologists and sociologists must go further than this. They must learn to consider relationships *between* persons in the light of field theory. He also thinks that the study of such relationships is of vital importance. An individual he said, probably responds automatically to buffets from his outer physical environment 99·99 per cent of the time, but just occasionally there is what might be called a leak in this close system of time-space-energy contact between the two. Suddenly, in, say, a card-guessing experiment, a percipient casually makes an astonishing series of correct calls. (We remember Lillian Levine.) Then, equally suddenly, "having proved itself, having had its fling, the odd capacity departs, and scoring goes back to its former humdrum level ..." In Murphy's view there is good reason to believe that these flashes of ESP indicate an enduring capacity at some deeper level to make contact with all of space and all of time. But what causes those flashes from that deep level to break through to our surface consciousness? The greatest factor, he suggests, is relationships between persons. And the reason such flashes break through so seldom—in the modern Western world particularly—is our psychological insulation from each other. We have become what he calls encapsulated entities. It has often been noted that an individual seems to get flashes of ESP more easily and more often the less he feels himself to be sharply separate from his fellows. And these are liable to come through when he is in a state of profound relaxation, when awareness of self has faded away to the fringe of consciousness. It is, moreover, a widespread and ancient belief that loss of self-awareness tends to bring a man into paranormal contact with his fellows.

This idea of subconscious merging between human beings at some deep level, towards which Murphy and other psychical researchers seem to be driven, is not one likely to be popular in our highly individualistic Western world. We do not apparently wish to be members one of another. But Murphy's reasoning seems to fit in with the techniques of the Eastern Yogis, of the seers of antiquity, of the crystal gazers and sensitives of today. And total absorption in a task or problem is well known to release subconscious knowledge as such. It is in a brown study that the fountain of song will flow for musician or poet or isolated facts unite in new relationships for the mathematician or man of science.

Murphy points out that on his hypothesis there is nothing to prevent the switching of consciousness backwards or forwards in time, provided that individuality is not completely absorbed in the physical or biological present. What may be a case of such switching backward in time, or retrocognition, has recently been investigated in detail by the S.P.R. Two ladies, both young and one of them trained in the W.R.N.S. to observe and time events accurately, were sharing a room at a seaside hotel near Dieppe, which during the war had been occupied by German troops. They were both awakened in the early hours of the morning by the sound of bombing and got up and stood at the window together. They heard the bombing change to gunfire, the firing come from different locations, the sound of shouts and cries and they timed these changes as they occurred. To their surprise, they found on enquiry next day that no one else had been similarly disturbed, and so they reported the incident to the S.P.R. Reference to unpublished War Office records, to which they could not have had access, disclosed that the timing of their impressions of bombing, gunfire and shouting tallied with the bombardment, landings, etc., of the Dieppe raid, as these had occurred on the beach below their hotel.[1]

Retrocognition, according to Murphy, may also explain collective visions of dead animals, of which he quoted an example reported to the S.P.R. in 1923. A blue Persian cat, Smoky, was much loved by its owners. After its death it was seen by four persons, sometimes by two of them at once, at intervals of about half an hour on a July day. It appeared in the garden and the kitchen passage, so clearly and so close to them that they finally had the body dug up to convince themselves that Smoky had not really been there.

Murphy, then, put forward three basic suggestions. One, that it may be a principle running right through nature that a complex organised whole cannot be fully understood in terms of its ingredient parts. Two, that the field principle may hold in psychics as well as in physics and a psychic field may extend backwards and forwards in time as well as outward in space. Three, that we may be hampered in the study of ESP by our acceptance of an absolute cleavage between individuals, for it is probable that this cleavage is no more than a matter of biological organisation.

In Murphy's view the model of field theory, as applied to psychical research, neither demands nor disproves survival, but it does suggest that any possible continuing psychical activity which might survive the death of the body would tend to merge more closely into the complex structural whole (field) of which it is an aspect. This does not mean that it would cease to exist. But it might mean that it was less easy to separate as an individual out of its context. It is hard, he said, "to know what a living poet, or an Eastern mystic, or a communicator through a sensitive, really means when he uses phrases about the gradual merging of the individual into some sort of cosmic whole. Indeed they may all mean different things and they may all be wrong. What they say does, nevertheless, seem to have much in common with the implications of field theory."

[1] *Journal* S.P.R., May-June 1952, Vol. XXXVI, p. 607 et seq.

He points out, too, that we can hardly conceive of a rigidly fixed entity continuing unchanged in a totally other environment. Such lack of change is against the dynamic principle of interaction as understood by science and, in the light of relativity, impossible to define. A field is not just an environment; it is the pattern of individual-in-environment, each acting on the other. And the pattern changes even throughout this life, as contacts change.

The traditional question is: Does personality survive death? In Murphy's view that is not a reasonable one to ask. If any psychical activity survives, he says, it will become an aspect of different fields and will thus take on new qualities and new structural relationships. Looking back at the cross correspondences, for example, we should have to ask, not only: How much is the purported Myers being modified by having to use the personality of Mrs. Willett or Mrs. Holland as a channel of communication? but also: If there is a communicator at all, how like or unlike is he to the Myers we used to know? What points of continuity can we find? And do individual memories and purposes continue active after death?

He thinks that the discoveries of psychical research make it clear that an answer to these questions can hardly be attempted until we know more about the paranormal powers and interrelationships of the living. Can we, for instance, find out if it would be within the subconscious powers of a living person to have worked out the cross correspondence patterns and caused the scattered automatists to produce their own fragments at the right time? We must set out to discover whether the field conception of interpersonal powers is true or not. One first step would be to study the effect of investigators and sitters on the statements of mediums. Another, since we already believe the subconscious influence of the living upon each other to be enormous, would be to search for collective veridical visions of persons long dead, as these would be less likely to originate in the minds of the living and would therefore suggest continuing psychic activity after death.

But the best evidence for survival, according to Murphy, is of the type supplied by Mrs. Willett in the *Ear of Dionysius* case, for this seems to indicate a surviving interpersonal relationship between Dr. Verrall and Henry Butcher. Furthermore, could subconscious activity on the part of a living person explain the rôle of Henry Butcher? Or could telepathy from the living account for a purpose apparently formed by the mind of Dr. Verrall after his death? Murphy thinks it would be very difficult, for the communications seem to be a joint expression of the two friends and they make sense in terms of a plan worked out by them *post mortem*.

It is evident that all personal activities are constantly changing context and interacting with those of others, and in Murphy's view it may be that each one becomes part of the cosmic process. If that is so, the simple question: Do we survive? cannot reasonably be asked or answered. But he thinks it possible that after death personality continues to be, as it is now, an aspect of an interpersonal reality, even though it is unlikely to survive as an encapsulated entity.

(iii) Dr. R. H. Thouless

In 1947 an original idea about the *psi* process was put forward by the psychologist Dr. R. H. Thouless and the bio-chemist Dr. B. P. Wiesner.[1] It seemed not only to fit together certain facts unearthed by psychical research which had hitherto been scattered about like an unmade jigsaw puzzle, but also to fit these facts into a pattern not very different from the one accepted by the more orthodox sciences of psychology and physiology.

They began by comparing normal sensory perception with ESP. What does an outsider, A., know about B.'s sensory perception, whether B. is an Einstein or a newt? No more than this: that B.'s behaviour changes in response to an impact

[1] R. H. Thouless and B. P. Wiesner, *The Psi Process in Normal and 'Paranormal' Psychology*, Proceedings S.P.R., Vol. XLVIII, pp. 177–96.
  Also *Journal of Parapsychology*, Vol. XII, pp. 192–212.

from the environment conveyed to him through his senses. And that is exactly what A. knows about B.'s ESP: that his behaviour changes in response to an outside impact. The only difference is that this time the impact does not seem to have reached B. via his senses. Now in both cases B. behaves as if he were aware of the impact. But is he? In the case of a human being, we can say that the answer is, usually yes, occasionally no. It is no, for instance, when a card-guesser has made a significantly high number of correct guesses but has himself no idea whether they have been right or wrong.

Now turn to PK. Thouless and Wiesner accepted the evidence for this, indeed Thouless was one of the two people in this country to obtain positive experimental results in 'willed' dice-throwing. They therefore divided *psi* into two types, which they called incoming or cognitive = ESP and motor or outgoing = PK. Both, they said, were generally considered unusual, perhaps abnormal. But was this true? Or were they merely unusual examples of processes which in other situations are so usual as to be universal, being part of both normal perception and normal out-going or motor activity? In normal perception a chain of material causation can be followed from an object to the sense organ of a living creature. Sound, for example, travels through the air and impinges upon an ear. This stimulates the electrical activity of the physical brain. And now comes the question of all questions: What happens then? How does a material process in a cerebral cortex produce something different in kind, a conscious mental event? Again, on the out-going or motor side, how does a conscious act of will start off the material changes in the motor area of the brain which are the material cause of a willed action?

The two authors did not try to answer these tremendous questions directly, but they deliberately advanced a stimulating notion to be tilted at. As regards the incoming side, they suggested that in normal thinking and perceiving I am in the same sort of relation to what is going on in the sensory part of my brain and nervous system as the successful clairvoyant is to some external event, and both are established by ESP. Similarly, on the outgoing side, I control the activities of my nervous system, and thereby my movements and thoughts, by the same means that some people are able to use to control the fall of dice or other objects, and that is by PK.

Thouless and Wiesner pointed out that PK has so far only been studied experimentally in objects which are mountainous in relation to the size of a body cell. But the ideal mechanism to study would be one in which minute systems were very delicately balanced. If these systems, while still protected from accidental disturbance from outside, could have their balance changed by tiny forces, and if this change could be magnified automatically to a larger energy charge in a larger system, then we might have the ideal mechansim to demonstrate ESP. Man has never managed to make such a mechanism, but evolution has created one for him in the human brain. That is an ideal instrument for distributing impacts received from outside via the senses, and for translating will and intention into action.

But now comes the eternal snag. What is receiving the impacts from outside? Who decides what to do about them? What name can we give the I? The word mind will not do, for it is now generally used, not for that which thinks and decides, but rather for the whole system of thoughts and decisions. Also we commonly talk of my mind, your mind. This also applies to the word self. At this point Thouless and Wiesner grasped the nettle. The word, they said, which best expresses their meaning is. undoubtedly soul. Their basic hypothesis is that the soul learns about impacts on the senses by ESP and controls the body's motor activity by PK.

It must have needed courage to revive the word soul in the world of orthodox psychology, where consciousness is normally described as "how the organism experiences its own brain happenings", and the two authors hastened to rename it by a harmless Hebrew letter, Shin. This avoided any appearance of prejudging such tricky questions as: Do souls survive? Do animals other than human beings possess them? Are they entirely separate entities?

There is one resemblance between ESP and normal perception which cannot show in the direct hit or miss of card-guessing tests. They are both symbolic. To common sense, of course, this is not true of sensory perception, which appears to give an immediate reproduction of an exterior object. But it is now well known that here common sense is suffering from an illusion, for the immediate material ancestor of a sense perception is not the exterior object itself, but a process in the physical brain. And what we perceive is not the actual brain undergoing that process, but the symbols by which it interprets the exterior object which has set the process going. So, too, ESP will interpret an outside event symbolically, rather than try to represent it.

Thouless quoted a typical case of symbolic ESP which was recorded by a talented sensitive, Miss Phoebe Payne. When talking to a friend she 'saw' a beam of golden light shoot from him in an arch over her head and fall beyond. Its colour and composition conveyed to her that it was of an intellectual order, its direction conveyed that it concerned her, its fall beyond her that it was concerned with the future. Her friend admitted when asked, that he had been thinking about her future intellectual work. But ESP is hard to understand for those who have never experienced it. I was present when a group of investigators asked Miss Payne to try and describe her own ESP. She quoted this incident, and I commented, "Of course you do not really mean you saw a beam of light." "Of course not", replied Miss Payne. This was very naturally received with bewilderment by the logically minded investigators. Similar difficulties face the mescalin guinea-pig who tries to communicate some of the unusual forms of awareness induced by the drug. He too, like the sensitive, has to use the imagery of sensory perception to describe experiences for which it is not designed. They are both driven to paradox.

Thouless and Wiesner believe that an extra-sensory perception by-passes the sense organs altogether. Obviously, then, the actual mode of awareness will be different and thus hard to express, and the perception itself will not be limited, as those which come via the eyes or ears are limited, by the position of those eyes and ears in relation to the exterior object that has made an impact on them. If B. hears A. call, the sound will reach him when waves in air have had time to travel from one to the other and will be more or less audible according to whether or not an aeroplane is drumming overhead. But what are the limits or the channels in the case of *psi*? How have the percipient's guesses been determined by one particular pack of cards, rather than by any other pack that ever has been or ever will be dealt out? What enables a mother to 'see' her own distant child at a moment of crisis?

The answer suggested by Thouless and Wiesner is that in the case of experiments *psi* appears to be focussed by the intention of the experimenter and this idea is in harmony with other hints and clues. In what is known as psychometry, A. appears to get on to the track of a stranger, B., by touching an object with which B. has been in contact. In spontaneous cases of *psi*, emotion, such as mutual love between agent and percipient or frustrated love of percipient for agent, seems to be a factor. And sometimes persons who habitually work together have apparent telepathic experiences. Carington suggested that mutual conscious thought of the same 'K.' object might help. There may be many focussing factors, but so far we can only guess at what they are.

Thouless and Wiesner considered various possible patterns of telepathy in the light of their hypothesis. Telepathy could be one 'mind' acting directly on another 'mind', or, as they put it, one Shin acting on another. In that case we are not yet in a position to know anything about it. It is extremely unlikely to be one physical brain acting on another by some form of material radiation. But there is a third possibility. This is that Shin A. can interact directly with B.'s brain and nervous system in the same manner as it interacts with its own. If this is so there can be two kinds of telepathy. Shin A. could set going a motor activity in B.'s nervous system by PK. This process fits both experimental card-guessing and experiments where the percipient draws the right object, as if impelled to do so by the agent's Shin, but interprets it wrongly and gives it the wrong name. Conversely, Shin B. could perceive something via A.'s nervous system. This fits the many occasions when mediums seem to contact latent memories in sitters or other people.

A further hypothesis by the two authors was that what is known as psychic healing need not, as is usually supposed, be merely a matter of suggestion, but may sometimes be achieved by the healer's Shin directly affecting the patient's nervous system in the same fashion that it affects his own. And it may be possible, they said, to relate normal growth and healing with the curious apparent *psi* phenomenon of materialisation in physical mediumship, for which they think there is some quite strong testimony. It may be that growth and regeneration are not entirely determined in a material manner by physico-chemical forces within an organism. They may be initiated by Shin acting upon the organism, and materialisation may be another case of the same thing.

The theory thus relates three pairs of phenomena: ESP with normal perception; PK with normal will; and materialisation and psychic healing with normal growth and regeneration. ESP and PK, the two functions of Shin involved in these processes, normally relate a Shin to its own body, but the same two functions can occasionally relate it to other bodies or to physical objects. The truth of one of these hypotheses does not entail the truth of the others, but they all grow out of the plausible idea that so-called paranormal processes are not as odd as they appear, but are, on the contrary, familiar processes occurring in unusual circumstances.

It is interesting that Myers, with his astonishing insight, began feeling his way towards such an hypothesis as far back as 1886. "Perhaps when I *attend* to a thing, or *will* a thing", he wrote, "I am directing upon my own nervous system actually that same force which, when I direct it on another man's nervous system, is the 'vital influence' of mesmerists (hypnotists) or the 'telepathic impact' of which Mr. Gurney and I have said so much." [1]

[1] F. W. H. Myers, *On Telepathic Hypnotism. Proceedings* S.P.R., Vol. IV, p. 172.

Professor C. D. Broad and
Professor H. H. Price

A FEW contemporary philosophers have been prepared to incorporate the fact of *psi* in the material from which they draw their conclusions. Among them are Professor Ducasse in America and Henri Bergson and Gabriel Marcel in France. In this country the two most distinguished figures are Professor C. D. Broad and Professor H. H. Price, and in the younger group are Professor C. W. K. Mundle and Professor Anthony Flew.

The work of Broad and Price is the most serious attempt yet made to devise a metaphysic which is partly based on, or finds a place for, *psi*.

Professor Broad's original training was in physics. Then he turned to philosophy and eventually became Sidgwick's successor at several removes in the Knightbridge Chair of Moral Philosophy at Cambridge. He retired in 1955. (His rooms in Trinity were once occupied by Isaac Newton, who used to descend from them by a little private staircase to the green below to supervise the progress of his alchemical experiments.) Price is Wykeham Professor of Logic at Oxford. It is an ironical trick of Fate that so fine a thinker and so retiring a man should often be confused with the late Harry Price, who pursued *psi* in a somewhat unreliable fashion with trumpets blowing and journalists in attendance.

Both Broad and Price have made a general study of the relation of man to his environment and they have both rendered great service to psychical research in particular. Broad's contribution has in the main taken the form of a minute and lucid analysis of *psi* phenomena and a clarification of the problems they present in relation to orthodox knowledge. In

206

his latest book, *Religion, Philosophy and Psychical Research*,[1] he starts from the fact that, as the framework within which all our practical activities and scientific theories are confined, we unhesitatingly take for granted a number of basic limiting principles. He defines these as the general principles of causation, the limitation of the action of mind on matter, the dependence of mind on brains, and the limitations of ways of acquiring knowledge. Of all the phenomena of nature, only the various forms of *psi* will not fit into that framework. In consequence, he says, *psi* is of extreme interest to philosophers, for its implications call for very radical changes in a number of those principles.

In the same book he makes a stimulating comparison of normal sense perception with what has so far been observed of telepathy and clairvoyance. He argues that telepathy between two persons need not imply that they are both receiving the same sensory impact from the outer world, or that they are both visualising the same image. For this reason he prefers the term telepathic interaction to telepathy, as it conveys better the fact that although A.'s thought or experience may be a cause of B.'s they are not sharing the same experience and their experiences need not resemble each other at all closely.

If that is so, telepathic interaction may be as common as daisies on a lawn, or even continuous. But this fact, says Broad, may escape notice, for B. does not necessarily realise that an event in his mind has been telepathically induced by A. He may only feel a change of mood. To be noticed by B., the impact from A. must be discontinuous with the immediate past and so surprise him. And this seldom happens. Broad says that he often finds himself aware of an image which has no apparent connection with his own experiences or usual trains of association. Yet he tends to dismiss it without surprise although he is professionally interested in such things. And for people usually concerned with practical things an experience would have to be very odd before they would seriously question its normality. Moreover, B.'s experience would never be caused solely by

[1] C. D. Broad, *Religion, Philosophy and Psychical Research* (Routledge and Kegan Paul, 1953).

A.'s but in part by his own past and present, and this too would tend to make it less surprising and discontinuous. And, to observe the telepathy, the two would have to be acquainted and one of them would have to feel enough interest in his own experience to describe it to the other.

The important point thus emerges that although telepathic interaction may be constant, it will be noticed only in special conditions. Broad finds analogies for this in the physical sciences. Magnetic forces, for instance, are all-pervasive and important factors in the physical world. Yet, although they are operating everywhere all the time, they might never have been discovered if the earth had not been a natural magnet and had not contained both iron and lesser magnets or lodestones. As it was, for centuries magnetism was only observed as freak behaviour on nature's part in connection with iron and lodestones, and that freak behaviour masked its real nature almost as much as it revealed it.

At the end of his comparison of ESP with sensory perception, Broad tentatively allows himself to envisage the possibility that a person's experiences can modify something which is neither his mind nor his brain. He calls this something a substratum—perhaps some kind of extended pervasive medium—and he finds no reason to suppose that words such as mine or yours can be applied to it as they can be to minds or bodies. All we can say is that the modifications in the common substratum made by A.'s experience afterwards normally affect A. alone. But it can happen that an experience or interest of B.'s will activate a modification in the substratum made by A., and in that case B. too will be affected by it.

Professor Broad has also discussed the questions of the separability of mind from body and of human survival of death —a possibility that he clearly envisages with distaste. When he first considered these matters his view was that some *psi* phenomena did suggest that something which carried memory traces and personal traits might persist at least for a while after bodily death. But he did not think there was any conclusive evidence for genuine survival in the sense of a life of active thought and of intentions fulfilled. He suggested that what we know as a mind—or one might say a person—might be a compound of two factors, neither of which separately had the characteristic properties of a mind. These two he called the psychic factor (after the word *psi* came into use he changed this to *psi* component) and the bodily factor, and it was the *psi* component which he thought might persist, anyway for a time, after death.[1]

He developed this line of thought many years later in a lecture on *Human Personality and the Possibility of its Survival* which he gave at the University of California in 1954. A human person, he said, differs from an animal in being aware of himself as a person and in having behind him a great number of memories. Most, though not all, of these are memories of events that actually took place. He also possesses an elaborately organised system of mental and emotional dispositions and, like other living creatures, he has a body. The minimal condition for anything like survival to be possible is that something carrying at least a part of this system of organised dispositions shall persist after the death of the body. Broad postulates the *psi* component as something answering to this minimal condition. Nowadays we find it very hard even to conceive of such persistence, since it is through the body alone that the *psi* component normally appears to interact with its environment. Dualism is thoroughly out of fashion. This, said Broad, is a mistake. Such a disembodied existence is not only conceivable but need not be inconsistent with what we know of physics, physiology and psychology. It is both theoretically and factually possible.

To record Professor Broad's philosophical arguments is beyond the scope of this book, but he used some illuminating analogies which help to provide an escape from the habit of conceiving any survival of a *psi* component to be hopelessly at variance with information acquired through the physical sciences. We need no longer suppose, he said, that although a surviving *psi* component may be bodiless, it is necessarily unextended and unlocalised, for we are nowadays well accustomed to such phenomena as electro-magnetic fields

[1] C. D. Broad, *The Mind and its Place in Nature* (Routledge and Kegan Paul, 1925).

which cannot be called bodies in the ordinary sense but which still have structure and definite properties and dispositions. Again, a piece of broadcast music may be said to exist in the form of modulations on the waves of a transmitting beam, whether or not there is a receiver to transform it into a pattern of sounds. It may be that the *psi* component of a deceased human being exists in some equivalent manner. Perhaps the notion that no part of a *psi* component can persist after the destruction of its associated body is equivalent to imagining that nothing corresponding to the performance of an orchestral piece could exist anywhere in space after the station that broadcast it had been destroyed.

Professor Broad warns us of the danger of old-fashioned analogies when considering the *psi* component of a personality. We must not think of it as something on which an experience makes an impression as a seal does on a ball of wax. That is cramping. We must rather consider analogies with vortices, stationary waves and so forth. Then we can envisage a number of interesting possibilities of partial coalescence, partial annulment, interference and so forth between the *psi* components of several deceased individuals. There are mediumistic phenomena and pathological mental cases, not ostensibly involving mediumship, which seem to fit this. (It is interesting to consider the cross correspondences, the Willett scripts and the Piper and Leonard phenomena in the light of this speculation.)

Professor Broad also discussed how much of a personality as we know it might be expected to survive, and in what condition. Would it remain in a state of dreamless sleep or would it have experiences and memories? If it had memories, would they include those of life in a body? And so on. In 1954 Professor Broad was inclined to think it unlikely that a *psi* component persisting after death would have experiences of any kind, and most unlikely that it would have any stream of experience at all continuous with life in a body. But in a broadcast given in 1957 he said that he has come to think that a very small number of *psi* phenomena—some of Mrs. Willett's scripts for example—do suggest a greater degree of survival than the mere persistence of an inactive *psi* component. They make it very hard, he said, to resist the conviction that the mind of a certain person has survived the death of his body and is continuing to think and plan.[1]

Professor Broad's views about the physical brain tally with those of Bergson and H. H. Price. "I have an impression", he says, "that we should do well to consider much more seriously than we have hitherto been inclined to do the type of theory which Bergson put forward in connection with normal memory and sense perception."

Bergson's theory was that the brain is an organ of limitation. He developed this idea in relation to psychical research in a Presidential Address to the S.P.R. in 1913, as well as in his book *Matière et Mémoire*.[2] The brain, he said, limits man's conscious awareness of the exterior world to what is practically useful to him, to what he can act upon to his own advantage. It keeps his attention fixed on those limited aspects of the world. It is the organ of *attention à la vie* and of action. It also causes man to perceive all things as divisible objects which he can take to pieces and remake to suit himself. Hence it is from the nature of the physical brain that the mechanistic interpretation of Nature arises. But in fact man unconsciously perceives far more than he realises. He may be potentially capable of remembering all that has ever happened to him and of perceiving everything that is happening anywhere in the universe. It is when his brain barrier is working inefficiently and his *attention à la vie* wavers that some of those other perceptions slip through, to be labelled, perhaps, telepathy, clairvoyance of mundane events, or subjective hallucination.

Bergson, then, did not agree with the current view that every mental state has its corresponding brain state, or that memories are stored in the physical brain. The brain's job, he said, is to keep out useless memories, and at times it does this less efficiently, when over-taxed, for instance, or in illness. He believed that when loss of memory occurs through damage to the physical brain, the memories still exist. It is the brain channel

[1] Since this book was written Professor Broad has developed these ideas in the thirteenth Myers Memorial Lecture. This is entitled *Personal Identity and Survival* and is published by the S.P.R.

[2] Henri Bergson, *Matière et Mémoire* (Félix Alcan, 1908).

between them and the level of conscious action which no longer works.

Both Broad and Price consider that the facts of psychical research are of great importance to Bergson's theory. Moreover, in Price's view, Bergson's is so far the only type of theory which can include the astonishing fact of clairvoyance of physical objects, as opposed to telepathic awareness of mental states.

To Professor Price the whole problem of *psi* is of vital interest and he does not hesitate to express himself strongly about it.[1] It seems likely, he says, to throw entirely new light upon the nature of human personality and its position in the universe. He believes that in time it may transform the whole intellectual outlook upon which our present civilisation is based, but he does not believe that psychical researchers will get much further towards this transformation unless they make vigorous attempts to include *psi* within the orbit of scientific thought. They must venture on hypotheses, however mistaken these may turn out to be. In his view it will be the timidity of our hypotheses and not their extravagance which will provoke the derision of posterity, and he is even prepared to postulate unverifiable entities and processes if we cannot get on without them. "The task of philosophical deflation, or removing unnecessary metaphysical entities," he says, "comes at the end of a science's progress, not at the beginning; if such writers as Hume and Mach and the modern Logical Positivists had lived in the early seventeenth century, physics would never have got itself started. In short, we must not be deterred by the thought of talking nonsense ... Moreover, in our search for a comprehensible hypothesis, we must not mind taking hints from quarters which are accounted scientifically disreputable ... It is well to remember that in India and the Buddhist countries men not necessarily inferior to Europeans in intelligence have been devoting themselves for very many centuries to the deepening and extension of human consciousness. The theories

[1] The following summary of Professor Price's views is taken from: *Presidential Address* to the S.P.R. (*Proceedings* S.P.R., Vol XLV, pp. 307–43). *Psychical Research and Human Personality* (*Hibbert Journal* for January, 1949). Two articles in *Enquiry* for July and September, 1949.

which they have been led to frame may have got mixed up with all sorts of dubious theological and cosmological dogmas. Nevertheless they may give us some help in framing a more adequate and genuinely scientific theory for ourselves. I even think that the humble savage may have something to teach us . . . Anthropologists have collected a whole mass of material which falls within our province, though their scientific orthodoxy has usually led them to assume that it *must* somehow be explained away as fraud and delusion." [1]

Professor Price himself has not failed to practise what he preaches in the way of setting up adventurous theories. One of these is about the nature of mind itself. He looks on the dualism we have inherited from Descartes as a grave obstacle to progress in psychical research. Descartes divided the universe into two, a material half composed of one ubiquitous substance, matter, and a mental half composed of many separate substances, individual minds. We believe this to be common sense. But it is not, says Price. It is a very brilliant theory which has been most useful in the past but is now a nuisance. A more adequate theory is to divide human nature into three parts—body, mind and the fundamental 'I', the pure ego, the Atman of the Hindu philosophers. This 'I' is not the concern of psychical research but of the philosophy of mystical experience or metaphysics. Our business is with mind, or what the Neoplatonists called the soul or *psyche*. (Price is not happy with these terms. But unfortunately for the philosophy of psychical research there are as yet no better ones.)

What then is a mind? Price thinks that we make a basic mistake in supposing it to be an indivisible entity or separate from other minds. He does not think that its essence is consciousness or that Descartes was necessarily right in saying that the only piece of matter which a mind directly acts upon is its own brain. This is a question of empirical fact. In his view such unity as a mind does have is precarious, unstable and a matter of degree, tighter at some times and looser at others. It has two aspects, internal and external. Internally, as facts of abnormal psychology show, it can at times split into two or

[1] Presidential Address, *Proceedings* S.P.R., Vol. XLV.

more parts, as in cases of multiple personality. And the facts of psychical research show that, externally as well, its unity is a matter of degree. One mind is not separated from another by any hard and fast line; two minds may overlap.

In short, Professor Price does not think that the concept of individual minds as basic units is the right one to work with. The unit he suggests is what, lacking a better word, he provisionally calls an idea. Ideas may be the ultimate elements of the mental world. Out of them various grades of psychical entity can be built. They can be the components of not very purposive ghosts and complexes at one end of the scale to a healthily integrated human mind at the other. Yet not even the waking healthy mind is completely autonomous or coherent; it too has ragged edges and its internal unity is unstable. Price does not, however, disintegrate human personality as Whately Carington does. He still distinguishes the mind from the spirit or 'I'. For Carington there was no 'I'.

Price points out that one way in which an idea can manifest is in the form of a mental image. Many people, especially the young, the uneducated and the primitive, think mainly in images rather than words. Images tend to emerge more easily in sleep and in states of relaxed attention and mild dissociation. It may well be, he says, that image thinking is going on in all of us all the time, but that in the highly educated it has got dissociated from the main stream of waking consciousness. And there is some evidence that to concentrate on verbal thinking reduces the power to make use of *psi*, though there are a few striking exceptions—Socrates, perhaps, and Swedenborg (and he might have added Gilbert Murray.)

"The intellectual and abstract thinking man", says Price, "is something of a split personality, a little mad, if you like; a conclusion which need not surprise us. As some philosopher has said, 'We live on the surface of our being.' The thing for us to do, then, is to reassociate our image thinking with the main stream of our waking consciousness: to break down a barrier which cuts off a fully active faculty from our view, rather than to revive by toilsome exercise one which has become atrophied through long disuse. Not that even this removal of barriers is an easy task; but experience shows, I think, that it is a practicable one."

There are certain physiological states—fatigue is one—in which images emerge more easily into consciousness. Fasting can temporarily induce such states. So can the special breathing and postures of Yoga or the auto-hypnosis of crystal gazing and other similar practices. And to release images, Price suggests, may be indirectly to release *psi*. If the highly educated could in some reasonable way learn to reassociate their image thinking with the main stream of waking consciousness, we should be in a position to learn a great deal more about *psi*.

Another of Price's contributions has been to suggest a possible habitat for minds. He argues that there may be something intermediate between mind and matter as we ordinarily understand them. That something would be material in the sense that it was extended in space (though not necessarily in physical space) and yet it would have some of the properties commonly attributed to minds. *Psi* phenomena had already driven Myers and a past president of the S.P.R., Professor C. A. Mace, to envisage a 'something' upon which could be recorded the pattern of events. Mace labelled it the psychic ether. And the idea, of course, is widespread in the mystical philosophies of the East.

To try and form a conception of this psychic ether Price first considers the nature of a mental image. Philosophers and psychologists have always supposed it to depend for its existence on the mind and perhaps also on the brain of the person aware of it. They have also assumed that it is private to that person and only exists during the time that he is aware of it. But suppose these assumptions are untrue. Suppose that an image, once originated, has a tendency to persist in being independently of the mind that created it. That mind might summon it up into consciousness from time to time or it might surface of its own accord. Or conceivably its whole career might be passed in the unconscious. Suppose again that it need not be private to the mind of its author and can even operate independently of him. A mental image may be dynamic. It may cause things to happen.

Here Price is thinking more of telepathy than of what

psychologists call ideo-motor action or the association of ideas, although, he says, this sounds absurd, since telepathy is commonly regarded as a relation between two minds or personalities. But that relation may be secondary. It may be that the basic relation is between two mental contents. Take images, which are an important kind of mental content. Perhaps one image can modify or even generate another. Perhaps it can do so from one mind to another, which would be what we call telepathy. Perhaps all images are endowed with a kind of telepathic charge. Such a charged image might vary in all sorts of ways. It could be weak or strong, it might endure but for a moment or even outlive its author.

To think of images in this way, as persistent dynamic independent entities, helps us to form some notion of a psychic ether. For this might be an ether of images. If it were, it would have the kind of properties which we require it to have. "It would be something intermediate between mind and matter as we ordinarily conceive them; while, if we were prepared to stretch these conceptions a good deal, then we could either call it mental or material as we liked."

As regards its mental properties, such an ether of images could be looked on as a range within the common unconscious, a range wherein the distinction between 'You' and 'I' no longer exists. In this range images could persist and interact more or less freely, no matter in whose mind they began their career. But this interaction would take place according to psychological, not spatial, laws, for the unity of the common unconscious is not spatial but causal. It is a unity of law, of interaction.

Price points out that the hypothesis of a common unconscious is only another way of saying that at their deeper levels all personalities are in complete and continuous telepathic rapport. But the idea of such rapport raises many questions. How extended is it? Does each person's subconscious interact with everyone else's or only with some? Can interaction be more or less intense as well as more or less extended, complete perhaps between Mr. and Mrs. Smith, slight and intermittent between Smith and Jones? Could Smith's unconscious affect

Jones's, but remain unaffected itself? Perhaps we should not ask: Are personality A. and personality B. altogether united or quite separate? but: How much of a unity is there between them?

So much for the mental properties of such an ether of images. Price then asks in what respect it could be said to have material properties as well. Naturally, he says, they are not the same as the properties we ascribe to ordinary matter, but they may be somewhat like them. The fundamental point is that images are, in a curious halfway-house manner, extended in space. This is at first disconcerting because we so seldom reflect on them. We think by means of them rather than about them. Take the visual image as an example. It has extension, a shape, sometimes even a stereoscopic one, and one item in it is located in relation to another. In an image of a room a cat can be located on the hearth rug. But the whole image is not located anywhere in physical space. Nor is it of any particular size. The cat in the image can be smaller than the arm chair, but we cannot say it is larger or smaller than someone else's image of Mont Blanc.

Different image fields, then, are not inter-related in one common space, though each possesses a space of its own. What unites them in one single ether of images are causal, not spatial, factors. Yet there may be some relation between separate image fields, consisting of greater or lesser degrees of telepathic affinity, which is a faint analogy to nearness or farness in physical space. A.'s body might be pressing against B.'s body, but if there were little or no telepathic affinity between them their respective images could be very distant from one another. Conversely, there might be most intimate telepathic rapport between A. and B., with the body of one in Hong Kong and that of the other in New York.

An ether of images, then, says Price, can have both material and mental properties. It is "either a queer sort of mental world or a queer sort of material world, as we like, though neither the word 'mental' nor the word 'material' can be applied to it without a certain misfit or discomfort. Indeed, all this talk of an ether of images or of a psychic ether may well seem like sheer nonsense when considered in cold blood. But this is only to be expected. Any theory of this difficult matter is bound to give our ordinary language habits a pretty violent tweak. If it does not, we can be sure there is something wrong with it."

Professor Price has propounded further hypotheses which all stem from the basic conception that ideas and images may persist in something intermediate between mind and matter as we understand them. Out of it, for instance, he builds an intelligible theory of hauntings. He also uses it, in an interesting lecture, *Survival and the Idea of Another World* to give a meaning to the survival hypothesis, quite apart from its truth or falsehood.[1] Nowadays, he says, many intelligent and reasonable people find the very conception of survival unintelligible and a discarnate human personality a meaningless phrase. In a long and intricate argument he shows that the hypothesis of an ether of images helps to solve this dilemma, and that in its light a physically disembodied existence, whether or not it is a fact, is an intelligible conception. He further suggests that ideas (including mental images) may not only persist independently of their author, but may have an inherent tendency to express themselves to some consciousness. They may achieve this by embodying themselves in matter, usually through the nervous systems of man and other animals, but occasionally, perhaps, by PK. Or they may do so by emerging directly into the consciousness of any person whose threshold they can cross, in other words, by telepathy. The collective unconscious is like a vessel with numberless lids against which its contents are perpetually pressing.

To Price, as to Bergson, the function of the lid or threshold of consciousness is to exclude all mental images, beyond those which serve a man's immediate interests at any particular time. That is one reason why telepathy is comparatively rare, because ideas which have not originated in a person's own mind find it harder to cross his threshold than those which have. Price does not think that this seething multitude of ideas, all struggling to emerge into consciousness, is held down by our little lids alone. Most ideas are cancelled out by their opposites.

[1] *Proceedings* S.P.R., Vol. L, p. 1 et seq.

"That is one reason", he says, "why telepathy and PK are relatively rare occurrences, because of mutual inhibitions. It is also a reason why they may fail to occur if there are sceptical spectators. Indeed the sceptics need not even be spectators. It will be enough if the general climate of opinion is sceptical. But this is itself just another manifestation of the self-expressive tendency of ideas. The negative idea, the idea that 'such things do not happen', expresses itself by preventing the phenomena from occurring, or at least by making it more difficult for them to occur. In an age of faith, when the general climate of opinion is credulous instead of sceptical, it is presumably the other way round. It really is easier for 'queer events' to happen, just because everybody thinks they do happen."

Price points out that if there is any truth in this hypothesis, thought is a very dangerous thing. "It is said that hard words break no bones, but they may sometimes do so if there are hard thoughts behind them. For it follows from what I have said, that what anybody thinks has some tendency to come about in fact, just because it is thought of; and it still has that tendency even when the thought is no longer in anybody's consciousness. If it does not, that is because there are other contrary thoughts which are opposed to it. Ideas are dangerous things, because they have a tendency, however slight, to come true."

APPENDIX II

Further Exploration

THIS BOOK was written fifteen years ago, a fifth of the average human life but no more than the fraction of a second in man's age-old search for an answer to the question: What am I? During that fraction of a second, has the study of *psi*, and of ESP in particular, helped his search?

Most psychical researchers would answer cautiously "Yes, perhaps, a little." By this they would mean that movement has been forward, not backward. No old findings have been disproved; many have been repeated; new experimental techniques are being devised (tests for telepathic reaction with a plethysmograph, for example), and there have been signs of a growing awareness that the conditions, both physical and psychological, which seem to favor ESP need more careful study. Moreover, the progress of physics has been so swift that the idea of *psi* in general is becoming slightly less unthinkable to open-minded scientists than in the days when classical physics held the field.[1] Not that any dramatic breakthrough has convinced all and sundry of *psi*'s existence; on the contrary, its opponents, though perhaps fewer in number, are becoming more vocal, almost as if they felt they were playing a losing game. Nor as yet can evidence of it be produced by anybody, to order. But many more statistically assessable experiments in ESP have been done, not only with card guessing, but with dreams and hypnosis, and a number of these have given positive results, although only one or two have been striking. Also more subtle methods of statistical assessment have revealed different *patterns* of scoring in different types of people, which in itself suggests ESP.

[1] See article "ESP in the Framework of Modern Science" by the physicist, Professor Henry Margenau, in *Science and ESP*, edited by Dr. J. R. Smythies (Routledge and Kegan Paul, 1967).

Turning to less strictly experimental fields, certain analysts who are prepared to envisage the idea of ESP continue to come across signs of telepathic interaction between themselves and their patients, though obviously it is seldom easy to report these without giving away identities. However, interesting examples have been recorded, and in his autobiography, *Memories, Dreams, Reflections* (1963), C. G. Jung gave a number of typical cases as well as many instances of *psi* in his own life.

Next, take automatic writing. Here, two sets of unusually interesting scripts have been published. One, "The Palm Sunday Case," contains long sections of the cross correspondences, which, as reported earlier in this book, had to be kept private until all persons concerned with the material in them had died; the other, *Swan on a Black Sea*, automatically written by Miss Geraldine Cummins, purports to be postmortem communications from the cross correspondence automatist, Mrs. Willett, and contains information which seems to have been unknown to Miss Cummins. Some account of these cases will be given later.

As regards spiritualist mediumship, an example of apparently paranormal knowledge of a death, which has survived the most meticulous investigation, will also be given later. It is known as the Vandy case and is of particular interest because four different mediums independently made similar statements, some of which were not apparently in the minds of anybody living.

Finally—and this may turn out to be the most fruitful advance of all—renewed interest is being shown in spontaneous ESP-type experiences, which fell so badly out of favour when success in statistically assessable experiments alone came to be looked on as legitimate evidence pointing toward ESP. Encouraged by such eminent psychologists as the late C. G. Jung, and Professors Sir Cyril Burt, C. A. Meier, and Gardner Murphy, who is constantly emphasizing the importance of parapsychology as a tool for understanding the human mind, a small number of investigators are becoming more willing to study spontaneous experiences, not—and this is the point—simply as evidence for ESP, but *as psychological phenomena of interest in their own right.* For instance, such experiences suggest that the relation of subconscious levels of the psyche to space and time may be different from that of the conscious self, and this is of peculiar interest at a moment when the attitude of physics toward these phenomena is also changing.

Moreover, spontaneous ESP-type experiences illustrate the varied and curious fashions in which material in general emerges to consciousness from subconscious levels of the psyche—the levels, it will be remembered, which appear to receive what may for convenience be called ESP "signals." All subconscious material, whether it happens to originate "inside" or "outside" the psyche, floats into consciousness "out of the blue," sometimes straightforwardly, sometimes disguised or in an oblique or symbolic manner. The pattern can be seen again and again in dreaming, daydreaming, phantasy, ESP-type experience—and in creative work.[1] One would scarcely, for instance, expect to find this passage in Bertrand Russell's autobiography—and what seems odd is that he does not appear to have thought it odd:

> During the summer of 1915 I wrote *Principles of Social Reconstruction . . .* I had had no idea of writing such a book and it was totally unlike anything I had previously written, but it came out in a spontaneous manner. I did not, in fact, discover what it was all about until I had finished it. It has a framework and a formula, but I only discovered both when I had written all except the first and last words.[2]

Obviously no complete account of all the work done in several countries during the last ten years can be compressed into one chapter, but I shall try to give a bird's-eye view of the present position by summarizing in a litttle more detail

[1] Examples of some of these varied methods of emergence and the resemblances between them are given in chapters II and III of *The Infinite Hive,* by the present writer (Chatto and Windus, 1963 and Pan Books, 1966). In the U.S.A. it is published by E. P. Dutton under the title *ESP: A Personal Memoir.*

[2] *The Autobiography of Bertrand Russell,* Vol. II (Allen and Unwin, 1968), pp. 19–20.

one or two examples, including those mentioned above, from each line of advance. Take the experimental work first. Much of this has been done in the U.S.A. and, apart from becoming more sophisticated, has not differed greatly in kind from previous work, except for some plethysmograph experiments and for Dr. Montague Ullman's dream experiments which will be described later.[1] Nonetheless, new types of analysis of the *shapes* of scores obtained even in monotonous card-guessing experiments has thrown some interesting new light on the subconscious mental processes involved. It has shown, for instance, that in certain experiments where the *total* guesses in a series of runs were at chance level, the *distribution* of hits suggested that ESP had been at work. To give a simplified illustration: the average chance number of hits when guessing through a pack of twenty-five Zener cards is five. But if, say, two packs are guessed through, and the scores pooled, this average can be obtained by making ten hits for one pack and none for the next. In long series with many packs it has been found that different types of personality in different conditions may incline toward one or other of these extremes, which means in effect that scores which in the aggregate give a chance number of hits can provide indications of ESP when studied by the new techniques.[2]

In Europe, interest in *psi* seems to be rising on the far side of the Iron Curtain, and some dramatic experiments have been reported from the U.S.S.R. and Czechoslovakia. The late Professor L. L. Vasiliev was allowed to add the study of parapsychology to his Department of Physiology at Leningrad University, and in 1963 there appeared an English translation of a book by him which claimed that he and

[1] For the general reader an interesting account, mainly of recent American work, is given by Dr. J. G. Pratt in *Parapsychology: An Insider's View of ESP* (Doubleday, New York, 1964). A more technical study of experimental work can be found in Dr. Ramakrishna Rao's book *Experimental Parapsychology* (Charles C. Thomas, Springfield, Illinois, 1966). The experimental psychologist, Dr. R. H. Thouless, paints an illuminating picture of problems posed by such work in *Experimental Psychical Research* (Penguin, 1963).

[2] *Parapsychology Today*, edited by J. B. Rhine and Robert Brier (Citadel Press, New York, 1968).

his colleagues had repeatedly succeeded in putting hypnotized subjects to sleep and reawakening them to order by mental suggestions at a distance—a distance on occasion as far as from Sevastopol to Leningrad.[1] Vasiliev did not, of course, use the word telepathy in connection with his "mental suggestions," for it has too many associations with such "unscientific" concepts as the possibility of "minds" being separable from "bodies." It is interesting that he got the impression that such mental suggestions were immediately received by the subject, but that his conscious or unconscious resentment at being hypnotized might delay the suggestion being carried out. On one occasion when an agent, Joseph Franzevich, was instructing a subject to wake up, Vasiliev says that she remarked, "Joseph Franzevich says, 'Wake up,' but I want to rest . . . I want to rest—'Sit up, sit up!' Oh, how he shouts—what a voice—don't worry, I will soon get up—you will strain yourself." Eventually she said, "That's enough. I'm getting up." And she did. On another occasion she said, "I am fed up with him—he won't let me rest in peace . . . ," and this time too, after a few more words, she woke up.

Vasiliev started with the working hypothesis that ESP could be explained by known principles of electromagnetic radiation, but after many experiments in which both agent and percipient were screened from such radiation in metal (Faraday) cages he came to the conclusion that this screening "does not in the slightest degree affect the mental suggestion from the brain of the sender to that of the percipient." It will be noted that he still used the word "brain" and not "mind," for his materialist orthodoxy was not shaken by this discovery. He merely postulated that one day a type of radiation would be discovered which could effect communication between brains.

In the early 1960s in Prague a Czech scientist, Dr. Milan Rýzl, decided to try to train persons who had previously shown no sign of ESP to acquire it under hypnosis. The result has been impressive. Early on he had some success in

[1] L. L. Vasiliev, *Experiments in Mental Suggestion* (Galley Hill Press, Church Crookham, Hants, 1963).

teaching a number of people to get mildly positive results when guessing cards under hypnosis, but eventually he came on an outstanding percipient, Mr. Pavel Stepanek, a genial man with no pretensions to being psychic, who, after hypnosis, left the others standing. Quite soon, for instance, he dispensed with the aid of hypnosis and settled down to produce a slight but steady positive deviation from chance expectation, which, with a few interruptions coinciding with difficulties in his private life, has continued ever since. He has, in fact, already had more success over a longer period than any other known percipient. Moreover, he has produced repeated significant scores, not only for Dr. Rýzl himself, but for a number of trained foreign investigators when Rýzl was not present. In the summer of 1967 the Czech authorities allowed him to visit the well-known American experimenter, Dr. J. G. Pratt, at the University of Virginia, and there, under the supervision of Dr. Pratt, Professor Ian Stevenson, and five other scientists, he produced positive results in a further series of eighteen tests.[1] The improbability of these results being due to chance is of the order of 10^{50}; so great in fact that a referee of the account of the experiments in *Nature* commented, "I can see no way of avoiding the conclusion that, in the situation described, a particular verbal response was being elicited by a concealed stimulus object, even though this object could not have been recognized by the use of any known sensory mechanism. The general interest and importance of such a conclusion speaks for itself."

Still, even though Stepanek has got more correct "verbal responses" with more experimenters over a longer period than any previous percipient—and may, who knows, do better yet—monotonous guessing in unemotional conditions does not give us as much insight into the conditions which

[1] For details of Dr. Rýzl's experiments with Stepanek and other percipients see *Journal SPR*, March 1962, and subsequent articles by Rýzl himself and others in the *Journal* of the American SPR, *Journal of Parapsychology*, *International Journal of Neuropsychiatry*, etc. The recent experiments in Virginia were reported by Pratt and Stevenson in *Nature* for October 1968 and by Dr. John Beloff in *The New Scientist* for October 5th, 1968.

favour ESP as accounts of "real life" ESP-type experiences. Yet "real life" experience cannot be statistically assessed and so can always be ascribed to chance. A new attempt to break out of this vicious circle has recently been made at the Maimonides Medical Center in New York by Dr. Montague Ullman and his colleagues. Anecdotal evidence suggests that dreaming may be a state which favours the emergence of ESP, so Dr. Ullman's group set about trying to induce telepathic dreams experimentally. Roughly, the design is that a volunteer goes to bed with electrodes attached to his head to record the various stages of his sleep. He is then awakened after every bout of rapid eye movements (REM), which, it will be remembered, indicate that a sleeper is dreaming, and is at once asked to report his dream. During the night in a distant room an agent looks at a target picture which has been chosen at random, and after the experiment independent judges as well as the dreamer rank the dreams or items in them against the targets. In a number of these experiments the results have been significant enough to suggest that the telepathetic transfer of information from agent to sleeper can affect the content of his dreams.

Finally, in the *Journal of Parapsychology* for June 1969, and in *The New Scientist* of October 18th, 1969, appeared reports of some new experiments which seem to be among the most impressive of all so far designed to demonstrate ESP. The experimenter was Dr. Helmut Schmidt, whose particular interest is statistical physics and who was at the time a senior research physicist at the Boeing Research Laboratory at Seattle. The object of the experiments was to "guess" *beforehand* which of four coloured lamps would light up first, their sequence being determined by single quantum processes which represent the most elementary source of randomness so far known. This source and the design of the experiments appear to have eliminated fraud, yet their results were highly significant. For example, in the first main experiments three subjects made a total of 63,066 trials, and the probability of their scoring rate being achieved by chance is reported as being less than one in 500,000 million. In the second main experiment there was a dramatic change of aim. Here three subjects tried to make *fewer* hits than were to be expected by chance alone and, in spite of this reversed aim, their success was of a similar astronomical order. "Thus," says Dr. Schmidt, "the subjects obtained what they were aiming at—a large or small number of hits respectively."

There seems little point in listing further experimental work for the simple reason that most sceptics admit that *on the face of it* the existence of ESP has been demonstrated. But only on the face of it, for they continue to argue that all the results reported by all the experimenters *might* be spurious—in other words, in each case somebody *might* have cheated. (It must be remembered that in many experiments that would have meant several respected scientists in collusion.) Therefore sceptics continue to insist that until ESP can be demonstrated *to order* in absolutely watertight conditions by any experimenter, however hostile, there is *no* evidence for its existence.[1] Late in 1968 a sceptic put forward this type of argument on television, and the well-known psychologist, Professor H. J. Eysenck, replied that he did not think it was valid. "Most experiments in psychology and physics," he said, "are not satisfactory in the sense you say . . . nearly all are faulty in one sense or another. I think one must judge on the accumulation of evidence, even though a single experiment is never absolutely convincing. The evidence is now so strong that we must either face that there is such a thing as extra-sensory perception or alternatively that there is a large number of very reputable professors and other people who are simply falsifying the evidence. I find this so incredible that I prefer the other alternative."

In a letter to the *British Journal of Psychiatry* Professor Eysenck also refers to another point in favour of ESP, over and above the statistical significance of so many scores. That

[1] In a book entitled *ESP: A Scientific Evaluation*, Professor C. E. M. Hansel has put forward a number of ingenious suggestions as to how cheating could have been carried out in certain well-known and apparently watertight experiments. But Professor Ian Stevenson and others have pointed out that the facts—position of doors, etc.—which he gives as bases for some of these suggestions seem to be inaccurate. See in particular Stevenson's review of the book in the *Journal* of the American SPR, July 1967.

is the *shape* of the scores *within* individual runs. "What has impressed me more than simple numbers," he writes, "has been the lawfulness of certain events occurring within runs, such as the fall-off of scores, which is reported again and again and which resembles what is often found in vigilance experiments. This is particularly impressive because it was not originally looked for and was found on going back over some of the older records when this effect was not even thought of and could therefore hardly have been faked." [1]

Another behavioural psychologist, who, although non-committal as to the existence of ESP, still seems to think that parapsychologists try to do their experiments scientifically is Dr. Robert Rosenthal of Harvard. When discussing attempts to minimize experimenter-subject contact in general he remarks:

> It is striking that so many of these efforts at greater control occurred in what might be called "borderline" areas of psychology. Even today it would be a rash parapsychologist who would not make every effort to minimize the contact between experimenter and subject in a study of extra-sensory perception. And this is all to the good. Also to the good is the fact that non-parapsychologists would be outraged if such controls against expectancy effects were not employed. But *not* all to the good is the fact that some of these same workers might be outraged if in their own less "borderline" areas of inquiry they were required to institute the same degree of control over their own expectancy effects. Clearly we have a double standard of required degree of control . . .[2]

The onlooker gets the impression that the widespread scepticism about the authenticity of experiments in ESP is greater than would be expected even in the light of the scientific rethinking which so novel a phenomenon might involve—and naturally enough ideas which may upset the prin-

[1] *British Journal of Psychiatry*, 1968, pp. 114, 1471.
[2] Robert Rosenthal, *Experimenter Effects in Behavioral Research* (Appleton Century Crofts, New York, 1966).

ciples on which one's life work may have been based can hardly be popular. But to give time and energy to try to *disprove* an idea one believes to be false, and to suspect one's fellow scientists of fraud because they put it forward, rather than let its falsity ultimately prove itself, suggests a further hidden motive. There are sometimes hints that this could be subconscious fear of the apparently irrational. Take, for instance, this extract from an otherwise laudatory review in *The Guardian* of July 12th, 1963, by Professor D. W. Harding, of C. G. Jung's autobiography, *Memories, Dreams, Reflections*. The book, it will be remembered, is scattered with incidents which Jung accepts as due to *psi*. Professor Harding wrote:

> A streak of superstition runs through the whole book; precognitive dreams, apparitions of the living, hauntings, poltergeistery, premonitions, magical coincidence ("synchronicity"), the lot. Here, inescapably, one sees that he really believed it all (turning, for respectable cover, to J. B. Rhine's inference from the statistics of guessing games). Some may feel compelled to believe in these things, but, if so, nothing stands between them and the morass of superstition, soothsaying and witchcraft out of which educated people have dragged themselves in the last few centuries.

As it seemed obvious that "these things" should be believed or not according to present evidence for them rather than to past superstitions about them, I showed the above extract to a friend, an elder statesman of science. He commented with a smile that when he was a young man at the beginning of the century he would often hear the following kind of remark: "A streak of superstition runs through all the writings of Rutherford. If we believe that atoms can be split, that unknown forces exist within them more powerful than gravity, that one element can be changed into another, nothing stands between us and the mass of nonsense which made up medieval alchemy and astrology: we shall shortly be talking of sending people to the moon as Kepler used to do."

Now to turn to the new material connected with the automatic scripts known as the cross correspondences (see chapters VIII and IX). It will be remembered that when those chapters were written only a proportion of these scripts had been published, for some of them prophesied future events and others dealt with the intimate private lives of a group of persons, some of whom were then still living. On his death in 1944, one of the group, Gerald, Earl of Balfour, who had charge of the scripts, left them to his daughter-in-law Jean, Countess of Balfour. The last of the group, whose pseudonym was Mrs. Willett, died in August 1956, and in the December number of the *SPR Journal* for that year appeared her obituary, which disclosed that she was actually none other than an apparently different type of personality, Mrs. Charles Coombe-Tennant, who had been the first British female delegate to the League of Nations and was well known for her efficiency in public affairs. With her death the need for secrecy as regards a large section of the scripts was over, and this section was edited by Lady Balfour and published in 1960.[1]

The Palm Sunday scripts referred over many years in a cryptic and symbolic fashion to an early love affair between Arthur Balfour and Mary Lyttelton, who fell ill just as he was about to ask her to marry him and who died shortly afterward on Palm Sunday, 1875. Scattered references to this private matter, of which they were apparently quite ignorant, were made in early scripts by Mrs. Verrall and her daughter and by Mrs. Holland, and some were signed M. or even M.L. But this signature meant nothing to the automatists at the time. Later on, more and highly specific items appeared in Mrs. Willett's scripts, and these scripts themselves ultimately insisted that Arthur Balfour, by now an old man, should himself come and sit with Mrs. Willett. In her previous scripts for years there had been scattered remarks which it was afterward realized could all apply to

[1] "The Palm Sunday Case," *Proceedings SPR*, Vol. II, Part 189. There is a summary of the case in an article by the present writer, entitled "Death and Psychical Research" in *Man's Concern with Death* (Hodder & Stoughton, London, 1968, and McGraw-Hill, New York, 1969).

Mary, among them, for instance, mention of a lock of hair, something purple, a metal box, and a periwinkle. When Arthur Balfour came, Mrs. Willett wrote a long and moving script, referring to these items and other previous statements applicable to Mary, and insisting that death had made no difference to her love for him and that she was with him always. According to Lady Balfour, Arthur Balfour now disclosed to his brother Gerald for the first time that he had had a box made, lined with purple and with periwinkles and other spring flowers chased on it, in which to keep a lock of Mary's hair. In fact, he had never got over Mary's death and these apparent messages in his old age were a great comfort to him. The story as told in detail by Lady Balfour is a very moving one and the paranormal nature of the scripts is hard to explain away, though whether they come from a number of living persons via fantastic ESP or from the dead is a matter every reader must decide for himself. And it should be added that *some* information about the Balfour-Lyttelton love story was given in Blanche Dugdale's biography of Balfour published in the 1930s.

In 1963 Mr. W. H. Salter edited a further series of scripts which contain what appear to be obvious references to the forthcoming birth and early death of Mrs. Willett's much loved baby daughter, although they were written before those events occurred. Since then, in the Lake District, Oxford, and elsewhere, Mr. Guy Lambert has unearthed further apparent sources—some from the far past—for statements in Mrs. Verrall's scripts which seemed meaningless at the time they were written. We know no more than when this book was written ten years ago what the origin of all this may be, but the new material makes the puzzle even more intriguing. And it looks more likely than ever that *something* paranormal was going on, whether or not it was connected with the dead.

Five years later an equally puzzling postscript to the cross correspondences was published. In 1957 Mr. Salter had asked a well-known automatist, Miss Geraldine Cummins, to try to get some communications from the deceased mother of a friend of his, Major Tennant. This resulted in a long series of scripts purporting to come from the most forceful personality Miss Cummins had ever "felt" writing through her. Six of them were written *before* Miss Cummins heard that Major Tennant's mother was, in fact, the famous Mrs. Willett, but fortunately these already contained much authentic information about her life and character. The scripts were edited by Signe Toksvig, the author of a well-known life of Swedenborg, and are preceded by an exhaustive analysis by Professor C. D. Broad, which is of great help to the reader who is trying to form an opinion about them.[1] Professor Broad appears impressed by the accurate characterization of Mrs. Willett, whom he knew, but Miss Cummins did not, and the book makes clear that some of the information in the scripts about Mrs. Willett's early life was unknown even to her sons until some old diaries were read through and confirmed it as authentic. There is here a puzzle as good as any in science fiction.

Professor Broad has also analysed an interesting case of mediumship which was meticulously investigated by a member of the Council of the SPR, the Hon. Mrs. Cyril Gay, and which shows apparent paranormal knowledge of the death of a young man, Edgar Vandy, by four independent mediums.[2] The following is a summary, but the case is far more impressive when read in detail.

Edgar Vandy was a clever engineer whose death occurred by drowning in 1933 at the early age of thirty-eight. At the time he was engaged in designing a new type of machine to reproduce lettering, etc., by electromechanical means. One Sunday morning he was taken by a friend, N.J., to visit an estate in Sussex, where N.J.'s sister was secretary to the owner, who was away at the time. As the weather was hot, the two men decided to go and bathe in the swimming pool which was somewhat cloudy and slippery, being fed from a stream. They undressed behind some bushes, and N.J. stated later that Edgar was ready about three minutes before him

[1] *Swan on a Black Sea* (Routledge and Kegan Paul, 1965).

[2] C. D. Broad, *Lectures on Psychical Research* (Routledge and Kegan Paul, 1962).

and went off alone to the pool which was out of N.J.'s sight. Edgar was a bad swimmer and could not dive and was later found dead in the pool. The essence of N.J.'s evidence at the inquest was that on reaching the pool he saw Edgar lying face downward in the water splashing and fluttering his hands. N.J. jumped in, but by the time he reached Edgar he was sinking and N.J. could not keep a grip on him. When Edgar finally sank N.J. rushed for help.

In the doctor's opinion the medical evidence—bruises, lack of water in the lungs, etc.—suggested that Edgar had dived in, struck his jaw, lost consciousness and so drowned, but Edgar's two brothers, George and Harold, were not satisfied, for Edgar could not dive and they found it hard to understand why the attempts to help him should have failed. George did not believe in survival, but was a member of the SPR, and he thought it just possible that a medium might become aware of the manner of Edgar's death by means of ESP. To this end he arranged for six strictly anonymous sittings with four different mediums, of which one was a proxy sitting to be taken by Mr. Drayton Thomas with Mrs. Osborne Leonard. Mr. Thomas was told no more than Edgar's name and that the relatives were in some doubt as to the cause of his death. The other five sittings with three other mediums were taken by George and Harold separately, under assumed names. George sat with all three of them, Harold with two.

Two main topics were mentioned by all four mediums: Edgar's death and the machine he was working on. As regards the death, Professor Broad points out the remarkable fact that two themes were common to all six sittings: (a) that Edgar fell on his head which was hit and damaged, and (b) that one or more persons were present, that it might be thought that they had failed to save his life through cowardice or incompetence and that he wished to shield them from blame. In five of the sittings there were references to water and drowning, and to Edgar's death being a strangely unlucky event which could easily have been avoided. In four the mediums said that it was not due to suicide or culpable carelessness and that there was a feeling of dizziness connected with the accident. In three there were references to a large scar which Edgar had said would always identify him. As regards the machine: in three of the six sittings and also at a later one taken by Harold Vandy there were a number of references to a machine, to something that Edgar had invented. Some of these were inaccurate, others correct and even specific to an extent surprising in women who knew nothing about engineering.

To demonstrate the improbability of chance coincidence being an explanation for the many "hits" made by the four mediums, Professor Broad asked three questions:

(1) What proportion of the male population of England are drowned per annum in open-air swimming pools, after falling mysteriously and getting a crack on the head?

(2) What proportion of them are skilled technicians devoting themselves to inventions in general and to the type of machine being designed by Edgar in particular?

(3) What proportion of them fall into both these categories?

Professor Broad appears to think fraudulent collusion between the experimenter, George Vandy, and the mediums equally improbable—and, indeed, all their successes did not convince Mr. Vandy of survival. In this case, then, it seems hard to avoid some kind of paranormal hypothesis. Professor Broad thinks that the minimal one to fit the facts would be that the mediums acquired the various items of information by telepathy from a number of living persons and dramatized them subconsciously as coming from the dead. In that case, he asks, why did certain very relevant items which would presumably have been in N.J.'s mind fail to appear? The maximal paranormal hypothesis, he suggests, would be that Edgar Vandy's personality had survived the death of his body and was deliberately communicating some of its thoughts and feelings telepathically to the various mediums. Professor Broad does not pass judgment either way. Nor does he comment on the possibility that, although no verbal help was given by the Vandy brothers, unconscious changes of expression on their faces might have conveyed hints which the mediums consciously or unconsciously picked up—on the principle that animals pick up clues from their masters which the masters are not aware of having given.

Finally we come to the natural-history side of psychical research, the study of spontaneous ESP-type experiences. Nowadays, even among the sophisticated, there are hints of renewed, though cautious, interest in them, excluding of course those persons who "know" that the answer to every case can only be human frailty or chance coincidence. However, so distinguished a psychologist as Professor Sir Cyril Burt has suggested that more progress is likely to be made by studying such experiences simply as psychological phenomena, as well as asking the question: could there be a paranormal explanation for them? And during the 1960s attempts have been made to do just that. In England, Europe, and America the Societies for Psychical Research and kindred bodies have made new collections of mainly contemporary cases and have analyzed them in detail, and in America Dr. Louisa Rhine has already been at work along those lines since the 1950s. She has received over 10,000 cases and has achieved the Herculean task of classifying and analyzing them. Fresh reports by her still continue to appear in the *Journal of Parapsychology* and from these scientific reports she has written two books for the general public which include interesting comparisons between patterns in spontaneous cases and laboratory experiments.[1]

The interest of the psychological aspects of ESP-type experience shows up vividly in Jung's autobiography, including the marked effect it had on his whole life and work. There is room for only the briefest comments on such aspects here. First of all, Myers and Gurney would have been

---

[1] L. E. Rhine, *Hidden Channels of the Mind* (W. Sloane, New York, 1961). *ESP in Life and Lab* (Macmillan, New York, 1967, and Collier–Macmillan, London, 1967). The present writer has also described and analyzed a number of ESP-type experiences *as seen from the percipient's point of view*, in *The Infinite Hive* (Chatto and Windus, 1963, and Pan Books, 1966). The book has also been published under the title *ESP: A Personal Memoir*, by E. P. Dutton, New York, 1965.

happy to see the extent to which resemblances in cases from all over the world support the conclusion they came to in the 1880s—that the factors in common in such cases look incredible should each one have occurred by chance or been separately invented. They thought it incredible too that hundreds of people should draw "the same arbitrary line between mistakes and exaggerations of which they will be guilty and those of which they will not." For us the hundreds have become thousands. Moreover, as we saw earlier, anthropologists find similar patterns among primitive peoples, though it is hard for even the most sympathetic "white" to get on terms intimate enough to learn much about them. I heard not long ago of an anthropologist who asked a tribal medicine man whether his people believed they could speak with the dead. "Of course," said the man as if it were as simple as telephoning to Brighton.

"Then why do you tell us nothing about it?"

"Oh, that is not the kind of thing one would talk about to white people."

There is less time than ever to understand the minds of primitive people to whom ESP-type experience, whatever its nature, seems to be normal, before it is apparently discouraged by a life of serving highballs and steaks to tourists in a worldwide Hiltonia. And yet it is increasingly clear that similar experience comes to Western man—less, perhaps, the greater his sophistication and consequent tendency to think in verbal terms rather than in images, but at all levels to a greater extent than the present mental climate allows him to admit, or at least to volunteer. But there are hints here and there that the climate shows faint signs of change. For example, books on psychical research are more often reviewed in serious, even scientific, publications, and to an increasing extent psychical researchers are asked to lecture to serious bodies. Not long ago, after I had been giving a talk to a group of head teachers, one headmaster said to me: "It may interest you to know that we have all been comparing notes as to how many of us have experienced or observed at first hand such incidents as you have been describing, and everybody in this room has come upon at least one." Yet none of them appeared to have mentioned these incidents previously and there was a distinct atmosphere of pleasure and even relief at being able to talk about them as easily as about football or politics.

One may guess that this kind of unconscious taboo may imply possibly undesirable repression of whole areas of the psyche. It may also help to account for the devious fashions in which ESP "signals" emerge into consciousness. As Professor Broad has pointed out, such a "signal" need not *reproduce* its related event. It usually appears "out of the blue," often obliquely, perhaps in symbolic form, or via an associated idea, or distorted, or as an apparently pointless urge to action, or an impulse to which the conscious mind gives a plausible though false objective. It is possible too that a person trained to verbal thinking may not conceive that his subconscious can still think in images, and will thus ignore an image floating into his mind from "nowhere"; whereas a primitive, like the Australian aborigines mentioned in chapter XVIII, who recognized a plover as a "mind bird" come to tell them of a relative's death, will find such symbolic means of information as natural as we find the words "John has died" on a telegraph form. Still, sophisticated creative minds do get useful information symbolically from the subconscious. Everyone knows, for instance, of the dream or daydream about a serpent biting its own tail which led Kekulé to the idea of the benzene molecule. But such inspiration, of course, is scientifically respectable since it need not imply ESP, but merely subconscious incubation of observations made earlier *via* sensory perception.

There is no room here for examples of the many oblique routes by which recent study is showing that ESP can work its way up to consciousness, but I will summarize two examples from Dr. Louisa Rhine's collection which suggest that it may often be blocked on the way or even cut off altogether, perhaps by the attitude toward it of modern man. In the first case the percipient's conscious mind concocted a spurious meaning to induce her to take an apparently pointless action which in fact saved a life. She was about to set out for work and did not want to be late when she felt an urge to go down through her landlady's basement kitchen and take in some clothes from the garden line—clothes which she knew could very well wait. The urge was so overwhelming that she gave in to it, hurried downstairs and saw her landlady sitting at the kitchen table, waving a glass and surrounded by empty beer bottles. But she also saw water splashing in the bathtub with the tap turned off, and hastened across the room to find out why. The landlady's ten-month-old baby was in the tub, completely submerged except for his feet which were splashing the water. The drunken mother said, "Oh, I was giving baby a bath and forgot about him. How funny he looks." The percipient applied first aid and the baby was saved.

The second case is one of simple compulsive action the meaning of which was apparently blocked beneath the conscious level. A Mr. C. who lived in New York was in the habit of visiting friends forty miles away at weekends only, but suddenly at a midweek evening party he felt that he had to go to them *at once*. So, without even fetching nightgear from his hotel, he took the first possible train, thinking, "This is the craziest thing I have ever done in my life." But he was wrong. On arrival he found his friend's house in darkness, so he asked the taximan to wait and walked toward the front door. Then he saw something lying on the ground. It was his friend's wife. She had had a stroke. Her husband was away, and had not Mr. C. followed his hunch there would have been no one to help her.

These spontaneous actions came "out of the blue" like Kekulé's dream and Russell's book. So, as recent studies of creativity have emphasized, do the inspirations of many thinkers. Gauss, for instance, once said, "As in a sudden flash of light the problem was solved." And it is the same with the arts. *"On ne travaille pas; on écoute,"* said de Musset. "I declare my tongue spoke by its own impulse," Dante wrote about the beginning of a new poem. "I may praise my poem," said Blake, "since I was none other than its secretary." Examples of the process are legion and their resemblance to the emergence of ESP, whether it takes the form of a spontaneous experience, automatic writing, or mediumistic utterance, is obvious—whatever the origin of ESP may be. But the resemblance at least suggests that it is a natural phenomenon and worthy of a place on the map of science.

Two other subjects which may be looked on as coming under the heading of *psi* should perhaps be mentioned, as there appears to be growing interest in them although they are hard to verify. The first is reincarnation. In 1966 Professor Ian Stevenson of Virginia University published a remarkable account of his research into evidence for it, having travelled in many countries, mainly in the East where, of course, the conception is taken far more seriously than in the West.[1] And yet in the West, as Professor C. J. Ducasse points out in his foreword to Stevenson's book, "Some of the most eminent thinkers have given it attention. Among them in antiquity have been Pythagoras, Plato, Plotinus, and Origen; and in modern times Hume, Kant, Fichte, Schopenhauer, Renouvrier, McTaggart, Ward, and Broad." Stevenson has made a census of reports of nearly 600 cases suggestive of reincarnation, of which he and his colleagues have personally investigated about a third. In his book on the subject he examines twenty of these in detail and the impression it gives is that whether or not reincarnation is the answer to them, some unknown factor is at work which needs to be discovered.

The second subject is known as out-of-the-body experience. In this the person concerned feels as if he leaves his physical body, at which he can look from another point in space. He also appears able to journey through what, for want of a better expression, may be called other realms and occasionally he reports events he has observed in our normal world during his "journeys"—events which were far beyond the range of observation by his physical senses. C. E. Green has recently written an interesting study of this phenomenon

[1] Ian Stevenson, *Twenty Cases Suggestive of Reincarnation* (American Society for Psychical Research, 1966).

and also of another related to it, known as lucid dreams.[1]

A final cause for encouragement to psychical researchers is that the map of science itself is altering at amazing speed and in a fashion which may make a place for *psi* less hard to find, since its edges are becoming more blurred and its contents more mysterious. "My own suspicion is that the universe is not only queerer than we suppose, but queerer than we can suppose," said J. B. S. Haldane, and in an article in *The Times Literary Supplement* (December 1968) entitled "The Queer World of Quanta," the author remarks that to get a true picture of science nowadays the first thing to abandon is that it equals common sense. Even the man in the street has come to accept that he does not live, as he once believed, in a world of certainties, but in one of probabilities; that in the spheres of the very large and the very small the classical notions of space, time, and matter no longer hold, and that ultimate particles can behave in a fashion far odder than the Red Queen.

Moreover, the dogma of classical materialism, that the brain *generates* consciousness, that mind is no more than an epiphenomenon of matter and can be adequately explained by chemistry and physics alone, is being questioned by some of the first neurophysiologists of the day, such as Lord Adrian, Sir John Eccles, and Dr. Wilder Penfield. As the great psychologist Professor Sir Cyril Burt has put it, "the structure of the brain suggests a mechanism designed to detect or transmit conscious activity rather than to generate it." [2]

[1] C. E. Green, *Lucid Dreams and Out of the Body Experiences* (both published by The Institute of Psychophysical Research, 118 Banbury Road, Oxford, 1968). There is a short survey of the subject by the present writer in a chapter of *Man's Concern with Death,* by Arnold Toynbee and others (Hodder and Stoughton, London, 1968 and McGraw-Hill, New York, 1969).

[2] Discoveries about the nature of the brain come so fast that the reporter can scarcely keep up. In 1969 appeared Dr. Grey Walter's Eddington Memorial Lecture, *Observations on Man* (CUP). When discussing brain function he writes:

. . . there is objective evidence that spontaneous impulses to explore and the evocation of imaginary experiences are preceded and accompanied by electric events [in the brain—R.H.] as clear and substantial

APPENDIX II

At the moment what it all seems to come to is this: during the last ten years psychical research has made a few halting steps forward along a trail which is not only continuous with the past but seems to be opening out slowly toward the future. But no dramatic breakthrough has been made which forces the determined sceptic to accept ESP as proven. That of course may be partly due to the attitude of the sceptic. John Stuart Mill once said: "A man who knows may tell me what he knows as far as words go. . . . But if I would know it I must place my mind in the state in which he has placed his: I must make the thought of my own thought. I must verify the fact by my own observation or by interrogating my own consciousness." To do that is obviously beyond the men who look on the idea of ESP as so absurd that they prefer to believe that their colleagues who produce evidence of it are dupes or liars, rather than that it is possible.

Still, a number of great scientists hold such an attitude to be a leftover from the past, and as we are told that the world of science gets queerer every day and is apparently becoming almost as elusive as the world of ESP, it seems justified to hope, indeed to expect, that before long the two will meet. So the ending of this book can still be that of ten years ago: If we do not cease from exploration, if we follow humbly wherever nature leads, it may be that:

---

as those I have described in relation to interactions with the outside world.

It is an eerie experience to discern through an electric machine the genesis of a person's intentions, to predict his decisions before he knows his own mind. Even more impressive is the experience when one can influence external events without movement or overt action, through the impalpable electric surges in one's own brain. Not surprisingly, perhaps, the repeated exercise of such effort requires the attainment of a peculiar state of concentration, a paradoxical compound of detachment and excitement. As a physiologist I am embarrassed to introduce here such a word as willpower, which I can define only within these crude empirical limits. Of course, there are more sophisticated terms with classical etymologies, but they explain no more and describe less vividly what we feel subjectively when we say, "I wish and I will." It may be the fate of physiologists that they can merely provide increasingly detailed corroboration of faculties which the wise have always known we possess. Nonetheless, I find it particularly reassuring that we can identify objective accompaniments of spontaneous volition and creative reflexion.

APPENDIX II

. . . the end of all the exploring
Will be to arrive where we started
And know the place for the first time.[1]

Note

Since this book was revised, *The New Scientist* of June 24th, 1971, has reported that Dr. Helmut Schmidt has conducted a new series of experiments—this time in psychokinesis—at Durham, North Carolina. Moreover, a further advance of parapsychology toward recognition as a scientific discipline has been the acceptance of the Parapsychological Association as a member by the American Association for the Advancement of Science.

---

[1] T. S. Eliot, *Four Quartets* (Faber and Faber, 1944).

Index

INDEX

INDEX

INDEX

Senses and Sensory Perception, 9–11, 13, 15–17, 22, 34, 49, 95, 111, 144, 178–9, 185, 194, 200–1, 203, 207–8, 211

Servadio, Emilio, 193–4; article in *To-morrow*, 193

Shackleton, Mr., 158–60, 170

Sidgwick, Henry, 14, 27–31, 33, 36–7, 39, 43, 48, 50–1, 53–5, 69–70, 81, 87–8, 105, 122, 133, 164; Mrs. Sidgwick, 31, 37, 49, 51, 55, 63, 67, 69, 72, 90, 106

Sinclair, Upton, and Mrs., 5, 140–2, 146, 155; *Mental Radio*, 5, 140

Soal, Dr. S. B., 88, 126, 145, 152, 158–60, 164, 170

Socrates, 214

Spencer Brown, G., 169–70; article in *Nature*, 169; *Probability and Scientific Inference*, 169

S.P.R. (Society for Psychical Research), 5, 7, 36–52, 62–6, 68–70, 72, 78–9, 81, 87, 108, 112–13, 117, 120, 126–7, 130, 145, 150, 153, 161, 174, 193, 197–8, 211, 215; *Journal*, 16, 130, 189, 198; President and Council of, 5; pamphlets, 118, 140; *Proceedings of*, 40–2, 49, 54, 60, 65, 70, 75, 80, 86, 91, 122–3, 127, 132, 142, 189, 200, 205, 212–13, 218

Spiritualism (*see also* Mediumship), 19, 22–3, 25, 29, 32–4, 36–8, 107, 112, 114, 174–5; Fox sisters, 23

Stepanek, Pavel, 228

Stevenson, Professor Ian, 228, 242

Stewart, Mrs., 158–60, 170

Survival of Death, 52–63, 67–9, 73, 85, 88–91, 93, 116–17, 124–6, 177, 195, 198–200, 202, 208–11, 218

Swedenborg, Emanuel, 21, 214

Symbolism, 17–18, 187, 202–3

Table-turning, 22–5

Talbot, Mrs. Hugh, 122–3

Telepathy, 10–11, 13, 16, 19, 33, 40–1, 44, 48–9, 51, 54–5, 58, 63, 65, 68, 71, 78, 82, 84, 87–8, 96–8, 100, 106, 118, 120–4, 133, 138–9,

140, 142, 144, 151, 154, 157–9, 161, 164–5, 170, 173, 176, 179, 185, 187, 189, 190–1, 193–4, 200,, 204–5, 207–8, 211–12, 215–19, 227, 229, 240

Thomas, Rev. C. Drayton, 118–20, 123–5, 236

Thomson, F.R.S., Sir George, 5, 166–8; *Foreseeable Future, The*, 5, 167–8

Thomson, Sir J. J., 14

Thought Transference, 33, 36, 142; *Experiments in Thought Transference* (Miles and Ramsden), 142

Thouless, Dr. R. H., 147–8, 162, 200–5

Three Faces of Eve, The (Thigpen and Cleckley), 109

Toksvig, Signe, 235

Trance, 22–5, 33, 38, 62–4, 66–8, 96, 100, 107, 112, 118, 120, 174

Trevelyan, G. O., 27

Troubridge, Lady, 122

Tyrrell, G. N. M., 46–7, 49, 71, 127, 148–52, 154, 156, 159, 161–2, 170, 185–7; *Apparitions*, 49, 185; *Personality of Man, The*, 46–7, 127; *Science and Psychical Phenomena*, 150

Ullman, Dr. Montague, 226; his dream experiments, 226, 229

Universities (attitude to *psi*), 23, 145, 164

Vandy case, 223, 235–7; Vandy, Edgar, 235–7

Vasiliev, Professor L. L., 226–7

Verrall, Dr. A. W., Mrs. and Miss, 69–71, 74–9, 81, 83–4, 86–9, 91–2, 95–6, 98, 116, 118, 133, 139, 200, 233, 234

Visions, 19, 45–6, 56, 92, 105, 113–14, 199

Wallace, Alfred Russel, 32

Warcollier, René, 142, 172; *Experimental Telepathy*, 142, 214

INDEX